UNDEFEATED

ALSO BY MIKE FREEMAN

Bowden: How Bobby Bowden Forged a Football Dynasty

The All-Time Biggest Sports Jerks: And Other Goofballs, Cads, Miscreants, Reprobates, and Weirdos (Plus a Few Good Guys)

Jim Brown: The Fierce Life of an American Hero

ESPN: The Uncensored History

Bloody Sundays: Inside the Dazzling, Rough-and-Tumble World of the NFL

UNDEFEATED

INSIDE THE 1972 MIAMI DOLPHINS' PERFECT SEASON

MIKE FREEMAN

itbooks

AN IMPRINT OF HARPERCOLLINS PUBLISHERS

HarperCollins books may be purchased for educational, business, or sales promotional use. For information please write: Special Markets Department, HarperCollins Publishers, 10 East 53rd Street, New York, NY 10022.

FIRST EDITION

Designed by Shannon Plunkett

All photographs courtesy of the Associated Press.

Library of Congress Cataloging-in-Publication Data is available upon request.

ISBN 978-0-06-200982-1

12 13 14 15 16   OV/RRD   10 9 8 7 6 5 4 3 2 1

TO ELLA . . .

THERE IS NO END TO MY LOVE FOR YOU AND

LIFE'S POSSIBILITIES ARE ENDLESS

Aim at perfection in everything, though in most things it is unattainable; however, they who aim at it, and persevere, will come much nearer it than those whose laziness and despondency make them give it up as unattainable.

—LORD CHESTERFIELD

He can take his'n and beat your'n, or he can take your'n and beat his'n.

—FORMER HOUSTON OILERS COACH
BUM PHILLIPS ON DON SHULA

CONTENTS

They enthralled presidents, charmed a city, intimidated a league, and challenged racial norms. There has never been a team like them. There may never be again. Many have forgotten just how good they were. It's understandable. What the Miami Dolphins did happened forty years ago . . .

PRESIDENT NIXON ON THE LINE

Seven days before the Miami Dolphins played Super Bowl VI against the Dallas Cowboys, President Richard Nixon placed a phone call at an indecent hour. He had a suggestion, and it couldn't wait until morning.

When the phone rang at 1:30 A.M., Don Shula picked it up only to hear a voice on the other end say, "This is the White House calling." Shula initially thought his players were engaging in another annoying prank, like the time they stuck a bullfrog on the podium where Shula was addressing the team and covered the poor creature with a towel. Shula unsuspectingly removed the towel and the bullfrog almost jumped down his throat. And, of course, there was the time when players spliced scenes from a pornographic film into the beginning of game footage that was to be reviewed by the team. When coaches turned the projector on, and the shock registered across their faces as a different sort of contact sport appeared on the screen, everyone laughed—including Shula.

The players were more than capable of executing a Nixon ruse despite the uniqueness of Nixon's persona and mannerisms. Except it didn't take long for Shula to realize the man on the phone was no impostor. It really was Nixon.

It was January 1972. That month, not long before calling the Dolphins coach, Nixon ordered the development of the Space Shuttle program. The first handheld scientific calculator was introduced. Price: $395. Recluse Howard Hughes emerged from his rabbit hole to denounce a biography on him as a fake. But Shula wasn't focused on spaceships or billionaire recluses; he was focused on the Super Bowl. Then came the call from Nixon's office. Shula covered the receiver with his hand and whispered to his wife, Dorothy, who was still awake and celebrating the conference title win over the Baltimore Colts. A few minutes later, Nixon came on the line. He first congratulated Shula on making the Super Bowl and then quickly turned to football strategy. There would be no lubricating of the conversation.

It wasn't unusual for presidents to speak with football coaches after a Super Bowl victory, and certainly there were post–Super Bowl visits to the White House for the winners. But a call in the middle of the week *before* the Super Bowl?

There were some who believed that Nixon's obsessive interest in sports was a stunt, a public maneuver to soften his image as one of the most disliked people in the country. Yet his sports infatuation was likely genuine. He had played three sports at Whittier College, including football, and now as president, he thought of himself as the "coach in chief." Or, perhaps more accurately, the "sports fan in chief." He became the first sitting president to attend an NFL game, hand out college football's glossy national championship trophy, and attend the Kentucky Derby (with a massive Secret Service contingent). His fanaticism about sports sometimes reached maniacal levels. Nixon once stopped a crucial meeting of his budget advisers so he could watch Michigan play Ohio State (tax dollars at work), and he seriously considered putting the legendary Vince Lombardi on his 1968 presidential ticket.

Politics hadn't dulled his love of the NFL. If anything, the bloody sparring in politics enhanced it. Nixon talked football with NFL coaches and players whenever possible, which was flattering to some and irritating to others. Indeed, despite the initial shock of hearing from Nixon and suspicions it was a prank, Shula probably should not have been so surprised by the call. Nixon was obsessed with Shula. He once tried to phone Shula after a loss, but the phone lines at the stadium were busy. Nixon would also phone in to Shula's Miami-based, call-in television show, surprising the coach after the team beat Kansas City. Shula had a presidential stalker.

Earlier in Shula's career, as coach of the Baltimore Colts, then president-elect Nixon wrote Shula a touching letter, after a crushing loss in the Super Bowl to the New York Jets, saying he was confident Shula would turn his career around the way Nixon did his. Nixon had lost the 1960 presidential election to John F. Kennedy and the 1962 California gubernatorial race before winning the 1968 presidency.

As president, he later became close friends with Washington Redskins coach George Allen. Nixon invited Allen to the White House on various occasions (Allen declined in some instances, telling the president he needed to focus on the season) and followed the team closely. He'd listen to the games on the radio and scream during them in front of elder daughter, Julie, as if the Redskins players could hear his orders: "Hit him! Hit him! Goddammit! Son of a bitch."

"That bad, huh?" Julie would say.

Nixon's telephone call to Shula was simply another link in the evolutionary chain of the president's football obsession.

"The Cowboys are a fine football team and Coach Landry is an exceptional coach," Nixon said.

"You're right, sir," replied Shula.

"Coach, I think it would be a great idea for you to use a pass that you throw to Warfield."

"What pass, sir?"

"You know, that slant-in pattern where Warfield starts down and then breaks into the middle of the field."

Such pass routes are common in football—suggesting a down-and-in route to star wide receiver Paul Warfield was like telling Mick Jagger to sing "Satisfaction" while the Rolling Stones were on tour—still Shula continued to listen patiently. This was, Shula thought, the president of the United States, after all. Hunter S. Thompson would later remark on Shula's apparent disdain for Nixon. True or not, Shula wasn't about to disrespect the office of the presidency.

"Yes, Mr. President, we do plan on using that slant-in pass to Warfield against the Cowboys."

"I think it can work for a big gain."

"Yes, sir, it can."

"Well, again my congratulations on a fine victory."

"Thank you for taking the time to call and for your interest in professional football, Mr. President."

The two men hung up the phone.

In a way, at that moment in time, Nixon and Shula—one man a president, the other a coach in a game that would be watched in many corners of the country and world—were two of the most visible men in the nation, both about to suffer painful losses. One would emerge as a cautionary tale. The other would recover and become a legend.

PART ONE

WRECKAGE

"I DON'T EVER WANT TO FEEL THIS WAY AGAIN"

A story about perfection begins with a blunder seen around the world.

On a 38-degree night in January 1972, one week after Nixon's late-night phone call, the Miami Dolphins piled into their locker room. Theirs was no different from many other locker rooms of the day, concrete and bland. But it seemed emptier and colder than when they'd departed it several hours before. Uniforms stained with blood and the wear and tear of violence were peeled away slowly by some of the men who wore them. It was a deliberate exercise at first, and then some stripped faster, as if taking off their shoulder pads and jerseys would make the pain of losing a Super Bowl easier. Or at least go away more quickly.

Others sat in complete stillness, refusing to remove a single piece of equipment or article of clothing.

There were dozens of people in the room, yet the only sound, at first, was the barely audible shuffle of football cleats on the floor.

Then a cough. A helmet landing on the ground. A hushed, quick conversation. Some players were so stunned by the game's outcome they hadn't had time to deal with the aftermath of the blistering violence that only minutes earlier tormented their bodies. The stout middle linebacker Nick Buoniconti, known as one of the toughest players in the sport, sat in a back corner still uncertain about what exactly had just happened. Early in the second half, a head-to-head collision had left Buoniconti so concussed he was unable to remember anything from the final ten minutes of the game. On the sideline, Buoniconti turned to his backup, Bob Matheson, and asked if the score was still 10–3. Matheson responded dryly that the Cowboys had scored 24 points. Now Buoniconti's teammates were muddling about the locker room in their own discombobulated haze. Larry Csonka, the team's star runner and eternal talent, sat still in front of his locker. He lost a fumble during the contest—his first all season—and wrongly blamed himself for losing the game. Teammates approached him to speak. He said nothing, barely raising his head.

Defensive line coach Mike Scarry looked around and noticed a roomful of men who were almost zombies. There was a great stillness and it went on for five minutes. Then ten. Fifteen. It seemed like an eternity to him. Finally, someone took some tape off. Still, nothing was said.

Shula entered, and the heavy doors closed behind him with a distinctive shudder. He initially walked into the room standing tall. It was an attempt to project calm and confidence. On his march to the locker room, through the concrete bowels of Tulane Stadium, Shula had wondered what he would say to his team, which had just been so humiliated.

Shula's square jaw and handsome profile, right out of Hollywood central casting, was normally stern, and his expressions predictable. It was a face that projected authority and radiated uncompromising discipline. Once, Shula threw offensive lineman Jim Langer out of practice for running the wrong way on a sweep, doing so without guilt or second-guessing. Now Shula appeared not stern but haggard. His normally neat black hair was tossed to the side. He was sweating and his face was flushed, as if it had just encountered frigid air or a sudden collision. Toward the end of the game, with the clock winding down to zero, he'd stood on the sideline and bit his bottom lip securely as the thick white collar of his dress shirt squeezed around his neck.

This was unexplored country for Shula. He had lost games, of course. Hell, he'd even lost Super Bowls. His previous coaching job with Baltimore ended with a historic—and singularly painful—defeat to Joe Namath's Jets in Super Bowl III. It was the most crushing loss of Shula's career. But that game was at least close. This was an ugly blowout. The Dolphins were the first team in Super Bowl history not to score a single touchdown.

Many in that room remember differently Shula's first words to them after losing Super Bowl VI that night to the Cowboys. The heavy weight of time on memory has taken its toll, but one overwhelming sentiment shared by all about Shula's message was that it focused on something players at the moment didn't want to do: remember the loss.

"We all hurt right now," Shula said, standing before the team. "It's painful. It stings. But I don't want you to forget how this feels. Take it with you everywhere. Remember it now and when you leave here. Remember it when you go home. Remember it when you start training again. Remember it next season. Remember it so when we get back to the Super Bowl next year, the highs of winning it will feel even greater.

"I want all of you to remember how we feel right now and I don't ever want to feel this way again."

Shula pointed toward the locker room entrance. The press would be storming in at any moment. "They're going to open that door and we're going to be tested," Shula said. Paraphrasing Abraham Lincoln, he continued: "If we turn on each other, we become a house divided. I won't allow that. You shouldn't allow it either. So when they walk through that door, remember we're a team."

Shula ended by making a promise he knew was almost impossible to keep.

"What I'm telling you," Shula said, "is that we'll be back. I can promise you that. We'll be back because we're champions."

Actually, what Shula said was much more than that. What Shula said was somewhat more jarring.

"I don't know if Don remembers this," Csonka says now, "but he actually said in the locker room then, 'We're going to go one game at a time and win every damn game.' That's what he said. He wasn't speaking generally or in clichés. That's an important distinction. He meant: *We're going to win every damn game.*"

Shula had no way of knowing the veracity of his statements to the team as he stood before them in the locker room following the Super Bowl loss to Dallas. Guaranteeing they'd be back to the Super Bowl was risky. If they didn't make it, despite the passage of time, some players might remember Shula's promise and hold him accountable, weakening his position as the team's leader. Parts of Shula himself didn't even believe what he was saying, and he wasn't alone. One player listening to Shula was angry about his lack of playing time and questioned his coach's decision making. "The only time I got off the bench was for kickoffs and the national anthem," complained runner Mercury Morris to reporters immediately after the loss.

Shula should have known the Super Bowl would end strangely

for him since the week began that way. First there had been the call from Nixon. The flight from Florida was delayed because the cargo door on the charter plane wouldn't close. After arriving in New Orleans, Shula had to refute a radio report that star quarterback Bob Griese had broken his arm during practice. Still, Shula wasn't worried. By the time the Super Bowl began, Shula expected the Cowboys to see the precision he had methodically instilled in his players, and the city of Miami and all of those passionate fans, indeed the nation, would see just how good his Dolphins team was. Instead, Csonka fumbled a handoff in the first quarter. Instead, Griese was sacked for a 29-yard loss and threw an interception. Nothing had gone right, including Nixon's play suggestion, which fell weakly incomplete early in the game.

Shula himself transformed from a cool sideline presence to an angrier one as the game got out of reach. By the fourth quarter, a furious Shula, bewildered by what he felt were unfair calls by game officials against the Dolphins, started to argue every penalty. Officials warned Shula to be quiet, but he refused. One penalty in particular set him off, and Shula screamed so loudly it stunned coaches and players standing nearby.

"If you open your mouth one more time it's going to cost you," the official told Shula.

Shula didn't want to make things any worse, so he said nothing further to the official. He did notice one of Miami's defensive players was out of position, so Shula yelled to the player, "Hey, you dummy, move over." The official thought Shula was talking to him and penalized Shula. That was the kind of day the Dolphins were having.

Shula had worked tirelessly in preparing for the game but he had been outsmarted by Tom Landry. Outsmarted . . . that is a sentiment that would never be said about Shula ever again.

Landry had studied every piece of film on the Dolphins and devised a daring plan. It was a defense designed to remove Miami's receiving threats, mainly Warfield. Cowboys defensive backs would squeeze the two players on their favorite routes, shutting the routes down and giving them a chance to intercept Griese. It worked, as the Dolphins' passing offense struggled and Griese was under fire all night. "We also got Larry Csonka to fumble a couple of times, something he had not done in the previous year or two," remembered Dallas middle linebacker Lee Roy Jordan in the Peter Golenbock book *Cowboys Have Always Been My Heroes*. "And Bob Lilly, George Andrie, Pat Toomay, and the guys put a lot of pressure on Griese. I remember one play they trapped him thirty yards downfield. He ran one way, and we had three guys, Bob, Larry Cole, and another guy, chasing him, and he turned one way and couldn't get away, and so he turned back the other way, and he ended up thirty yards downfield."

"Against the Dolphins, Tom used the KISS theory: Keep It Simple, Stupid," Cowboys cornerback Mel Renfro recalled in the book. "He let us play football. We knew we had to eliminate Warfield. We had good talent at linebacker, so we could control their tight end, which allowed us to double their wide receivers. And Bob Lilly and the rest of them were all over Bob Griese all day. That was the key to defense."

The Miami postgame locker room was opened to the press after the defeat. Several cameras surrounded Griese, their lights making the glaze over his eyes more pronounced. Griese did something he rarely does and it demonstrated the magnitude of the loss as much as anything. Cameras rolling, Griese cursed. "This is a damn disappointing way to end a successful year," he said.

Shula started talking slowly to the writers. He raised his head high, but the shock was still like a heavy stone on his neck. "What's so sad is for a bunch of ballplayers to come this far," Shula explained, "so many sacrifices, so much sweat, so many great games, and then . . ." Shula's voice trailed momentarily, but suddenly it was back as if Shula realized he was displaying a public moment of weakness. " . . . to have it end like this."

When Shula was done speaking, one of the coaching assistants whispered in his ear that Morris was complaining about him to the press. While most of the other players sulked at their lockers, Morris had taken a chair, moved it to the middle of the room, and sat down with his arms crossed, knowing the constant flow of reporters would see him and stop to ask questions. Shula bit his lip and his face flushed. He was angrier at that moment than he had been on the field arguing with the game official. It was, in fact, the angriest Shula had been for some time, maybe years. Morris was publicly questioning Shula's coaching acumen only moments after a nasty Super Bowl loss. It was a personal attack at an inappropriate time. Morris's outburst was actually a continuation of what had started on the sideline during the final minutes of the game. Angry over his lack of use, Morris began kicking over tables, the drinks on top of them crashing to the floor.

When a second wave of reporters started asking Shula about the game, he ignored their questions and marched to the other side of the locker room, where Morris was still ripping Shula to shreds. Reporters knew something was wrong and followed. When Shula reached Morris, a group of reporters formed a small circle to see what would happen next.

Shula stood inches from Morris's face and their eyes met. Shula motioned to one side, signaling Morris to end his impromptu press conference and step toward a less occupied portion of the room and out of earshot of the writers.

"If you have anything to say about me," Shula told Morris, "you should say it to me first."

Morris was left temporarily speechless by Shula's blend of fury and bluntness. Morris said nothing back.

"Come to my hotel room tomorrow morning," Shula told him. "Be there by ten."

It wasn't the first time Shula was angered over one of his player's public words. As coach of the Colts, Shula became infuriated when running back Alex Hawkins vented to a reporter about his lack of playing time after Baltimore's 38–7 victory over Washington. The following morning, when the story appeared, Shula summoned Hawkins to his office. Shula started the conversation by pointing to the newspapers that contained Hawkins's off-the-record complaints that the reporter put on the record. "Is this your shit?" Shula asked.

"Yes," Hawkins said, "he wasn't supposed to have printed it, but those are my words." Credit went to Hawkins for taking his share of the blame. Shula was nevertheless unimpressed.

"Well, you asshole, we've got a good thing going and you try to screw it up with shit like this," Shula said. He was getting angrier by the second.

"He wasn't supposed to print that—" Hawkins said.

"What you're doing is second-guessing my decision and I won't have it," Shula said, now screaming. "Now get your ass out of here. I don't want to see you any more today. From now on, keep your mouth shut."

Shula didn't tolerate what he saw as disloyalty and someone undermining his authority. Years later, he'd see the actions of Morris in a similar light. Morris was indeed wrong to air his complaints publicly, but he was correct in one thing: Shula had erred. The Cowboys' linebackers were talented and had enough speed to track Csonka or halfback Jim Kiick, but Morris attacking the edges would have presented a challenge. Even the Cowboys wondered why Morris wasn't in the game more. "Our whole game was to stop the running game and Paul Warfield," remembered Dallas defensive back Cornell Green. "If they were going to beat us, they were going to beat us with Howard Twilley and Marv Fleming. They weren't going to beat us with Warfield, Jim Kiick, or Csonka. We geared up for Mercury, and Mercury Morris did not play in that whole game, and that was a blessing. 'Cause Chuck Howley could catch Kiick. If Mercury got in the game, that was going to be tough. I have no idea why Shula didn't play Mercury more. I don't know what Mercury did to piss Shula off. I wish I did."

Morris had not yet earned Shula's trust. Kiick and Csonka had. Shula wasn't going to hand the football to Morris if he didn't believe Morris had earned the right to carry it.

The owner of the team, Joe Robbie, stood in the back of the room weeping. Tears stained his black-rimmed eyeglasses. A television reporter put a microphone in front of Robbie. The light from the camera illuminated his smallish face. "I can't express how proud I am of this team . . ." he said. "It is unique. It will be here again." Robbie turned and walked away. Nearby, reporters gathered at the locker of Twilley, who gazed in the direction of Griese. "This is one of the few times that I'm glad I'm not the quarterback," he said.

It had been a massive buildup for the Dolphins players, who felt confident they would beat Dallas. The city of Miami had been equally excited. Some fans thought they'd never see the day. Some longtime black residents wondered what would come first: a Dolphins Super Bowl title or integration to Dade County. Both had been stubbornly elusive over time. The week the Dolphins prepared to play the Cowboys, a countywide integration plan was announced for all Dade schools. Some thirty-three thousand students were to be bused over the coming three to five years using 173 new buses. Reactions to the plan began to spread across Miami, and some of it was angry. The NFL's release of tickets for Dolphins fans didn't cause the same kind of visceral reaction, but it was still uncomfortable. The NFL allotted the Cowboys and Dolphins ten thousand tickets each to sell to fans. Miami fans gobbled up the tickets in just several hours, causing anger among the fans who didn't get the chance to purchase any. Some went to the Dolphins' downtown offices and protested. About forty staged a sit-in and demanded an apology from Robbie. "Two, four, six, eight—open up the stinking gate," some chanted. A small group of police kept order, including one officer who successfully chased down a man who had snatched two tickets from the hand of another fan and tried to run. He was tackled a short distance away.

Airlines added scores of extra flights to New Orleans, and, as you'd expect, Miami politicians jumped on the Dolphin bandwagon. Speaking at a prayer breakfast in West Palm Beach, the governor of Florida, Reubin Askew, read an unusual Bible quote to the group. Askew was considered a new politician for the South, and his support for the Dolphins was one way of connecting with a more modern constituency. He championed school desegregation and appointed women and blacks to key political and even judicial appointments. He also had a nice sense of humor, as was evident when he spoke at the breakfast. "You Dolphins and all water creatures," he read, "bless the Lord and exalt Him above all, forever."

"Nowhere," the governor explained, "do I find mention of Cowboys."

The letdown was devastating for all—a city and a team. Defensive lineman Manny Fernandez quietly escaped the gloomy locker room and walked alone to the team bus. Fernandez was one of the toughest men not just on the Miami team but in the entire NFL. He sported woolly sideburns that ran uncontrolled down to his chin. His neck resembled the middle portion of a fire hydrant. Fernandez played through numerous painful injuries, his body sometimes a network of slings, braces, and stitches. He'd play one season with no ligaments in a shoulder, torn cartilage in his knee, bone chips, and a deteriorating femur.

Fernandez also had no problem throwing punches when warranted. In 1974, after a brutal title game loss at Oakland, a drunken Raiders fan sprinted onto the field and sucker punched Buoniconti in the stomach before trying to run away. Fernandez saw it, and as the fan attempted to escape, he used his left elbow to smash the fan in the face. The elbow was followed by a right cross. If Fernandez hadn't been pulled away by a game official, he might have killed the man. "If Manny was ticked off, he hit people," Csonka remembered. "Friend or foe, he hit people if you made him angry."

Nonetheless, when his bus reached the hotel a short distance away from the stadium, Fernandez slowly exited as he had done many times before, but this time he stopped in front of a small car and his hulking frame slumped onto the tiny front bumper. Fernandez began to sob. He couldn't stop. This went on for several minutes. The reality of the moment finally breached his controlled, fierce demeanor.

The outside world wasn't helping either. The Dolphins weren't seen as being beaten by a better team. They were viewed as losers. There was a significant difference. "Super Bubble Bursts" read the *Miami Herald* newspaper on its front page. When the Dolphins' plane arrived at Miami International Airport just before eight that night, a fraction of the expected thirty thousand fans—some two thousand—were there to greet them. Shula left the Eastern Airlines jet first and waved timidly.

"To get to the Super Bowl and then get beaten so soundly, just without a doubt—what a humiliation," remembered linebacker Doug Swift in a book years later. "I don't think I've ever been more humiliated or depressed or just totally disconsolate after having played a ball game as I was that one. And that's the stuff you just never forget. So we had a lot to show, a lot to make up for . . . When you do things when you lose or when you make a mistake, [it's] sort of the way football is taught in practice. You just feel miserable for it. You just are very cruel to yourself, you're tough on yourself. I say cruel—you're tough on yourself to the point of cruelty."

Yet something started to occur. Shula's instructions not to forget what happened began to take root only a short time after the game. This theme didn't crystallize organically; Shula had smartly planted the idea in the heads of his players that making a return to the Super Bowl wasn't just talk—it was a requirement to make them whole men again. No, the notion didn't happen naturally, but it did happen with amazing speed. Cornerback Tim Foley found a snapshot of the final scoreboard—DALLAS 24–MIAMI 3—and taped it to his locker, where it stayed all the following season. He purposely glanced at it daily throughout that next year. Buoniconti read a quotation in a post–Super Bowl article and became infuriated. He chopped out the quote, underlined it with a yellow magic marker, and hung it on the bulletin board for all his Miami teammates to see. It was from Dallas player Cornell Green: "The difference between the Miami Dolphins and the Dallas Cowboys was that Miami was just happy to be in the game and Dallas came to win the game." Green was challenging Miami's toughness.

In football, there are few bigger insults.

CHAPTER TWO

TRUCE

The morning after.

The parking lot outside of the Miami team motel, the Fontaine-bleau Hotel, was quiet. The Dolphins were scheduled to leave New Orleans later in the day. The scene looked normal except the rental cars belonging to four members of the Dolphins organization were partially covered in garbage, empty cans on their side, their contents spilled across the hoods and windshields. Cowboys fans at work. Some of the cars had messages written in soap on the windshields. DOLPHINS NO. 2, one read. Inside suite 3D Shula's six-year-old son, Mike, cradled a soft pass from his dad, the football landing in his cupped hands. Mike then accidentally slammed into a thick cabinet, bounced off, and immediately got back up. He survived the collision unscathed and undeterred, but Shula still shifted the cabinet's position to better protect his son's hard head as well as the cabinet itself. "Here, we better move that," Shula said. "We'll push it flat against the wall. That way you won't bounce it around when you hit it." Shula returned to his comfortable chair. "Hut," he said. Mike scurried across the tan carpet, and Shula tossed a perfect down-and-in—the kind of pass Griese had such a difficult time completing only hours earlier.

The Shulas were close, and at home, Don was a progressive husband and father who listened intently to what Dorothy had to say even when it was difficult to hear. Dorothy was loyal and understanding and had come full circle in grasping what it was like to be a coach's wife. Earlier in their marriage, as Shula climbed the coaching ladder and spent more time away from home—many hours, in fact, with practices, games, travel, and film study—there was great frustration from Dorothy. "The first five years, I was almost envious of my husband," she once said. "I was tied down with babies. He did try to include me, but he was trying to prove himself as a head football coach. I felt football was getting more attention than I was. And when he came home, instead of letting him relax, I unloaded all of my problems. I had three in diapers at a time and he had all the glory, it seemed.

"I used to hate it," she said. "I was so alone. It's a very lonesome job, being a coach's wife."

Shula once told her, "You know, I think you're jealous."

"Maybe I am," she replied.

They reached a détente where Shula wouldn't talk football with her and she would be more understanding of his stresses, though Dorothy's occasional playful jabs at her husband would continue. "He won't smile," she explained in a 1973 interview. "He's afraid that iron jaw will break. He thinks laughing will hurt his image. It's the same with dancing. He's a good dancer, but someone might see him do it."

Dorothy was there for one of Shula's worst moments, another Super Bowl loss. She was almost as shocked as he was at the outcome, because she knew how hard Shula had prepared for the game. Indeed, the entire coaching staff remained stunned at the outcome, the chill of the morning air doing little to remove the pit in their stomachs. For a few Miami coaches, the sick feeling would last for weeks and even months. The five cans of game film remained unopened and stacked in a corner of the team facility. To some, they were a reminder of failure. "There they lie, like a contaminated corpse," offensive coordinator Howard Schnellenberger, often with smoking pipe in hand, would say.

Shula had his meeting with Morris. When Morris entered the room, he was less defiant than he'd been the night before. Shula's anger had subsided as well. The truth was, Shula needed Morris, and Shula knew it. He had to convince Morris that his way was the right way, and the process of persuading Morris would start now in this odd little hotel after a public and painful loss.

Morris pleaded with Shula that he wanted his playing time to increase and sheepishly apologized for his outburst. Shula accepted the apology and asked Morris to listen closely.

"If I bring you back next season—and right now there isn't any reason why I don't think you'll be back—the thing I want to do is find out whether or not you are capable of being a play in, play out full-time player." Shula was concerned Morris's slight build and injury problems would prevent Shula from allowing him increased playing time. Morris had suffered a hemorrhaged thigh one year and a severe ankle sprain in another—and Shula still wasn't certain if those were anomalies or if Morris was injury-prone.

Morris should have known a conversation like this was coming. Shula's uncertainty when it came to Morris was partly unfair but also partly the fault of Morris. He'd sum up at least a portion of the problem some of the Dolphins had with him this way in his autobiography: "I know my lifestyle while I was with the Dolphins had rubbed some people the wrong way. I had really enjoyed being a cocky son of a bitch. I drove fast cars. I dated the prettiest women I could find. And I always said what was on my mind. That if Shula had played me in Super Bowl VI we'd have beaten the Cowboys. That I should be starting in the backfield with Csonka because I was better than Kiick. That a state of de facto segregation existed in the Dolphins locker room." What Shula and others on the team wondered was between Morris's extracurricular activities and his jawing, how much did he care about football?

But at the time of his talk with Shula, Morris was nonetheless perplexed about Shula's attitude toward him. Morris thought of himself as someone who could carry a house up a thousand hills. Csonka was bigger at 6-3 and 235 pounds; Morris was 5-10 and 190. The difference was Csonka did his damage to defenders after gathering a full head of steam. He was a runaway beast at full speed between the tackles. Morris, however, could be just as powerful. Morris did his damage while building momentum and attacking the edges. His thighs were weaponized against even helmeted heads. "Mercury Morris had tremendous power even before accelerating," Ralph Cindrich, a former NFL linebacker who competed often against the Dolphins, once said. "If you hit his legs before he even got going hard, you felt it." Morris also prided himself on staying in superhuman condition. In the physical tests administered by coaches, Morris could routinely do 150 push-ups straight, more than any other player on the team. No Dolphin could match his 420-pound bench press either. Part of that drive to be the best began at a young age. When Morris was ten years old, he went to a local junkyard near his family's home, spotted a truck with a loose axle, and moved the axle to his house, where he converted it into a barbell.

Despite all that, Shula still wasn't sure. Morris would have to show him. It was Shula's way. Players were constantly under observation and being tested, like astronauts preparing for a moon launch. How they responded to this probing was an indication of their mental and physical toughness.

Shula already had some concerns long before the Morris outburst. He'd drive up Shula's blood pressure by lining up in the wrong spot on some formations. Shula also remembered a scene from a year earlier in a game against New Orleans, when Morris fumbled three times. There was the moment against San Francisco when, after Morris fumbled, he removed his helmet and threw it a solid 20 yards. Shula wasn't the only one worried. Some teammates had their questions as well. A few wondered about his toughness and whether some of his injuries were real or if Morris was milking them to get time off during practice. The reality was much of that talk was false. Teammate Norm Evans once saw doctors examining Morris's knees. The physician took out a tape and measured the healthy knee versus the injured one, and the ailing knee was 1.5 inches smaller. It had atrophied because of cartilage damage. Evans never again wondered about Morris's toughness after witnessing that scene.

Morris was just *different*. He didn't fit the mold of the alleged robotic NFL player. Morris did his own thing and didn't care what the NFL world thought. It was actually a brave position, since most players then didn't question authority. Morris also didn't care about protocol. A few years later, at the 1973 Pro Bowl, he'd meet the legendary defensive back Willie Brown, who played for the rival Oakland Raiders. Brown wore his trademark black armbands that fit snuggly across his forearms. Morris saw the armbands and liked them immediately. "Willie," he said, "can I have those armbands?" Brown didn't hesitate. He removed the armbands. "Here you go," he said to Morris. Morris wore the armbands the rest of his career and it didn't matter that they belonged to one of Miami's rivals.

No, some players weren't sure what to make of Morris initially, but like Shula, they realized there was great potential. Teammate Larry Little used to tease Morris, but behind the playful taunting was an attempt to show Morris the meaning of being a true professional as well as the trappings. On every team flight, Shula had the team leaders sit in the front of the plane, and on every flight, Little would ask Morris to come to the front, where he'd put his arm around the runner. "Now, Merc, I just wanted you to see this," Little would say. "This is what's known as 'first class.'"

Shula's evaluation of Morris was ongoing, but he was slowly becoming a Morris convert despite his past misgivings. By the time the ten-minute meeting was over, Shula had convinced Morris he needed Shula while all the while Morris had no idea Shula was slowly becoming convinced he needed Morris. Shula's instincts, almost all the time, were correct. This would be no different despite rumors in the media that Morris would be traded ("Morris is supposedly headed to Kansas City," wrote the *Miami Herald*). Shula's use of Morris as a starter would become one of the most significant personnel maneuvers in NFL history. Before the upcoming 1972 season, Morris never had more than 60 carries in a single year. That would change under Shula, who entrusted Morris with 190 carries for 1,000 yards and 12 touchdowns. Morris and Csonka would become the first tandem in league history to each gain more than 1,000 yards in a single season. Yes, Shula was right once again.

The morning after. Between his meetings with irritated players and watching his son attack hotel furniture, the game replayed inside Shula's mind. The questions came and went. The number of second-guesses, big and small, that confound a football coach. Shula thought back to strategy and preparation. Were the right plays called? The correct defenses? Did he push them too hard in the weeks before? Too little? Shula grasped for anything. He even thought back to a team dinner from the night before the game. Shula broke from routine and had the players—as well as wives and girlfriends—dine at a restaurant near the team hotel. Normally, the players had a snack of sandwiches and fruit at 9:30 P.M. followed by bed check at 11:30, but Shula decided a change might be good. The problem, Shula thought in retrospect, was that during the team's eight-game regular-season winning streak that propelled them to playoffs and then the Super Bowl, Shula kept the same routine. Every game, every week, every day. In football, many times, routine equals life, and Shula had violated this superstitious, if not mythical, edict.

The morning after . . . Shula initially found it difficult to get out of bed. Dorothy told him it would be okay. The day wore on, and he started to believe her. And as young Mike bounced off the freshly moved furniture and scurried across the hotel floor, and as Morris had been calmed and seemingly convinced, hope was returning, Shula began thinking about what he told his players after the game: The Dolphins would be back in the Super Bowl. Shula started to ponder the chances. His mind moved quickly. The plotting began.

One thousand miles away, shifting back and forth in his brown leather chair at the White House, the president had Shula on his mind. After the horrific Super Bowl loss, Nixon felt compelled to reach out to a man he now considered his friend. Nixon sat in the Oval Office, his desk area immaculate. A small notebook sat alone near a tall black pen standing in its holder. Behind Nixon was a bust of Lincoln situated near a picture of Nixon's family and two dimly lit lamps. The American flag was just behind Nixon's right shoulder.

He began the taped dictation of this compassionate note to Shula, a moment of tenderness that eluded much of Nixon's presidency and person, with two simple words: "Dear Don."

"I know how disappointing it must be to you and members of your fine team to have this season end on such a disappointing note." Nixon paused, and the loud sound of his weight shifting in a creaking chair echoed throughout the Oval Office. Nixon cleared his throat, shifted some more, and continued. "You can take a great deal of pride, however, in the fact that you brought the young Dolphin team to the very heights of pro football competition."

Nixon took a longer pause of almost 40 seconds. There seemed to be a trace of emotion but also a gathering of thoughts. As Nixon dictated, it was becoming strikingly clear he felt personally invested in Shula and the Dolphins. His words weren't like those of a president with an ego-driven interest. They were more like a grandfather watching a child slowly stand after a nasty fall. While the football world and much of America saw Shula and his Dolphins as failures, likely to never be heard from again, the president of the United States was one of the few men on the planet who believed otherwise. Nixon ended his dictation on a hopeful note a matter of hours after Shula's Super Bowl loss and five months before the break-in of the Democratic headquarters at the Watergate Hotel in Washington. The date of Nixon's dictation was Monday, January 17.

Nixon finished: "And I would not want to be on the other team the next time your young Miami players have another shot at the Super Bowl. Regards, Richard."

CHAPTER THREE

THE START OF REDEMPTION

The summer was spent thinking about the past. The recent past. Every weight lifted, every sprint, every workout—it was all dedicated to correcting it. The off-season was a quiet march toward fixing what many Dolphins felt was an embarrassing moment in the biggest game of their lives. The Super Bowl loss didn't truly represent the kind of players they were. "Everyone has had those times in their lives when something bad happened professionally and it didn't really represent their true ability," said Csonka. "It was an off day but it didn't represent you. That was us as a team. Except our bad moment happened in the Super Bowl with millions of people watching."

So they worked to correct a wrong. That's how they saw it. There were some in football who believed the Dolphins just weren't good enough and their Super Bowl run was a fluke. Reading this or hearing it only made Miami players angrier and Shula more relentless.

Shula was stern as he stood at the front of Miami's meeting room on the first day of training camp some six months after the Super Bowl debacle. No eye wavered. No one's attention wandered. Every player listened intently to Shula's opening message. They needed to know what he would say. No one would be disappointed.

"We won ten games in each of the past two years," Shula began. "In 1970, we went to the first round of the AFC playoffs. Last year, we won the AFC title and made it all the way to the Super Bowl. How many of you guys thought last year was a success?"

Shula waited for a response, knowing none would come. The pain from the Super Bowl loss was still firmly planted in the team's posterior. No one was eager to discuss it, let alone pat himself on the back for just getting there. Quite the contrary. The memory made most players want to vomit.

Shula waited for the silence to pass. "So, none of you?" he asked. "That's good, because last year wasn't a success. There is only one thing that counts in professional football and that is winning the Super Bowl. The rest of it means nothing. Absolutely nothing. If you don't win the Super Bowl, you're nothing but an also-ran, just like the team that finishes in last place. Well, this year will be different. This year we'll be successful. By that, gentlemen, I mean that we will win the Super Bowl."

The first game of the 1972 season started as it usually did with Kiick and Csonka. It also started with an insult. The Dolphins were at Kansas City for the season opener—the first game ever played at the new Arrowhead Stadium—and Shula walked into the Miami locker room with a newspaper clipping in hand. He posted it in the center of the room and players, in small groups, and sometimes individually, approached to read it. It was a quote from the coach of the Dolphins' Super Bowl nemesis, Tom Landry, in a Dallas newspaper. "It's only four months since the Super Bowl," Landry said, "but I can't remember the names of the Miami front line."

Arrowhead was spanking new and considered extravagantly priced at $51 million. Not all of the Kansas City players were impressed. Quarterback Len Dawson was asked the difference between the old and new stadium: "It means that now you can get booed by eighty thousand instead of fifty thousand."

In football, in Shula's time, excellence didn't come with a forewarning. Or a tap on the shoulder. Or suspenseful music. There were no power rankings. Quite often, greatness began immersed in intense heat on a practice field. Because of Shula's relentless preseason practices in the Florida humidity, the Dolphins were far more prepared than Kansas City players when they filed onto the Arrowhead Stadium turf, which was a stifling 110 degrees at kickoff. Practicing in the heat hadn't just armored the Dolphins more than most of their opponents, but they had also learned coping mechanisms unfamiliar to other teams. Shula allowed the players to soak their feet in trays of ice water along the sidelines during games. All these things—the heat toughness, the cooling strategies—allowed the Dolphins to physically and mentally outlast any opponent. To the Chiefs, the heat was like playing a second opponent simultaneously. To the Dolphins, it was no different from one of Shula's brutal practices back in Florida. They were so accustomed to the extreme heat that players joked about how they were ready to play a scrimmage on the surface of the sun. Kansas City wasn't so hot it could warm a solar system, but the difference in conditioning levels became quickly evident. The Dolphins jumped to a 20–0 lead, and as the game went on, they seemed to get more energy as the Chiefs became drained.

The Chiefs also became frustrated. The Miami secondary had

surprisingly but stunningly stopped what was a skilled receiving corps of Otis Taylor and Elmo Wright. Dawson had been blitzed and harassed and was unable to pass deep until late in the second half when the game was out of hand. Taylor became so agitated with the tight coverage that he punched one of the Miami linebackers, Doug Swift, in the face. Swift was wearing a birdcage-style facemask, so all Taylor did was injure his own hand with the punch. He was thrown from the game.

Miami's was a powerful display of force. It was clear the Dolphins had gotten even better than the last time they faced, and beat, the Chiefs the previous season in what would stand as the longest game ever played in professional football history. Kansas City runner Ed Podolak was the star in the first game, but in the rematch, his fumble led to Miami's first score. Wide receiver Marlin Briscoe scored on a 14-yard reception, kicker Garo Yepremian added two field goals, Csonka scored, and the rout was on.

It was Shula's move with Morris and Kiick that was the most discussed part of the afternoon by the press and players. Shula had inserted Morris into what had been, up until that game, a Csonka-Kiick backfield. The move worked brilliantly. Csonka was, well, Csonka. He brutalized the Kansas City defense for 118 yards rushing, but when Morris ran on the edges, using his speed to get past slower defensive linemen and linebackers, not only did Shula know the move worked, but many on the team, even those loyal to Kiick, knew it as well. He gave the Dolphins a speed dimension they didn't previously possess. Morris finished with 67 yards and had similar statistics in the second and third games of the season. Shula's system, mocked around the league initially, was now being studied and copied. Teams wanted their own Csonka and Morris, though it was clear there were few Morrises out there and only one Csonka.

"Everything is O.K. in Kansas City except the Chiefs," wrote the *New York Times*. "Opening the season in their magnificent new stadium, Arrowhead, before 79,829, the Chiefs were beaten thoroughly today by the Miami Dolphins, 20–10, who were an alive, aggressive football team. These were the teams which last Christmas Day played the longest game in pro football history, 82 minutes. Today's game was in regulation time; it merely seemed like the longest game."

The aftermath of the Kansas City game took its physical toll on some of the Dolphins, and not because of the Chiefs players. Running and hitting on the new artificial turf was like playing on concrete covered by a thin layer of carpet. Dolphins safety Jake Scott jammed his big toe so badly while making a cut on the surface that, several days later, doctors had to drill two small holes into the toe to relieve the pressure so he could get ready for Houston.

Shula would have a difficult time getting the Dolphins to believe the Oilers were an equal match for them. Houston had been average in the preseason with a 2-3-1 record and had been beaten 30–17 by Denver in the first game of the regular season. Still, Shula did everything possible to make sure his team wasn't overly confident. In one of the first addresses to the team that week, Shula emphasized how cockiness could kill the team. "Don't think because you beat Kansas City you can beat the world," he told the players. "This is how good teams prove themselves after a big win. Good teams don't let down. All right, Houston had problems in the preseason"—an understatement that made Shula's selling job more difficult, yet he continued undaunted—"but they are a very physical team, and they have got a young quarterback, name of Dan Pastorini, capable of being All-League when he finds out how good he is. Make sure he doesn't find out against us."

Shula should have known few players would become complacent under him. If so, they'd only need to search their memories. No Dolphins player was untouched by Shula's coaching bluntness, and if they were ever feeling superior, they knew Shula would be right there to remind them they weren't infallible. The season before, offensive guard Bob Kuechenberg stalled a drive because of his holding penalty. There was also an illegal man downfield flag called on him. After the game, and in front of the entire team, Shula blasted Kuechenberg. "You're on your way to qualifying for the Hall of Shame," Shula yelled. Shula then compared Kuechenberg to a former Colts player who Shula claimed cost Baltimore 5,000 yards and 27 touchdowns because of penalties. No, few players became overconfident under Shula.

The game was played in a harsh and driving rain on the slippery—and extremely dangerous—new PolyTurf surface. It was a merciless concoction of artificial grass and asphalt subsurface that wrecked knees and ended careers. PolyTurf was to some football players what a tar pit was to a T. rex. When PolyTurf became wet, playing on it was like trying to run in a bathtub. The Dolphins would learn the tricks of running on the frightful material (simply by practicing and playing on it) while other teams struggled. Miami pummeled Houston for 274 rushing yards. Csonka, Morris, and Kiick scored an impressive total of 4 touchdowns. Each player, with a different running style, taking turns shredding the Oilers. Shula's idea of a three-back system continued to work.

Pastorini would burn Miami late in the game with an 82-yard touchdown, but overall players would heed Shula's warning. The Dolphins set a team record with 17 rushing first downs. After the Oilers' loss, Houston's coach, in a truthful assessment of his team, said afterward: "I don't think we'll win one game the rest of the year." He was wrong. They did win one, and it was the sole victory of the year as the team finished 1-13.

After week two there were five unbeaten and untied teams in the NFL.

The hit on Bob Griese came hard and fast. Minnesota defensive lineman Bob Lurtsema, all 250 pounds of him, slammed into Griese seconds after Griese had thrown a pass. Griese wasn't seriously injured, but the game official had been watching closely and penalized the Vikings 15 yards for roughing the passer. "My momentum had carried me into Griese, who was falling down," Lurtsema would say after the game. "I've made plays like that for six years and nobody ever called me before."

It wasn't a crucial penalty, but it was one of those plays. One of many that season; the small plays, the ones that moved the football and set up the larger ones. The plays required to win, to go perfect. There were others in the third game against Minnesota, including a 14-yard sweep by Morris as part of the three-play sequence that led to a Miami scoring drive and come-from-behind win. But the game was significant for another reason. Yepremian made a 51-yard field goal, again proving his worth to Shula and his teammates. Yepremian's nickname was "Keebler" because he reminded some players of the Kellogg cookie elves, and indeed, his kicks were so accurate it seemed there was some magic at work. He was critical to the Dolphins more so than generally acknowledged at the time. Shula's plan was to rely on his running game and defense, keeping the number of Miami mistakes low and those of the opponents high, as well as the score low, and, if needed, he had a good kicker to win games for him. Yepremian certainly filled the last part of the Shula requirement.

The Minnesota game showed two other facets of the Dolphins. The Vikings had shut down the Miami running attack that had dominated and would later conquer the NFL. Griese took control of the game, showing that when he needed to, he could. Griese didn't always just hand the ball off to Csonka. He could be deadly accurate and at times even prolific when needed. Against Minnesota, two of his passes were perfectly thrown to Twilley, leading to a score. "The club came from behind," Shula said after the game. "When we had to get it, we got it, which gives us faith in the future."

Miami was now 3-0, the only undefeated team in football.

CHAPTER FOUR

THE THREE WISE MEN

The Miami of the 1970s was superficially tranquil. The city had not yet been *Miami Vice*'d. People commuted to work, kids went to school, shops pushed their wares. The Nixon family sold two Miami homes and moved on. A confidant of Nixon's, Bebe Rebozo, stayed in Key Biscayne and was elected president of the local chamber of commerce. The CIA had begun to scale back its once extensive efforts to destroy the Cuban government. Tourism bloomed.

The appearance was deceptive. Cocaine began to flow through the city and, as a result, the violence began to simmer. The U.S. Drug Enforcement Administration said the drug sales were extensive. Battles among distributors grew. So did the numbers of murders. It wasn't unusual for a *Miami Herald* editor, staring eastward over Biscayne Bay, the skylines and weekend regattas visible over the water, to spot dead bodies floating adrift.

Drug kingpins looked for ways to launder their money and used legitimate businesses as a front. Other smugglers tried to hide their money in more old-school ways. A Colombian man was arrested with ten cashier's checks in his shoe worth $500,000 each.

As the city became more brown and Cubans more insular—except for the Cuban-Americans for Nixon campaign organizers—whites fled. It was a great irony for the Dolphins. As they began a trek toward unity, much of it racial, the city around them became more segregated.

The drug violence wasn't the only violence. The Coconut Grove Rapist surfaced in 1971. He carried a homemade rape kit that held a wig, a can of Mace, a starter pistol, masks, towels, lubricants, and spermicidal jelly. He sported a purple leotard and leopard-skin cape and committed a startling number of double rapes on mothers and daughters, sisters, and roommates.

Miami has long been a city whose true core has been mostly obscured from public view, sometimes literally. "The general wildness, the eternal labyrinths of waters and marshes, interlocked, and apparently never ending; the whole surrounded by interminable swamps . . . Here I am in the Floridas, thought I," wrote John James Audubon to the editor of the *Monthly American Journal of Geology and Natural Science* during an 1831 expedition into what was then called the Floridas.

Miami's reputation for the subcutaneous was still intact more than a century later. The city emerged in the 1960s as the point around which conflict swirled because of America's Cold War with the Soviet Union and Cuba. The failed Bay of Pigs Invasion (and the Cuban Missile Crisis to come) was predictable, considering the rhetoric emerging from both sides just months earlier. "We must attempt to strengthen . . . anti-Castro forces in exile," stated a 1960 John F. Kennedy campaign statement. Three months following Kennedy's ascent to the presidency, his words would become reality when a CIA-trained force of Cuban exiles invaded southern Cuba in an attempt to overthrow Castro. The exiles were beaten in seventy-two hours. The Bay of Pigs cemented Castro as both a leader and a thorn in the side of the United States.

The failed assault didn't stop Miami's emergence as an anti-Castro hub. A series of military training camps was started in the Florida Keys and then later centered on the University of Miami campus. There were so many clandestine anti-Castro American forces in Miami that the CIA Miami base became the largest CIA installation in the world outside of the headquarters in Langley, Virginia.

Declassified documents later showed just how bloated it had become. There were between 300 and 400 case officers stationed at the Miami campus. Each case officer had between 4 to 10 primary agents, and those agents themselves had between 10 to 30 subordinates. This means there were at least 12,000 subordinate agents, with a maximum amount of 120,000. The true number was likely closer to the maximum. One wonders if they were football fans.

The CIA had a modest army in Miami, and it was also equipped with an accompanying navy. It owned a fleet of small ships, many of which were disguised as commercial vessels. One CIA source told the *Miami Herald* the CIA's arsenal of ships was "the third largest navy in the western hemisphere." The CIA also had an air cargo force and numerous safe houses across the city and various waterfronts.

This was Miami in the early 1970s. A city where revolutions were hatched on flotillas, where exiles clashed, and where races lived in a state of material distrust—all against a backdrop of tourists cuddling on the sand, of football, of beaches under a bright sun. Most who came to Miami were unaware of the conflicts. Desegregation came to South Florida at a stubborn trickle even behind other Jim Crow–hardened southern outposts. Well into the 1960s and slightly beyond, blacks did not swim at Dade County beaches. At the Dade County Courthouse, they paid their taxes in a separate window. In some high-end shopping centers, they were allowed to buy the clothing but—alas—could not try the clothing on, and the elevators were for white customers only. Then the riots came: 1968 in Liberty City; 1980 in Miami; 1982 in Overtown.

Stadiums were used for both sports and political games. Jacqueline Kennedy spoke at the Orange Bowl to Bay of Pigs veterans in 1962, lauding their bravery. John Kennedy later did the same. This was the Miami of the embryonic Dolphins, a franchise created in 1966. Much of this political and racial chaos would be the backdrop to the most significant accomplishment in team sports history, the Dolphins' beautiful season. So were the drugs. The drugs.

After Eugene "Mercury" Morris became one of the great comeback stories in sports history. After he changed the Miami Dolphins with his physical grace. After he fumed in the fourth game of a perfect season because Kiick had more carries. After he became a champion. After he dated a white woman in segregated Texas. After he starred in a blaxploitation film. After he did lines of cocaine. After he was a role model—then he wasn't, then he was. *Now he is.* After he was accused of running a drug-dealing operation, though he didn't. After Shula said he deserved forgiveness. After all of that, Morris sat in a prison, rotting. It was the drugs. The drugs.

Morris got his nickname Mercury from a local sports journalist who described his running style as mercurial. As Morris became known in college football as a massive talent playing in a tiny program, the attention grew. *Life* magazine came to West Texas State's campus in 1968 to report on Morris. That was a strange year followed by several more: Charles Evers, a black man, was elected mayor of a Mississippi town; a tragic accident following a night of drinking led to Senator Ted Kennedy's car crash and the death of Mary Jo Kopechne; Neil Armstrong took one small step; there was Woodstock; and American soldiers killed hundreds of women and children in the My Lai Massacre. But 1968 also featured Morris breaking onto the national sports scene, appearing in *Life* magazine in full uniform, wearing small wings on his helmet and feet and sitting on a fiberglass buffalo. The strange photo was an attempt to portray Morris as an unbeatable force sitting atop the football world, his speed the first line of offense. Indeed, Morris would continue to do things differently with little shame or remorse throughout college. There was genuine courage and strong confidence peppered with unfiltered arrogance.

He also defied the backward social norms of the country in general and Canyon, Texas, specifically, where West Texas State was situated. The town of about eight thousand people at the time was located some thirty minutes from Amarillo. Morris knew he was in a different world when he learned the name of the punter's horse. The horse, a deep shade of black, was named Nigger.

The black players were told by friends on campus not to date the white students. Morris didn't listen. It's not that Morris set out to date white women (or ignore them). He simply wasn't going to allow any social "taboos" to dictate his behavior, even if breaking those directives could lead to his lynching (a very real possibility). He met a woman who was literally a pageant queen, and they began to date. She was very beautiful and very white, and Morris was now a step closer to being very dead. Morris was defiant, but his fearlessness would go only so far. The two dated secretly for months until a deputy sheriff saw them kissing in a parked car. A short time later, one of the school's deans asked to speak with Morris in his office

and bluntly suggested that white women should be off-limits because they were trash. "His point seemed to be that any white girl
who would date a black man had to be trash," Morris once stated.
"I ignored him."

After one year of dating, Morris's girlfriend informed her father,
who, despite being married to a Mexican woman, became infuriated over his daughter's interracial relationship. He vowed to shoot
Morris the next time Morris scored a touchdown. Morris ignored
him too.

In between being distracted by horses named after racial epithets
and a father threatening to make appearances at his games, shot-
gun in hand, Morris spent a great deal of time obsessed with O. J.
Simpson, a star at USC at the time. In the world of Morris, he and
Simpson were in a tight race for best runner in football; Simpson
the All-American and Morris the honorable mention. Years later,
Simpson said he knew of Morris and respected him but didn't follow
him closely. That isn't completely true. In a moment of arrogance—
and an indication that Simpson was, after all, aware of Morris—the
USC star running back would make an unusual gesture. One day,
just before his team was to play in the Junior Rose Bowl, Morris
received a letter from Simpson. It was an autographed picture of
Simpson with a note: "Thought you might enjoy this."

Morris saw himself equal in talent with Simpson. That wasn't
exactly correct. Few runners, in college or among the professional
ranks, were close in ability to Simpson. In their final collegiate
seasons, Simpson won the Heisman Trophy while Morris finished
ninth. *So what?* Morris thought. *If I'd gone to USC and Simpson
played football in bumfuck Texas, I'd have won the Heisman too.*

In some instances, the wounds Morris suffered, both minor and
significant, were self-inflicted. This would be another pattern of
Morris as well. During his final days at West Texas State, he de-

cided to throw a cherry bomb into a courtyard where a group of students was watching *The Great Escape*. When the fuse on the firecracker burned far more quickly than Morris anticipated, he hurriedly tried to throw it out the window of the men's restroom he was occupying without first checking to see if the screen was raised. It wasn't. The firecracker bounced off and landed in a nearby toilet before exploding.

Morris's impulsive drive was not always rooted in the trivial. He despised bigotry in all its forms and felt a genuine passion to speak against it whenever the opportunity presented itself. This was the case in Morris's last days in Canyon. He was at a gas station in town refueling his Corvette. He noticed three older black men hovering over the opened hood of their vehicle, which appeared to have engine trouble. The scene was quiet until a group of kids drove through the gas station and yelled, "Hey, nigger." They were addressing the other men, but nonetheless Morris was infuriated. He kept gassing up as the car turned the corner, but then the kids returned, yelling racial slurs at the men again. Morris had heard enough.

As the car with the kids drove away, Morris followed in hot pursuit, and for some reason, they pulled over when he got close. One of the kids in the car recognized Morris and was friendly. Morris realized the irony in the situation. Only minutes earlier, they had called a group of black men "nigger," but they were friendly toward Morris because Morris was a famous football player. To the kids, Morris was a different kind of nigger. He was a respectable nigger.

Morris remembers in his autobiography what happened next this day. He instructed one of the kids to get out of the car and then slapped him in the face three or four times. The kids departed and Morris went home. The next day, he was charged with felony assault and battery.

The complainant stated in court documents that he didn't use a racial slur when addressing the black men with car trouble. He said he yelled: "Hey, Mercury." Morris took a lie detector test to prove he was telling the truth. He passed, and the felony charges were dropped.

That didn't stop Morris from being sued by the young man and his family for $25,000, a great deal of money in the late 1960s. When the civil trial began, Morris looked around the courtroom and saw an all-white jury, a white judge, and a white prosecutor. The only other black person he saw in the courthouse was a member of the janitorial staff. Morris thought he was pretty much doomed, and after hearing some of the testimony, where racial slurs were tossed around like pizza dough, he became disgusted. He left the trial before its conclusion. He didn't care.

A jury awarded Morris's accuser $2,500. He refused to pay it. He never did.

Morris was tough, particularly mentally, and he'd need that toughness to elbow his way into a cemented backfield. Early in the 1972 season, with memories of that Super Bowl loss still fresh in their minds, Kiick and Csonka set the tone for the team's comeback from the Super Bowl loss. Yet Csonka's acts of on-field brutality—both inflicting and enduring—had already transformed him into a legendary figure. Part of the reason why was that infamous Csonka nose. O. J. Simpson had known Csonka for years, since Simpson was nineteen years old, but out of all those memories, a handful stand out. Simpson doesn't recall the year, but it was after a game on his home field in Buffalo. Simpson moved toward Csonka to say hello and Csonka, recognizing Simpson, went toward him. Csonka took off his helmet, and Simpson says he immediately noticed Csonka's nose was askew. It was pointing in an unnatural direction. "Csonka was just talking normally and his nose was bent and there was blood all over his face," Simpson says.

Its various twisted shapes became a symbol of Csonka's indefatigable will and tolerance of pain. The legend began on that Ohio farm when Csonka first shattered his nose following a collision with a shocked bull. Csonka had set a large bucket of water down on the ground near the animal, frightening it, and the result was one of the few times he ever lost a physical contest with another living thing.

Csonka's nose, from that point on, was easily broken, and once he reached the pros, it was shattered so often it became almost a running joke to the Dolphins. Csonka's hard running style meant he was constantly hit hard, his face barely protected by the inadequate face mask of the period. It wasn't unusual for one or two teammates to be hunched over in the huddle only to see Csonka's blood all over their cleats.

Csonka relished his well-earned reputation for toughness, but he was also aware of the business side of the sport—a fact that would come into play just a few years later. For the moment, Csonka looked at football and at his own body, both sometimes causing moments of pause at the extraordinary violence players were enduring. He once had a frank conversation—partly joking, partly not—with a small group of writers early in the 1972 season. "My left leg is turning yellow," he said. "My back is turning blue. Sometimes I wish I'd studied harder in college so I could be a veterinarian and go around patting dogs on the head."

Csonka then became pensive, recalling memories of the physical beatings he'd endured. "What is the single most expendable item in the NFL?" he asked, then paused. "The players. They can run out of a lot of things, but they can always find more players." Csonka was reminded that there were few players in the sport of his caliber. "Who says you have to win every game? They always make money. And they can always find more bodies, which is all they need. The game goes on."

By August 1972, not long before they'd start the perfect season against the Chiefs, Csonka and Kiick were entrenched as the best one-two runner combination in the league and were quite possibly the sport's most entertaining characters. They were featured on the cover of *Sports Illustrated*, Kiick standing and leaning against a goalpost and Csonka seated on the ground. It seemed like a harmless photo until you noticed Csonka slyly raising his middle finger on one hand. The Smirk Brothers were at it again. (Csonka maintains the magazine took more than 150 shots and the one with the rogue digit was supposed to be a joke for his photo collection. Csonka received several dozen angry letters from the humorless and the self-righteous saying he was corrupting young athletes and his behavior was no way for a role model to act, but the bigger reaction came from collectors who wanted him to sign the magazine. In some ways, what Csonka said at the time of the photo controversy best spoke to his personality. He was no-nonsense, nonhypocritical, laid-back off the field, a killer on it, and he despised stupidity. "There are a lot of other things to straighten out and write letters about," Csonka explained then. "People are just not aware of the intelligence of today's youth. I don't see how displaying the middle digit of my hand will bring the nation down to rubble. Maybe I'm hard to understand, but I shouldn't be. I'm no extremist. I'm against players going around portraying themselves as nondrinkers and non-smokers and non-swearers in the belief that this is going to make all little children grow up to be fine, churchgoing men. I drink some. I smoke some. I swear some. But I try to live the right kind of life for myself and my family. I'm not going to try and pass myself off as a saint for the purposes of advertising . . .")

Csonka and Kiick's friendship was cemented by a similar sense of humor. They eventually became known to fans as Butch Cassidy and the Sundance Kid, after the heroic movie characters. Kiick and Csonka played up the imagery, posing for posters in western garb. Shula winced when the *Sports Illustrated* story was released, but Csonka and Kiick loved it. As much as Csonka had come to appreciate, even cherish Shula despite the harshness of some of Shula's rules, a part of him still loved to tweak his square coach. Csonka, like Shula, came from a Hungarian background. He inherited his toughness from a father who was a part-time bouncer at a movie theater and once tossed a rowdy customer through a door. Csonka referred to Shula and his father as "those crazy Hungarians," even though Csonka had an element of crazy spliced throughout his own DNA as well as a brilliant and prickly sense of humor. Shula once became slightly irritated when *Miami Herald* columnist Edwin Pope left Shula's press conference several minutes early to speak with Csonka. Shula publicly expressed his irritation, and Csonka put his arm around Pope and stated loudly (so Shula would hear him): "Don't worry about it, Edwin, you heard one hunky, you heard 'em all." Csonka was using the slang for Hungarian to poke a little fun at his fellow Hungarian

Csonka was different in other ways. Many of the Dolphins players lived in Miami out of both convenience and to take advantage of the rich social scene. Csonka lived in Plantation, Florida, about twenty-five miles away from the city and the Orange Bowl. Csonka despised the politics and infighting that occurred in NFL locker rooms, even locker rooms that were mostly unified like Miami's. Csonka once explained the decision to live away from teammates this way: "I enjoy every guy on the team. But I think your private life and your working life must be separated. When you're too close to people for too long you get on each other's nerves. Petty things are magnified. In Plantation, my neighbors aren't people I work with every day. I can have a party without having to worry about hurting the feelings of the guy next door because I didn't invite him and he was a teammate."

Csonka's physicality was only matched by his sense of humor and penchant for the perfect prank (part of the reason why Shula initially suspected Nixon's late-night phone call was a joke). No one pulled them off better than Csonka. One of his best came when the team was staying in a hotel in Cleveland. The legendary broadcaster Howard Cosell was staying on the same floor as Csonka, Morris, and Kiick. When the noise got too loud for Cosell, he knocked on Csonka's door. The problem was Cosell's toupee was askew. "Keep the noise down," Cosell said. Csonka grabbed the toupee and tossed it fifteen feet down the hallway.

Kiick was equal parts smart-ass and thorn in Shula's backside. He derided the idea of Shula's conditioning run, a twelve-minute monster that most players simply gritted their teeth and completed without complaint. The idea was for players to run as far as possible in the allotted time. It was brutal, since the run happened during Florida's ugly summer heat. Shula wanted his players to be like Dick Anderson, who ran two miles farther than any player Shula had coached to that point. What Shula didn't want was Kiick's approach to the run. "If I wanted to run cross country," he told Shula, "I would have gone out for it in high school." Then he ran the damn thing.

Kiick described his and Csonka's running styles perfectly: "I like to run where there are holes; Larry likes to run where there are people."

"To say Csonka was tough is an understatement," Simpson remembered to the author. "I truly believe some guys on defense were scared of him." Before Simpson became an acquitted double murderer, and before people named their anal polyps after him, he was one of the best running backs in NFL history. He remembers the beginning of the 1972 season: "Teams worried about Csonka, Jim Kiick, Griese; they had some star power. I liked how Mercury ran. Going into that year, you thought the Dolphins were a good team, but no one was scared of them. Most people I knew in the league thought them making the Super Bowl was a fluke. They didn't buy them as a great team. I did buy into Csonka."

Kiick was the higher profile of the two, but it was Csonka who made the impression on Simpson. He remembered a game when a smallish Buffalo defender had a clear shot at Csonka as Csonka was beginning to approach full speed, but the defensive player tripped just before attempting to make the tackle. Except to Simpson, the trip was no accident. It was done to avoid a painful collision with one of the most feared men in football.

But as tough as Csonka was on the field, and as biting as his humor could be, Csonka was introspective off of it. He was the prototypical rugged back with the nonconventional football mind-set. Csonka wasn't a braggart or a loudmouth. He enjoyed a good party and stiff drink but preferred the predictability of moderation. He was seen in the locker room by the black Miami players as an open-minded and intelligent teammate. Csonka even took on Nixon, criticizing the president for pushing youth to play football without also relaying the risks. "What I object to is that when it comes from him, from the President, it's as if he has sanctioned *all* of football, that football is just naturally wonderful for everyone," Csonka told *Sports Illustrated* in August 1972. "Parents start pushing a kid toward the game without realizing the dangers in it. You see it in these Little Leagues. Poor equipment, poor coaching. Some 25-year-old frustrated jock making kids run 8,000 laps. And *gassers*! A kid gets his nose broke, and the coach yells at him and calls him a coward and shames him. Hey, kids listen to adults, especially if he is a coach. They start to believe. Maybe a kid believes he can't compete, that he *is* a coward. If a kid's not ready to hit or be hit, he shouldn't have to."

Like Csonka, Kiick had high capacity for playing through extreme discomfort. Kiick in one game suffered a bruised elbow and a hip injury, and if that wasn't enough—even worse—he played in that same game with a broken toe and finger. The pain had to be debilitating, and as the team trainer wrapped the elbow, he asked how Kiick was feeling. Kiick brushed off the question. When the wrap was removed after the game, the elbow had swollen substantially.

The two men's ability to play through pain is where the similarities ended despite a close friendship. Csonka was a serious student of the game, examining all of its intricate details. He was also football royalty: a first-round draft pick with a $100,000 signing bonus and consensus All-American background who had to work to be good. Kiick was a natural talent who was drafted in the fifth round and was never interested in learning about football's finer points the way Csonka was. Csonka respected authority and appreciated structure while Kiick sometimes hated both. Just a few years after Csonka and Kiick became one of the best running tandems in history, Kiick summed up the differences between the two runners at the beginning of the 1972 season:

"I've always been what you might call lackadaisical. It makes for a bad appearance," he told *Sports Illustrated*. "For example, I hate exercise. I hate sit-ups. Larry thrives on hard work. Raised on a farm, up at 5:30, milking cows, getting the work done. I was lazy. Or looked lazy. Shula yells at me for the way I do exercises. I just like to loosen up. I don't worry much about form. I don't knock myself out on the unnecessary stuff. Why run back to the huddle? Conserve your energy. Pick your spots." He added: "I'm not a student of anything. I stopped growing mentally at 17. I know absolutely nothing about football. I don't know how to read a defense. I'm always afraid they'll quiz me on something I'm supposed to know."

Csonka was the opposite. As a young player, he was always studious about the game and pushing himself to extremes. When Csonka was just twelve years old, he weighed a stupendous 150 pounds. Csonka never took his size advantage for granted, and throughout high school and college, he used weights and some unorthodox means to improve his already formidable strength. At Syracuse, a teammate told Csonka one way to strengthen his arms, particularly the forearms, was to bang them against heavy objects. Csonka resorted to hitting them against solid walls. Csonka's physicality, persistence, and skill led to him rushing for more yards than some of the great backs in Syracuse history, including the best runner ever at any level, Jim Brown.

Why Csonka and Kiick became close is as simple as opposites attract. Csonka respected Kiick's desire to have fun and Kiick appreciated Csonka's precision and professionalism. When they met at a College All-Star Game, Csonka was taken aback at how poorly the coach of the team, Norm Van Brocklin, treated Kiick. Van Brocklin refused to play Kiick in the game, calling Kiick fat and slow. Csonka saw a different player, one who had heart and more skill than Brocklin or many people in the NFL had seen. When Kiick came to Miami, it was Csonka who made a prescient statement to the beat writers who covered the team. "Maybe you never heard of him," Csonka told them, "but he's going to be a hell of a player."

Yes, Csonka and Kiick were close, and they were formidable and extremely successful together—Kiick's favorite play was Ride 34, where he followed Csonka's lead block—but that didn't stop Shula from pondering an important change. You see, there was another difference between the 1972 game against the Chiefs and the one a season before it. Shula had done the unthinkable—he had broken apart the duo of Csonka and Kiick. The duo had become a trio.

What always made Shula special in the annals of football history was being ahead of his time. Only his idol, Paul Brown, was more inventive. In that rematch against Kansas City, Shula unveiled the 53 Defense—an alignment never before seen. But it was Shula's benching of Kiick and insertion of Morris as a starter that was one of his more resourceful ideas. Every team in football used a static set of starters, and at running back, it was a one- or two-back offense. Shula began a regular rotational system involving three runners. Such design seems simple enough today, but at the time, it hadn't been done before. It was an ingenious maneuver that would later become commonplace.

Kiick and Csonka had started together in forty-nine of their fifty-six games together in Miami. Nevertheless, Shula had been impressed with Morris and never forgot that conversation at the Fontainebleau Hotel after the Super Bowl. Morris had kept his promise to work hard and respect Shula's authority, and Shula decided Morris needed to be rewarded. Shula also made the move for more practical reasons. He felt the offense needed an injection of speed and Morris could certainly provide that. Morris remains one of the more underrated offensive players in league history.

Kiick, in some ways, knew what was coming. In addition to the fair and practical reasons for the switch, there was also perhaps an element of vindictiveness. Shula was brilliant and eternal, but he was also not above striking back at a player who defied him, and Kiick defied Shula in almost every possible way. He mocked a portion of Shula's Saturday-night road itinerary, in which players were required to have a mandatory snack at 9:30 and be in bed for 11:30 curfew. In 1972, Kiick told one of the writers covering the team that the mandatory snack was "childish, like we have to be on a leash." Beer was served during the snack and players were allowed to drink as much beer as they liked, but Kiick complained that wasn't the case. "Reach for a third can and the coaches start looking at you funny," he said.

Kiick's somewhat strained relationship with Shula was vastly different from the warm one he had with former Dolphins coach

George Wilson. Kiick's father, George, played college football at Bucknell and professionally in Pittsburgh. Wilson once wrote a letter to George that read in part: "As one father and ex–football player to another I just want to express our pride here in Miami that Jim Kiick wears a Dolphin uniform."

It was the conditioning run more than anything that would lead to Kiick sharing time with Morris. Kiick and Csonka wrote about Kiick's benching in their book *Always on the Run*. In previous years, Kiick had begrudgingly completed Shula's twelve-minute gauntlet, but at the beginning of the 1972 season, Kiick decided to effectively tell Shula to fuck off.

Eight minutes into the run, Kiick stopped, saying he had shortness of breath because of a chest cold. Since Csonka was loyal to his friend, Csonka stopped too. Shula saw them and hurried over as quickly as possible, running by the other players who were conducting the run without imagined diminished lung capacity. Once Shula reached the two men, he was, as usual, quite succinct. "Are you trying to defy me," he said, "in front of the rest of the team?" Kiick and Csonka explained they were tired, but everyone in the conversation knew the truth. They were thumbing their noses at Shula.

"You can't have a team where one set of rules applies to certain guys and another set of rules to others," says Shula now.

Shula did try to live up to that mantra, but it should be noted that Csonka went basically unpunished. Shula wanted to set an example, but he wasn't suicidal. Disciplining both Kiick *and* Csonka would have crushed the Dolphins. Besides, Shula knew that Csonka was one of the true professionals on the team. Hell, in the entire league. And Csonka's actions were more a product of backing his friend than being a mutineer.

It didn't take long for Shula to take action against Kiick. Just a short time after the twelve-minute rebellion, Shula informed Kiick that Morris was getting the bulk of preseason snaps. Kiick didn't think anything of it, believing the fact he had combined for 1,000 yards in rushing and receiving in each of his first four years would put him out of hailing range of Morris no matter how fast Morris was. When Shula started Morris in that opening game against the Chiefs on September 17, 1972, Kiick fumed. The rotational runner system had begun, as did the end of Kiick's perennially costarring role with Csonka.

Kiick would complain publicly and Shula would fume privately. Kiick still got his carries, sometimes more than Morris, and then Morris would complain to the papers again, causing Shula to become quietly angry. It was a frustrating experience for all of them—though there was a part of Morris who loved the idea of stirring the pot—with Csonka caught in the middle. Csonka wanted to publicly back his friend, but he was respectful of Shula's authority. Besides, Csonka thought, the system was working well. Indeed, Shula had created something that moved with elegant proficiency despite driving the three participants insane. Only Simpson would have a better season running the ball.

This was the Dolphins' eclectic backfield. A talented bruiser in Csonka. A white guy with a chip on his shoulder. A black guy with a chip on his shoulder. They began to coalesce into a formidable if not dysfunctional unit, with Csonka as its leader and Morris as an outspoken intellectual force and quirky personality. After the Oilers game, the second of the season, and before the Dolphins were to play the Vikings, Morris walked into the training room where Csonka was talking to a reporter while performing his morning ritual of icing his aches and soaking in the whirlpool. On the speakers was the music of Andre Kostelanetz, one of the gurus of easy listening music. Morris twisted his head toward the speakers and his face contorted. He turned to equipment manager Danny Dowe. "This will never do," Morris said. Morris switched the channel to a rock station, turned up the volume, and settled in. Morris did his own thing.

On the field, and outside of the training room, Csonka was viewed as such a threat that he occasionally made for a wonderful decoy. In that crucial third game, played on October 1 in Bloomington, the Vikings had an 8-point lead in the fourth quarter. The Vikings were a cunning and dangerous team that would make four Super Bowl appearances in the decade. They were led on defense by Jim Marshall, a strapping defensive lineman, who was feared as much for his intellect as his physical prowess. The Dolphins' tight end Jim Mandich entered the game as a substitute, not knowing in that moment he'd help save the contest.

The matchup was close and it had been a brutal game up to that point. Fran Tarkenton was one of the league's premier quarterbacks, and the Dolphins had mangled him for 5 sacks. Very little worked offensively for the Vikings. One of the plays late in the game—Slide Power 21—went for a short gain like so many of his other play calls. After one series, Tarkenton walked off the field with a slight limp and glanced over at the Dolphins' defense with a look that said: *Who the hell are those guys?*

Csonka again displayed heartiness in his galloping running form, but he also took another nasty hit. While launching upward to catch a pass, he was smashed in the back. Csonka's body bent backward, and many fans in attendance could be heard gasping. The tackle on Csonka became national news, momentarily emerging from the sports universe and entering into pop culture. The hit was replayed on *The Tonight Show* and Johnny Carson was as taken aback as anyone else who saw it. (Csonka would later join Carson on the show's 1,280th episode along with Bob Hope.) Other Dolphins players moved toward Csonka, fearing he had suffered serious or even permanent damage to his back and spinal column. Csonka could have, without question, died on the spot.

Csonka had landed not far from the Miami bench and literally crawled off the field. He reached the sideline, where Shula was waiting. "Get up," Shula said, "the Vikings are going to think you're hurt."

Csonka looked up: "I am."

Shula remembered the scene. "There are few people who could've endured that kind of hit," Shula said, "but that's him."

There was 1:20 left in the game with the Dolphins still down, but they were sitting at Minnesota's 4-yard line. The Dolphins knew the entire Minnesota defense would be looking for Csonka. It was a smart assumption. The Dolphins were close to the goal line, and when the offense was that close to scoring, Csonka was like a large automobile that only went in one direction and at one speed. He plowed ahead. He scored. That was the normal course of things.

This time, Griese called for a play-action pass. The ball was faked to Csonka and Griese dropped back to throw. The entire Minnesota defense swarmed Csonka, thinking he had the football, except for one person: Marshall. He wasn't fooled, and Marshall anticipated the play. Marshall knew that if he knocked Mandich down, the play was basically dead. So Marshall launched his 250-pound frame into Mandich, easily toppling him. Mandich stayed slightly stunned on the ground and watched as Marshall, thinking Mandich's part in the play was over, hurriedly joined his Vikings teammates pursuing Csonka. Every player on the field ignored Mandich after Marshall pummeled him. Every player except Griese.

Griese had hoped for this all along. As he had all season, Griese called his own plays and could visualize every possible outcome, like a scientist who studies alternate universes. Griese waited patiently for Mandich to get up, and he knew Mandich would because very little could keep Mandich down. Not even a forearm from Marshall. One second passed. Another. And another. Finally, Mandich crawled to his feet and ran a short distance. When he turned, the football was already in the air. Griese knew where Mandich was supposed to be and the ball was thrown to the exact spot. Miami scored and the team won.

Something was happening with the Dolphins and that fact was becoming clear across the entire sport even at that early point in the year. The Dolphins were coming off a Super Bowl appearance, albeit a disastrous one, but a showing nonetheless. Now they were 3-0. At the Monday press conference following the win, Shula stood before several of the usual beat reporters: Bill Braucher of the *Miami Herald*, Bob Sheridan of WGBS radio, and Bernie Lincicome of the *Fort Lauderdale News* and *South Florida Sun-Sentinel*, among others. Shula received the expected questions about how good this team could be.

"Are you beginning to think that this is one of those years where everything you do is right?" Braucher asked.

"A lot of people can win three games," Shula responded. "We're not letting it go to our heads."

Shula would make certain of that. Yet it was also undeniable the Vikings game showed what he'd suspected all along: This Miami team was good. No, you don't say that publicly. Not this early. But he knew. Deep down, he knew.

But Shula wouldn't even hint at this before the press. He didn't want his players' heads to swell after reading about how good they were in the papers. So Shula refused to play along with the praising newsmen. "You guys have the easiest jobs in the world," Shula told them during the press conference. "You always get to celebrate everything before it happens. We're going good, sure, but say the same to me after it's all over. Any team that makes it through to the Super Bowl . . . must have a lot of depth. I don't know if we've got enough of it but we'll see. It's a forty-man game."

"Going into these first four games," one of the writers asked, "would you have settled in advance for a 3-1 record?"

It was a trick question. Shula didn't fall into the bear trap.

"I tend to think in terms of winning them all," Shula responded.

The depth Shula spoke of was the most critical part of his statement. It was true. Shula knew that in order to win, he'd need a team that was two or three deep at most of the key positions. Now the Dolphins had a hardened mantle of formidable talent, but it surrounded key figures who didn't always get the headlines or fat contracts. This is one way the Dolphins would transform the sport. Shula was the first coach and the Dolphins the first team to emphasize depth as much as stardom. Shula stockpiled the castoffs and transformed them into a cemented group. The defense from the unbeaten season would put only one player in the Hall of Fame. There was no Lawrence Taylor or Ray Lewis on the Dolphins. Some of the players were so nondescript they earned the perfect nickname: the No-Name Defense.

CHAPTER FIVE

REVENGE OF THE NAMELESS

Just how nasty and tough Miami's defense had become materialized in the fourth game of the season against Joe Namath and the New York Jets. Before the contest began, Griese patiently paged through a game-day program. Nothing caught his attention until he saw a feature story on Jets cornerback Steve Tannen. Griese hoped there was some information in the article he could use against Tannen on the field. There was.

In the story, Tannen admitted the two toughest receivers he'd ever gone against were Kansas City's Otis Taylor and Miami's Twilley. It's understandable why Twilley had caught Tannen's attention. Twilley was talented and resilient and, despite being just 5 feet 10 inches tall, weighing 185 pounds, and possessing limited speed, had turned into a highly effective receiving threat. Over the years, Twilley had also endured a jaw broken in two places and a fractured elbow.

Tannen's words were interesting to Griese. In making such an admission, Tannen was practically guaranteeing Twilley would attack him. It didn't take too long for exactly that to happen. The Dolphins got inside Jets territory, and Griese noticed Tannen covering Twilley one-on-one. Griese hit Twilley for the score.

Namath didn't have Griese's intellect (few did), but he was still far more studious than his girl-chasing reputation would have people believe. Namath studied defenses for tells and there were usually many. Miami safety Jake Scott did the same thing, except he studied quarterbacks, and the number of times a quarterback gave away a play with a certain eye movement or arm twitch was equally plentiful. Scott even discovered that Namath had seen one of Scott's tells.

One of Scott's favorite opponents was Namath. Their games would be an incredible brinksmanship. Namath recognized Scott's first step after the ball was snapped indicated the type of pass coverage the Dolphins were utilizing. Scott soon realized that Namath was reading that first move, so Scott began faking his initial steps and thus fooling Namath. When Scott initially suckered Namath, the Jets quarterback began cursing at Scott before the snap. "You're not getting me this time, motherfucker," Namath once yelled.

Namath threw 1 interception in the game and completed only 12 passes and failed to throw a touchdown. He also spent large chunks of the game scrambling from pressure. The Dolphins had stopped Namath. They had, in fact, slowed the entire offense: The Dolphins stopped the Jets at the 1-yard line on three straight plays and forced New York to settle for a short field goal. But that game represented much more than the shutting down of Namath. It was the start of Miami's use of the 53 Defense. Dave Anderson, the Pulitzer Prize–winning writer, described the simple but historic personnel maneuver in the October 9, 1972, *New York Times*: "Matheson, a linebacker, replaced Jim Dunaway, a tackle, while Lloyd Mumphord, a defensive back, replaced Mike Kolen, a linebacker."

The Dolphins used the 53 to shut down dangerous Jets tight end Rich Caster. Whenever Caster lined up wide, at his most threatening position, he was double-teamed by at least a linebacker and defensive back and more than likely two quicker defensive backs. No one had tried this—either the 53 or using a defense to double Caster. In the Jets' previous three games that season, Caster had torched defenses for a nearly 30-yard average on 11 catches. The Miami defense held him to 1 pass for 5 yards. Caster didn't stand a chance. Namath didn't either.

After the game, an almost defiant Buoniconti spoke of his defense to the press. "We're the no-name defense and we're proud of it," he said. "Nobody has been able to give us a nickname. We love it that way. We enjoy being anonymous."

Miami's defense under Shula was always talented; it just wasn't necessarily seen that way publicly. Before the Super Bowl against Dallas, some Cowboys players called the Dolphins' defense "Buoniconti and ten other guys," referring to the linebacker who had the largest profile of the group. Buoniconti becoming a visible Miami player was basically remarkable. The fact that Buoniconti was in professional football at all was also stunning. Buoniconti played at Notre Dame, but as a 5-11 linebacker weighing 220 pounds, he was considered smallish by NFL standards. Buoniconti's Notre Dame coach told NFL scouts: "He'll run through a wall, and he'll leave a hole, but the hole will be small."

How he ended up in Miami is interesting in itself. Buoniconti was never drafted by the NFL. He was taken thirteenth by the Boston Patriots in the AFL in 1962. He took a portion of his $1,000 signing bonus, went back to Notre Dame to finish his senior season, and while there spent a good chunk of his bonus on a beer party or two. Or three. But make no mistake: Buoniconti was no lazy partier. He was one of the most intelligent and physically zealous linebackers of his era. Buoniconti started law school at Suffolk University his second year as a pro player. He would later become a heroic symbol for paraplegics after his son, Marc, was tragically paralyzed while making a tackle playing football for the Citadel in 1985. Nick eventually became one of the well-known faces for a paralysis cure, founding the Miami Project to Cure Paralysis. He'd go on to own a Miami restaurant and graphics company (ownership of the latter would cause a rift with the players' union, causing him to give up his position as team player representative in protest).

Buoniconti was, among other things, extremely strong willed. When the Patriots traded him to Miami, he initially retired. He didn't want to play in the ridiculously hot conditions. Also, the Dolphins were seen as a farce by almost every player in the sport, and Buoniconti wanted no part of it. So he made Robbie an offer Robbie couldn't refuse. "I'll come down," he told the Miami owner, "if you give me a three-year guaranteed contract. I'm not moving my family from Boston all the way down to Miami unless I have a guaranteed contract." It was a bold request, and Robbie initially scoffed. Buoniconti didn't flinch. He submitted his retirement letter to NFL commissioner Pete Rozelle and began thinking about his life as an attorney when about three weeks later the impossible happened. Robbie relented and agreed to Buoniconti's terms. When Buoniconti was a teenager, he dreamed of having two things: a Buick and the financial prowess to pay off his mortgage. The deal allowed him to fulfill both.

By the fourth game of the season, well into an already memorable professional career, Buoniconti had become one of the more important players on the team. In his first game with Miami, the

Dolphins lost in the final seconds to Cincinnati. As other players left the field, Buoniconti stood there, tears streaming down his face. He despised losing. It was this type of dedication that earned the other players' respect, and he was named team captain.

Before the Jets game, the 53 had been used before in small doses, but now the Dolphins decided it was time to permanently unleash it. However, the 53 wasn't named after Buoniconti, the obvious candidate. The 53 was the brainchild of assistant Bill Arnsparger, a meticulous and inventive defensive coach, who was known as much for his chain-smoking as he was his brilliance. It wasn't unusual for Arnsparger to sport his dark sunglasses, headset, and cigarette during games.

The move Arnsparger would make was partly because of need. Buoniconti had been injured in the 1971 preseason, and the Dolphins were looking for insurance, so they traded for linebacker Bob Matheson. Before heading to Miami, Matheson spoke to Shula on the phone and liked what he heard. When he arrived at Dolphins camp, he and Arnsparger met at a Howard Johnson's restaurant on 163rd Street and stayed there for five hours, until three in the morning, going over Miami's defenses. Matheson soaked it all in, and by the summer of 1972, following a rash of injuries that left the Dolphins with just two healthy defensive ends, Arnsparger's creative juices got flowing.

Matheson was a linebacker but had experience playing on the defensive line. Arnsparger would change the defense drastically by shifting to a 5-2 alignment: defender over center, defenders over both offensive tackles, and four linebackers. Matheson would rush the quarterback. It was ingenious, and nothing like it had really been seen before. They called it the 53 after Matheson's number.

The defense not only covered up massive injury problems, but the genius of the 53 was that it forced offenses to be practically mistake-free to beat it. Since the Dolphins played zone defense in the 53, teams had to matriculate down the field slowly and carefully, since a zone mostly prevented huge plays either on the ground or through the air. Arnsparger knew his players well. They were both mentally disciplined and physically exemplary, so he figured his group could handle the extra mental strain. He wasn't wrong. By the end of the perfect season, the Dolphins' defense had made just nine mental errors total when it's normal during a season for a defense to make dozens if not a lot more mistakes.

The defense was confounding to almost every team the Dolphins played. Offenses just didn't know when the Dolphins would blitz, and they didn't know how many were rushing the passer and from where. It forced teams to keep backs and receivers in to block instead of wrangling free into the Dolphins' defense. In other words, offenses worried more about blitz pickup than going on the attack. The constant shifting of bodies and attack angles were confounding. Other teams blitzed. Other teams tried to confuse offenses. But until then, no team did both so well and possessed the high-functioning cerebrums to pull off practically mistake-free football. It would take two years for teams to fully decode the 53 and mount an offense against it.

The 53 worked so well that the Dolphins were able to use it effectively against even Simpson, which limited his ability to score. The Dolphins rushed on the weak side, forcing Simpson to stay in as a blocker rather than be utilized as a pass receiver out of the backfield. Against the 53, Namath had a difficult time, and afterward, when Shula was asked about the 53 by reporters, his answer was stunningly matter-of-fact. "We just call it our 53 defense," Shula said. "That's because 53 is Bob Matheson's jersey number." That's how history, at the time, was partially recorded for one of the great innovations in football.

CHAPTER SIX

THE DUKE OF EARL

During the Dolphins' fifth game of the season, played in Miami against San Diego, disaster struck. At the time, the raw emotions of the moment provided the best quotations. Griese would describe his situation to the media with typical and simple eloquence: "I didn't know how bad it was, but I knew right away I wasn't going to be playing any more football the rest of the day." Shula was blunter: "I looked around for a convenient place to throw up."

The play had started off simply. Griese rolled left and, like he'd done many times before, he looked to throw a deep pass to Warfield, who had two men covering him. No deal. So Griese, efficient and refusing to take unnecessary risks, went to the safer option, which was Kiick. The problem was in that one second it took Griese to make that decision, Chargers lineman Ron East was able to close in on Griese. It wasn't a clear tackle. It wasn't a hard tackle. It was in some ways the worst kind of tackle. It was desperate and lunging and clumsy. East's helmet hit Griese's right leg right around the lower part of the shinbone as East dove low on Griese. To make matters worse, at the same time, Deacon Jones, a 6-5, 270-pound defensive end, made it to Griese. Jones hit high as East was hitting him low. Griese's leg didn't stand a chance. The shin fractured. The ankle dislocated.

When Griese stayed on the ground, a hush went through a normally chatty Miami sideline. Shula immediately called for the backup, thirty-eight-year-old Earl Morrall. Morrall scrambled, searching for his helmet. He was prepared to play. He was always prepared to play, but the suddenness of Griese's injury still caught him by surprise. Where was that damn helmet again? Teammate Bill Stanfill, in those few seconds, had a message for Morrall. "Okay, old man, get those cataracts in motion, turn up your hearing aid, and let's go," Stanfill said.

It's the way of football. Body in, body out. There's no time for sympathy. Griese understood this. In 1967, as a twenty-two-year-old rookie, Griese replaced John Stofa, who severely injured his ankle. "Injured" isn't the right word. After Stofa was hit, he heard the ankle crack, and his foot dangled on the turf. Body in, body out.

Shula had signed Morrall for this exact moment. Morrall wasn't just an accurate passer with a powerful arm. Morrall was experienced; *Morrall knew football.* He'd been everywhere and seen everything. He was drafted by San Francisco at twenty-two years old and signed for $14,000 a season with a $2,000 bonus. He played behind legend Y. A. Tittle but was nonetheless irked he had to wait to play. Morrall was later traded to Pittsburgh for a player and two draft picks. There, he played for Coach Buddy Parker, who a short time before had been coach of the Detroit Lions. Parker resigned after declaring at a banquet sponsored by the team's most impassioned fans that he was coaching "the worst team in training camp that I have ever seen." He added: "I'm getting out of Detroit football and I'm getting out tonight." Parker did just that, and sixteen days later he was coach of the Steelers just as Morrall got there.

Morrall's adventures continued. Parker was so angry and impulsive, a Pittsburgh writer once referred to him as a "hot-tempered mule skinner." Parker traded Morrall to Detroit after promising he wouldn't. He'd throw for 24 touchdowns one season as quarterback of the Lions, not long after Parker said at a press conference that Morrall would never make it as a professional quarterback. He shared the limelight in New York, then was traded again, this time to Shula's Baltimore Colts. Before Morrall jogged onto the field to replace a writhing Griese, he had replaced a seriously injured Unitas and led the Colts to a 13-1 record, two playoff victories, and the disastrous championship game against Namath's Jets. Shula never forgot how Morrall saved his season in Baltimore, and when he became coach of the Dolphins, he was determined to get Morrall in Miami. The Dolphins claimed Morrall off waivers for $100, and while Robbie winced at Morrall's $85,000 salary, he still told Shula to get him.

When Morrall replaced Griese, he had help from Miami's defense, which added 2 interceptions, 1 for a score. Morrall threw a touchdown pass himself, and the Dolphins won by 14 points. Csonka remembers Morrall literally drawing plays in the dirt. Morrall was confident in his ability to replace Griese, but to Dolphins players, it was a pleasant surprise. They breathed easier after watching Morrall. They saw what Shula had already known: Morrall wasn't just a substitute. He was the solution.

Griese and Morrall couldn't have been more different in their approaches to football. They were almost stereotypically opposite. Griese was the perfectionist who kept to himself. He had a keen eye and often saw things on film that coaches missed. As a kid, he was playful but also took athletics extremely seriously. According to the reporter Braucher, when it was too cold or dark outside to play basketball, Griese would hang a makeshift hoop (a hole cut out of a shoebox) inside the kitchen door. Once the tennis ball he used landed in a pot of chili bubbling on the stove. Despite the culinary disasters, Griese's parents were supportive of his sports. As a Little Leaguer, his uniform was washed for every game and there were no holes in his socks. His competitive nature and ability to break down defenses made him an All-American at Purdue and the fourth player selected in the 1967 draft.

Griese didn't fit into the Dolphins' hard-charging culture (or, to some degree, the NFL's for that matter), especially the locker room when Wilson was coach. Wilson wanted his quarterbacks to curse hard and drink harder. Griese was studious and quiet. Morris remembers Griese cursing just once. Griese came into the huddle, and many of the Dolphins players were chatting in their own separate conversations. Griese quickly grew irritated. "Shut up, dammit!" he said. The huddle was suddenly quiet.

Journalist Dave Hyde wrote of the time the extremely private Griese was asked one night to hang with teammates by Terry Cole, an old high school friend who had joined the team as a fullback but spent much of the 1972 season hurt. Griese hesitantly agreed but the next day told Cole: "I'm not doing that anymore."

In the book *But We Were 17 and 0*, teammate Larry Seiple said of Griese: "[He] was kinda' a strange person. He wanted to stay away from everybody so he could be the leader, so if he had to be the asshole he could be the asshole. If he had to be the nice guy he could do that, too, without having any personality conflicts involved."

It was actually a wise way to approach the quarterback position, especially in an era when many quarterbacks called their own plays, but it was also Griese's personality. Griese enjoyed the intellectual challenge of football more than machismo camaraderie. He spent most of his time studying the game, dissecting defenses either when he was on the field of play or sitting in his living room watching hours of film. Griese wouldn't hang, but he had the respect of his teammates and not just because he was a winner. In practice, he sought their input on almost everything, and in games, he'd ask some of the linemen for a few "attitude plays," which was Dolphins code for physical plays that set the tone for the game. He also had a grasp of the Dolphins' complex playbook that made him popular on the team because he had an answer for almost every query about a play or game situation. (The Miami offensive linemen were extremely intelligent as well. They were coached by Monte Clark, who would go down as one of the most underrated assistant coaches in NFL history. Clark initialized an audible system that allowed the quarterback to change the called play just seconds before the snap of the ball. Later, this system would be commonplace. Griese mastered it.)

Griese was naturally intelligent, but there was another factor at work. Griese had to overcompensate for his moderate arm strength, and he found extreme preparation was the way to do it. Criticism of Griese's arm strength was common, and a story that circulated when George Wilson was head coach would stick to Griese for years afterward. Wilson had gotten into a near brawl with *Miami News* reporter Jim O'Brien. Wilson exclaimed he'd have one of his players throw him in a nearby pond. O'Brien later told writers he hoped one of the players wasn't Griese, because if Griese was doing the tossing, O'Brien would land short of the pond.

By 1972, Griese was becoming nationally known for his efficient play, and questions about his arm strength were no longer relevant. The way Jake Scott knew quarterbacks and their tendencies, Griese knew defensive backs and theirs. "In a game, I think of myself as looking down on a situation from above, like a chess player," he told *Time* magazine. "I can see moves coming and I'm ready to make them. When you're a rookie you feel just like another one of the pieces. You can't see everybody because you're down among them. But when you have a total grasp and knowledge of what's going on, then you feel you can effectively maneuver people around, manipulate your offense to take advantage of what the defense is doing."

Griese was once asked if he did anything to take his mind off football. "If you mean do I play tennis," he said, "no. I just study football."

Morrall was different. He absorbed football; he didn't study it like he was pursuing a doctorate the way Griese did. He played more by feeling and instinct. Morrall once described Griese as the most prepared quarterback he'd ever seen. Morrall wasn't known for being prepared, but as players witnessed on October 22, during the Dolphins' sixth game, one week after Morrall had replaced the injured Griese, he was just as resilient. In the game against the Buffalo Bills he threw 1 interception but also 2 touchdowns in that 1-point victory. The win was an odd one and it took the Dolphins a great effort to get it. The Bills led 13–7 at halftime despite not getting a single first down. "Well, we couldn't have played any worse," Shula said at halftime, "and we're still in it."

One of the things that helped the Dolphins win that game was the quickness of defensive lineman Manny Fernandez, who stole the football during a handoff attempt by the Buffalo quarterback and stumbled short of a touchdown. After the game, Fernandez joked with reporters that he could have scored, but his 20-200 eyesight prevented it. "I was afraid I'd run into the goalpost," he said.

The offense almost derailed the season's perfection in that game, but a blend of skilled coaching and player talent stopped it. Buffalo entered the contest with a defensive game plan the Dolphins hadn't seen before. The Bills put their defensive ends in a wider alignment than normal, and for much of the game, the Dolphins coaches had no answer for it. Shula had rarely been more frustrated. He became so angry at one point in the game that he grabbed the arm of one of the game officials and was penalized for it.

So the Dolphins adjusted their offense on the fly. They plotted in huddles before the snap, and line coach Clark broke out a blackboard on the sideline and solved the puzzle just in time for Miami to win the game.

It was a strange game indeed, the kind that kept Shula awake late into the night. He couldn't sleep and neither could daughter Sharon, so they talked in the kitchen, each drinking a glass of milk. Shula's gut knew the turnovers and chaotic nature of the game were because of the change in quarterbacks, but he spent extra time just making sure. Later, at the office, he studied the film, looking for anything else—a lack of effort, a flaw in tactics, an unprepared line—and didn't see it. The restlessness receded a bit, but there was a private moment, a few of them actually, when Shula wondered if the team could truly win consistently with Morrall. He didn't tell a soul.

On October 29, Unitas, still with the Colts, and his onetime backup, Morrall, shook hands moments before the Dolphins and Colts were to play in Miami's seventh game of the season. They exchanged the usual pleasantries until Unitas, age thirty-nine, asked Morrall, age thirty-eight, a question. "You're getting too old for this, aren't you?" Unitas said with a smirk. Morrall didn't hesitate. "Well, you're a pretty old buck yourself," Morrall responded.

Unitas and Morrall had a close relationship, but Unitas's notoriously prickly attitude was always present. Morrall had achieved a large degree of success in relief of Unitas, and Morrall was beginning to build a lengthy and gorgeous career arc of his own. It's not certain if Unitas felt threatened, but he didn't hesitate to establish the hierarchy publicly. When Unitas missed all of the 1968 season, and Morrall led the Colts to the Super Bowl, Unitas was once asked if he was concerned about getting his job back. Unitas was incredulous. "Whaddya mean?" he asked. "I'm the quarterback of this club."

Unitas perhaps had the best description of both Morrall and himself: "I like to score in six seconds. Earl wants to take six minutes." That was true when Morrall faced his old team. In that game, Unitas was benched by the Colts' general manager, and his statement about Morrall's desire to kill a defense slowly with a tedious drive proved prophetic. The first drive went 80 yards in ten agonizing plays, with Csonka and Morris dominating. The Dolphins did not allow the Colts' offense to pass Miami's 35-yard line, and they won in a route, 23–0.

After a slower start, Morrall had now taken complete control of the offense in Griese's absence. The Dolphins players had come to fully accept him and they had good reason. The defense had been equally, if not more, dominant to the offense, but not only was Morrall winning games, but he was picking up exactly where Griese had left off that horrible day when his leg went in several different directions. In three games, Morrall hadn't lost and completed 65 percent of his passes. After beating the Colts, he was awarded the game ball. "I think they felt sorry for the old quarterback," Morrall joked with the media afterward. "It could have gone to a dozen other guys. I'm just happy they came back here and won with me at quarterback. This is the tenth time I've been in the visitors' locker room, and I spent four years over in the other one. It's tough to look across the line and see all the other guys you know so well, but you also know they'd like to kick the hell out of you every play."

Shula was one of the few in football (if not the only one) who knew at the time what history would later comprehend. Morrall wasn't just a career backup, a disposable part. He was someone to be counted on.

The win over the Colts meant the Dolphins had made it through half the season, seven games, without a loss. On November 5, in Buffalo, Morris would dazzle again. On his first carry, Morris followed blockers to the right on a sweep and ran for 33 yards. It was the kind of display of power and speed that had entranced Shula and turned him into a Morris convert. Later, Morris ran for a 22-yard touchdown. Csonka watched and shook his head. "He'd make that play that sometimes caused you to go, 'Wow,'" Csonka explained.

The game saw Morrall make one of his first big blunders when one of his passes was intercepted and returned 39 yards for a touchdown. Despite the miscue, Miami was still never in great danger of losing the game. Morris would help guarantee the win with a late score. O. J. Simpson was held to just 45 yards.

The Dolphins went to 9-0 on November 12 when they beat the New England Patriots 52–0. There were many moments of skill that helped Miami dominate the league, but there were, again, moments of luck. They were able to play the Patriots in Miami instead of Boston, and the Orange Bowl temperature was 85 degrees with 87 percent humidity. In Boston, it was a windy 49 degrees. Skill is mandatory, but luck helps. Just the week before, tight end Marv Fleming found a ten-dollar bill lying on the grass in the end zone after he caught a touchdown pass. He pocketed it. That same weekend, a two-year-old greyhound named Jake Scott won his third consecutive race at a Miami-area dog track. The Dolphins defensive back went to the track and placed a wager on his namesake, winning a small amount of cash. Luck incarnate.

"Miami has few, if any, weaknesses," wrote the *New York Times*, "even with the absence of Bob Griese, its No. 1 quarterback, whose injured leg could heal in time for him to make the playoffs, where it is possible the Dolphins could play host in both games leading to the Super Bowl."

The game was Shula's hundredth win, and this time it was his turn to get a game ball. At the time, eight other coaches in NFL history had won one hundred games, but Shula was the first to do it in just ten years. The team gathered in the middle of the locker room, and Little tossed it to Shula. "We know it's not the one you want," he said, "but we want you to have it anyway." Shula smiled but couldn't let even this relaxed moment go without making a point to his players. "You know the one I want," he responded. Everyone knew which game ball Shula was talking about. To the Dolphins, there was just one mission, outlined by Shula in that dank locker room after their Super Bowl humiliation. One mission, and one real game ball. This one was a nice impostor.

Shula met with the press and, again, talked about the larger objective.

"I'm happy about today and the game ball," he said, "but the one I want is at the end of the year."

Many Dolphins players say now they didn't really think about going undefeated until very late in the year. November was not the time to jump to that conclusion. Not even after 9-0. The press, however, began to hint at the possibility and to ask the questions. "The Dolphins could again wind up in the Super Bowl but this time emerge as champions," wrote *New York Times* writer Al Harvin.

"We don't feel any pressure," Shula told reporters. "Our goal is to win the world championship. If, during the course of the year, things like an unbeaten record fit in, fine."

Shula received one more congratulations. It was a telegram from Nixon. The president couldn't resist.

Heartiest congratulations on Victory Number One
Hundred. You have done something no other coach in
professional football has ever accomplished—one hundred
victories in your first ten years—and the Dolphins'
record this year is nothing less than sensational. This new
milestone is convincing proof of your superior coaching
ability and, therefore, I will do my very best to resist
suggesting any more plays should you get through the
playoffs and into the Super Bowl again.

The early moments of Shula's Dolphins coaching days sometimes
caused his blood pressure to launch into low orbit. Perhaps Shula's
worst fit of anger in those days before perfection happened after
Miami was beaten by the Patriots at Foxboro Stadium. Griese had
been sacked a nasty 7 times. Shula was furious during the game and
screamed at offensive line coach Clark. While Clark would end up
as one of the most respected at his position, the line had a nasty start
that day. After the game, Shula gathered his players and staff and
began to berate them, unaware the open windows of the room led
to the area where writers were waiting for Shula to speak to them.
They heard every word.

It was a classic rant. "You guys have got to be able to play better
than this," Shula screamed. "You don't even belong in this league.
You don't belong in the Atlantic Coast League. Now you've got to
go back to Miami. How're you going to like that? After a decent
exhibition season, you got to go back to Miami after getting beat
by this team." Shula emphasized the word "this," as if the Dolphins
had lost to a bunch of eighth graders. He continued: "You're going
to be the laughingstock of South Florida."

Writers made Shula aware they had heard every word, and he
threw up his hands, almost as exasperated with them as he was

with his players. "That's all right, coach," one told Shula. "You can't affect these guys by calling them a laughingstock. They've been the laughingstock of South Florida for four years." Shula was hot, but he still couldn't resist chuckling.

Now the offensive line was breathtakingly good. Morris was becoming one of the best backs in football. He scored twice against the Patriots in that 52–0 blistering, and in the tenth game of the season against the Jets, he scored the game-winning touchdown. That fact was particularly pleasing to Morrall, since there was little animosity lost between Morrall and Namath. It all started in 1969 before the Jets-Colts Super Bowl, with Morrall replacing Unitas. Namath made the remark to the press that there were at least three quarterbacks in the AFL who were better than Morrall.

Before playing the Jets during the perfect season, on November 19, Morrall was critical of Namath's partying lifestyle, saying he wouldn't want his son to be like Namath. It was an equally unfair statement. The animosity reached an apex at midfield, for the coin toss prior to the game. The four Miami team captains, including Morrall, met with the two Jets team captains, one being Namath. Everyone shook hands, except Namath refused to shake Morrall's hand; he wouldn't even look at him, causing Morrall to chuckle.

The most important pregame event came before handshake-gate. Shula had sent two of his personnel men to watch Jets linebacker Larry Grantham during warm-ups. There were reports in the press that Grantham was injured, and as the Dolphins staffers watched, it was clear the reports were accurate. He ran gingerly, and it was reported to Shula that Grantham was at best 50 percent. Shula told Morrall and the offensive coaches the news. Everyone stored the information away.

In the fourth quarter and trailing, the Jets inserted the injured Grantham. Alarm bells rang across the entire Dolphins offense, beginning with Morrall. The next play was a sweep with Morris, which singled him against a slow Grantham. Morris scored the game winner. It was another example of how during that unique season, the Dolphins had luck but also many times made their own.

The Dolphins won and Morrall won. Those were the two important victories, but it was a brutal game. Csonka's nose, seemingly in a perpetual state of fracture, was broken for the fifth time that season alone. But he wasn't just absorbing hits. He was inflicting damage as well. Collisions with Csonka led to severe injuries to three Jets players. The 28–24 win gave the Dolphins a 10-0 record, and they had such a comfortable lead in the standings that they won their division despite having four games remaining in the regular season. "At that point everything was clicking," Shula says now. "Our defense was playing great. Our offense was playing well. We were a very confident team. No one was talking about a perfect season. We were just playing hard and being smart. I think the biggest thing is we were a very close-knit group. We were very unified."

How that happened was no accident, and what Shula had to overcome—and did—remains one of the most underrated aspects of his legacy.

PART TWO

FROM THE ASHES

CHAPTER SEVEN

MELTING POT

In the late 1960s, before Shula came to town, a handful of black Dolphins players had made the final roster. They were among the first blacks to do so. They were on the team. They'd done it. That was supposed to be the hard part, but finding a place to live became the real battle. The black players knocked on doors and answered ads only to be told no blacks were allowed. On occasion, the language was blunter, as players were informed "niggers" weren't permitted to live there. That's what they were told. No niggers. The next ad, the next apartment, the next landlord . . . no niggers. This is how it went for a number of black players in those days. They looked for places to live for weeks and months. This was part of being a black NFL player in South Florida.

In the NFL, and on the Dolphins before Shula, black and white didn't mix. The South had perfected the art of bigotry, but even in the North, racial hostilities were still problematic in the sport. Across the nation, systemic segregation remained in football decades after Jackie Robinson broke baseball's color barrier. The Dolphins were no different. Once practices and games ended, black Dolphins went in one direction, and whites the other. They mostly ate separately, prayed separately, and partied separately. Marv Fleming saw this the moment he walked into the Dolphins locker room.

Fleming was traded from Green Bay to Miami in 1970. He was known as a gregarious and friendly teammate and one of the best tight ends in football. He won two Super Bowl rings in Green Bay, and if that wasn't enough, *Ebony* magazine named Fleming one of its eligible bachelors. Fleming once swore he'd only get married if the woman agreed to two prenuptial agreements: one for before the marriage and one for during it. In the meantime, he enjoyed all the delicious trappings of being a single, handsome NFL player. "*Ebony*'s 1970 bachelors have an eye for women who are well groomed, educated, poised and possessed of social graces," wrote the magazine in its bachelor issue. "They are not looking for beauty queens, but they put greater value on spiritual beauty— sincerity, and loyalty. Their ideal woman is a homemaker who is fond of children and believes in the capabilities and the changing destiny of black men."

"Marv Fleming, 27 . . . has substantial oil, real estate and stock investments, drives a '70 Eldorado and lives with his mother and brothers in beautiful Marina Del Rey, Calif.," the magazine stated. "Naturally, he admires sports-minded women, but they also 'must love to be loved.'"

Vince Lombardi, the iconic Green Bay leader, like Shula, tried to deactivate the explosive device that was race. Fleming would say that in Green Bay there were only three colors: gold, green, and Italian (gold and green being Packers colors and Italian meaning

Lombardi himself). He immediately saw that inside the Dolphins locker room there were two colors: black and white.

After Shula introduced Fleming in the locker room, Fleming immediately made his opinion known, as the book *Still Perfect!* reported, on the separation of races. "Hey, hey, hey what is this?" he said loudly. "All blacks over here?" He pointed to his left. "All whites over here?" He pointed to his right. Fleming was carrying a heavy bagful of clothes and dropped it purposefully in the middle of the locker room. His voice boomed even louder than before, almost near a scream. "You guys okay if I dress right here in the middle, near the Mason Dixon line?" Laughter erupted through the room and the tension broke.

Fleming wasn't the only person to speak publicly about the division. While Morris was full of bluster and sometimes spoke without a filter, his observations were cogent. In Wilson's last year, 1969, Morris penned a daily diary for the *Miami News* and didn't hesitate to discuss the racial practices of the Dolphins. He observed how in the dining area, black and white players never ate together. "There's a sticky situation here at Dolphins camp. I've been doing my best to get rid of it," he wrote. "There's a de facto segregation being practiced here and it's as much my black brothers' fault as anyone else's. The first day in camp I noticed it right away.

"In the dining hall there'd be a table with nothing but blacks sitting there, all whites at another table, etc. There aren't any signs on the tables saying anyone has to sit at any specific table, but it always ends up the same way . . . One day I walked into the shower and saw all the black fellas crowded into one area, and the whites off to another side," he continued. "I said, 'Oh, no, we can't have this stuff.' So I moved them all about mixing them up. I want us to be a team. All that dirty water rolls down one drain."

What Morris didn't write was this fact: White players utilized the part of the shower that had the properly functioning nozzles, where the water gushed out, and black players were relegated to the showerheads where the water came out much slower.

It wasn't unusual for music to become an issue as well. Kuechenberg tells the story of the Dolphins being on a team bus and Morris boarding with a portable radio that was loudly playing rhythm-and-blues music. Kuechenberg didn't appreciate having his mental preparation disturbed and grabbed the radio from Morris and threw it out the window. Morris says that entire scene never happened, but what is true is that as Shula attempted to pull the Dolphins together as a team, there were still some divisions and they happened along musical chasms. Twilley liked to put the country music station on the radio that played in the locker room. Morris would change the channel to the rhythm-and-blues station. Country. Rhythm and blues. Country. Rhythm and blues. On and on this would go until Morris would simply outlast Twilley.

In some cases, the players used humor to broach what might have been uncomfortable moments. One practice, Morrall gathered the offense into a huddle and a few players, including Morris, weren't moving fast enough for Morrall. "Come on, boys, let's get back to the huddle," Morrall implored. Morris looked at the other black runner in the huddle, Hubert Ginn, and gave him a purposely sarcastic look. "Hubie, did you hear what he called us?" Morris asked. "He called us 'boy.'" An exasperated Morrall replied, "Ah, dang it to hell, get in the huddle."

What was happening in the Miami locker room was reflective of the city. Before Miami became famous for its beaches and as a destination for college students to party, it was known for its extremely hostile racial climate. Outside of the Selmas and Biloxis and South Bostons, few places were as oppressive to blacks as Miami. "Race, of course, is the great American subject, the subtext of the country's passions and its politics, the hidden, yawning fault line in its discourse," wrote author David Rieff in his book *Going to Miami*. When Miami was initially constructed in 1896, 162 of the 368 voting residents were black. The migration of blacks from places like South Carolina created a large black population, with many settling in a segregated neighborhood called Colored Town (later Overtown). The ugliness and brutality against blacks would start in earnest and continue up to and beyond the Dolphins' perfect season. White soldiers from a local army base crossed into Colored Town and murdered blacks with impunity. Local newspapers, including the *Miami Herald*, blatantly referred to blacks as "coons" and "hamfats." The Ku Klux Klan grew. Long after the Emancipation Proclamation, blacks were the dominant race in Florida's—and Miami's—prisons, as inmates were used for labor in a system that closely resembled slavery or, at the very least, a mostly black penal system. Black prisoners were leased like automobiles, making the state and others wealthy. "There is no penitentiary; the convicts are hired to the one highest bidder who contracts for their labour, and who undertakes, moreover, to lease all other persons convicted during the term of the lease, and sub-leases the prisoners," wrote the 1911 *Encyclopaedia Britannica* in an entry about Florida. It later reports: "In 1908 the state received $208,148 from the lease of convicts." That year, of the 446 convicts sent to Florida prisons, 15 were black women, 356 were black men, 75 were white men, and none were white women.

Martin Luther King Jr. visited the city just a handful of years before Shula took over. In 1968, with the jobs for blacks disappearing and the frustration building, blacks rioted throughout the city, as Nixon was in Miami accepting the Republican Party nomination for president. Reporters covering Nixon in one part of Miami saw the smoke from the fires off in the distance. More riots came in 1970.

The hostility blacks faced in Miami, and their resulting outbursts at that hostility, would continue and intensify through the decades. In Liberty City, a centrifuge of racial confrontation, a group of blacks organized and approached the police about a troubled cop who had harassed the community. They were admonished like children by the Miami chief of police, who called them "silly." Just a few weeks after the complaint, the officer in question charged a seventeen-year-old black kid with possessing a concealed knife, forced him to completely disrobe, and then hung him by his heels from an overpass high above the Miami River. It was like a scene from *Scarface* except it was real. In Miami, black citizens were routinely beaten, falsely accused, and harassed by officers, yet court acquittals of police officers accused of these crimes were as constant as the sticky summer air. This led to an ever-present simmering among blacks and a deepening of the divide.

The Economist wrote in 1982 that "Miami is not a good city in which to be black." It was worse a decade earlier. The parallels between a segregated Miami and a segregated Dolphins team are difficult to ignore. The team was as separated as any other segment of Miami society, and Miami was a town divided along black, white, and Latino lines. "Desegregation had not just come hard and late to South Florida but it had also coincided, as it had not in other parts of the South, with another disruption of the local status quo," writes Joan Didion in her book *Miami*, "the major Cuban influx, which meant that jobs and services which might have helped awaken an inchoate black community went instead to Cubans, who tended to be overtrained but willing. Havana bankers took jobs as inventory clerks at forty-five dollars a week. Havana newspaper publishers drove taxis."

Football locker rooms were in some ways as racially pernicious as the city of Miami. To borrow a phrase from novelist and social critic

James Baldwin: to be black in the NFL "meant, precisely, that one was never looked at but was simply at the mercy of the reflexes the color of one's skin caused in other people." It was still believed that blacks lacked the cerebral necessities to play certain positions like quarterback. Blacks were also viewed as cowards and incapable of being leaders. Inside most NFL locker rooms, blacks and whites dressed in opposite corners. They often traveled in different sections of planes and buses. The two races rarely roomed together in hotel stays on the road. The racial problems permeated the sport from the players all the way to the top of ownership in most NFL franchises.

Many of the cities where NFL teams were located, including the Miami area, didn't help. Across the sport, players fought bigotry in the franchises for which they played and in the cities where they lived. In 1960s Dallas and its surrounding areas, the hostility to the handful of black Dallas players was palpable. Writer Golenbock in the book *Cowboys Have Always Been My Heroes*: "As late as the 1960s, the West Texas town of Stinett would not allow a black to remain in the town after sundown. Trains and automobiles pulling into the East Texas town of Greenville passed a large electrified sign that proudly boasted: 'Greenville, Texas: The blackest land, the whitest people.' In Mount Vernon, about a hundred miles east of Dallas, doctors' offices had separate waiting rooms for blacks and whites."

Tex Schramm, the onetime Cowboys general manager, remembers asking a powerful Dallas political group to change the segregationist culture at Dallas hotels so both black Cowboys players and visiting black players could eat and sleep with their teams: "When we came to Dallas, we had no hotel where any of our black players could stay, nor could any of the visiting players who were black. At that time, they had a very good situation in Dallas in which there was a group of businessmen that essentially had the influence in the town and ran things with good intentions. I went to them and said, 'Look it. We got a problem. We've got blacks on our team, and the teams coming in are going to have blacks.' They were very conscious and aware of the circumstances, because they had been working with the [black] leaders to prevent things that had happened in other parts of the South, having nothing to do with football, and so the Ramada Inn on the property of the airport said they would take all the players, but only if none of the other hotels would retaliate. Back in those days, if a hotel took a black in, the other hotels would get the word all around, and so the whites wouldn't go there. They got an agreement from the other hotels, and so that first year we stayed at the Ramada Inn, both the white and the black players. We stayed there after training camp and the night before games. We then moved to a Sheraton downtown, and that broke the hotel barrier, though Dallas still had a restaurant problem." Dallas had more than a restaurant issue. In the 1960s, as black players integrated, it had been nicknamed by people in other parts of the country as the "City of Hate." John Kennedy was called a "nigger lover" by right-wing Texans, and his running mate, Lyndon Johnson, was tagged as a socialist.

One of the main problems throughout the league was that a small core of bigots often pressured more moderate players to segregate themselves from blacks. Black players at the time had a phrase for this: "secondary pressure." Former NFL player Willis Crenshaw once described it this way to *Sports Illustrated*: "Here's how it works. We had two Negro rookies, Ted Wheeler and Jamie Rivers, and they were real good friends with two white players. In fact, they were all gonna be roommates together. But when they got settled in St. Louis the haters put so much pressure on these guys that it all ended. You can see this secondary pressure even in the Sideliners, our wives' club. At the beginning of each season the new white wives are always friendly to the Negro wives, but as the season goes on they become more and more aloof."

The St. Louis Cardinals perhaps epitomized the extreme difficulty in uniting a black and white locker room in the late 1960s and early 1970s NFL. Most teams had a handful of black players, and according to players and others familiar with the racial politics of that era, many team owners enforced an unwritten rule that only a certain number of blacks were allowed on the team, that number being between six and ten. "Teams wanted black talent but not *too much* black talent," said Hall of Fame running back Jim Brown, who played in Cleveland.

The extent that teams went to impose this racial firewall was diabolical. Even numbers of blacks were kept on the roster—an odd number meant a black player would have to room with a white one. If there was an injury to a black player that prevented him from traveling, leaving an odd number, sometimes teams purchased separate rooms, one for the black player and one for the white player. Thus, teams paid extra money to keep the races apart.

When Jim Brown played in Cleveland, he'd walk around the locker room on cut-down days (when teams reduced their rosters to a league-mandated number) and glance at the black faces in the room, knowing some of those faces would be gone not because they weren't talented enough but because there were more black players than the quota allowed.

On many teams, life for these players could be brutal, as their smaller numbers made them easy targets for bigoted teammates and coaches. In St. Louis, in 1968, black players spent as much time fighting their white teammates as they did battling opponents, as *Sports Illustrated* wrote. In one instance, a few black Cardinals players were walking through their locker room, wearing large medallions hanging from their necks. This caught the attention of several white players, with one asking what they symbolized. A veteran defender named Bobby Williams jokingly responded the medallions represented black power. They didn't, but Williams thought he'd try to lighten what was quickly turning into a prickly moment. "Bobby," the white player said, "if you're indicative of black power and all the other niggers are as smart as you, we whites will never have anything to worry about."

Sports Illustrated examined the turmoil inside the St. Louis locker room in what was a groundbreaking story on race and football. The Cardinals stood as a symbol for the status of race relations throughout much of football. "We kept 10 Negroes around here last year that don't even belong in football," one white player said. "They say they're being prejudiced against, and yet I can name you 10 of those guys—and I'll put $50,000 in escrow tomorrow that if any one of them ever stars for a team in the NFL you can have the money. That's how bad they are! Some of them couldn't make my college team. And yet these guys are in the upper 1 percent of the per-capita income of all Negroes, and if this is the way they're going to act with all that money, complaining all the time, just think what a miserable place this country's gonna be when the other shines catch up."

The racial split on the team reached an apex one night at a dinner for players and their families at the Falstaff Inn, which had become a favorite hangout for the Cardinals. Two players, the black Bobby Williams and the white Billy Gambrell, had quietly become friends, despite the insistence from white players they stay apart. The white and black wives of the two players were also friendly.

The dancing started after dinner, and Bobby unexpectedly asked Billy's wife, Kit, to join him. She wasn't going to embarrass Bobby, despite knowing what the reaction would be from the three-hundred-some people in the room. So she accepted his invitation with Billy's blessing. They started to dance. First, it was the boogaloo, and then the stomp, two nonsexual dances in which their bodies never touched. Still, outrage swept through the room like a fast-moving virus. The floor mostly cleared of other dancers and clumps of white onlookers stared and pointed. A handful of white couples left soon after the interracial dance began. "It hurt me so much," Kit remembered, "for people to act so small."

Willie West, a safety in St. Louis who had joined Wilson's Dolphins, stated the quota system cost him a job with the Cardinals. Wilson, admirably but clumsily, wandered into those difficult racial waters. "No Negro will be cut because he's a Negro on this squad," Wilson told the media, "and let me add that no Negro will be kept because he's a Negro either. My job is to find the 40 best football players around here and win games with them."

It was a noble gesture, but just a short time later, one of the Miami players that had been cut, linebacker Rudy Barber, said the Dolphins were utilizing the same quota system and he'd been released because he was black. Wilson denied Barber's claim and threatened to beat up Edwin Pope, the newspaper writer who wrote it.

It would get worse for Wilson. Pope was the sports editor of the *Miami Herald* and the city's most influential sports journalist, eventually becoming one of the top sportswriters of his generation. Pope's words carried massive weight, and when he wrote of Dolphins players' private concerns that the speedy Morris and another fast player weren't being used because they were black, it didn't bode well for Wilson. "It is patently absurd," Pope wrote in his column, "in the light of Morris's fantastic college career, to denigrate his general talents . . . Charges of racism seem exaggerated. Yet the suspicion lingers that somehow Wilson lacks the rapport with blacks that he has with whites . . . Excluding the gradual emergence of guard Larry Little, the Dolphins are the only team in pro football without a black offensive regular."

This was the racial nightmare happening across the NFL. This was the racial nightmare Shula was trying to avoid with his Dolphins team.

The NFL was in the early stage of becoming a great, gleaming apparatus, but its old guard fought to hold on to its rickety and bigoted ways. Shula was attempting to build racial tolerance among the Dolphins in a country that didn't seem ready for it and a city that openly fought it. Shula faced race the way he did a man or a team. He believed anyone or any obstacle could be beaten. Or, at least, mostly beaten. To Shula, bigotry was no different. If he couldn't eradicate it, he was determined to control it, to the point where its damaging effects were limited.

Interestingly, Shula's attitude toward women in sports was also tested. Jane Chastain was the first female sports broadcaster on both the local and national levels, the Jackie Robinson of women's television journalism, and she worked at a Miami television station regularly covering the Dolphins. Chastain faced as much discrimination as some of the black players. She wasn't allowed in the press box or locker rooms for a large swath of her career. Some athletes refused to speak with her. The Yankees great Joe DiMaggio once showed up to spring training in Fort Lauderdale and would not answer her questions. Chastain didn't hesitate. "Mr. DiMaggio," she said, "I'm going to go back and tell my boss that I didn't get the interview because I'm a woman. Would that make you happy?"

DiMaggio considered his untenable position and decided to submit. Afterward, he offered her a condescending review. "You know what?" he told her. "You *did* know what you were talking about."

For a lengthy time, Wilson wouldn't speak with Chastain, before eventually succumbing as well. Shula never had any reservations about talking to her and explained his position in an early 1970s magazine interview: "Jane is a girl who conducts intelligent, compelling interviews. She's not past throwing a controversial question at you either. There's no way you can just talk your way around her. She'll just come right back at you until she's satisfied you answered the question." Shula had heard from Dolphins players that Chastain was a true journalist, but he was admittedly skeptical. "I figured they were impressed because here was a good-looker talking about football, but Jane sure surprised me with her knowledge of the game. It only takes me two or three questions to see when a reporter's been doing homework."

Shula was asked his thoughts on women reporters, and the first portion of his answer applied to his thoughts on race as well. "You can't generalize," he said.

Shula noticed early during his tenure as Dolphins coach that he had inherited a locker room that was as racially segregated as Miami itself. Shula's Dolphins were in the middle of a city immersed in a vicious cycle of rioting and police brutality. Nonetheless, in the face of societal pressure to maintain the racial status quo, he made an interesting tactical decision. Shula decided to openly wade into the thorny racial politics of the time, and twenty-four hours after Fleming put the team on notice, players arrived at the Dolphins facility and saw a dramatic change. Shula had ordered the remodeling of the locker room so offensive players were on one side and defensive players on the other. There were no more individuals. There were to be only units, and those units would cohabitate peacefully.

Room assignments on the road also changed, as blacks and whites shared rooms when the team traveled. It was one of those quiet moments that have mostly gone unnoticed in sports history.

Shula wrote in his autobiography, "As a football coach I want to treat everybody the same and not worry whether a player is black or white, or whether he's Catholic, Jewish, Protestant, or whatever. The only thing I want to do is to be able to judge them objectively. I feel that unless I treat everybody the same, and this is in regard to rooms or seats on an airplane or whatever, I wouldn't be actually practicing what I preach. So, the first year together I decided to mix the blacks and whites on our rooming list and it worked out well. For example, Bob Griese and Paul Warfield roomed together; Marv Fleming and John Stofa; Otto Stowe and Jim Del Gaizo; Curtis Johnson and Tim Foley. A simple thing like rooming assignments helped create a feeling that everybody would be treated alike and that they were going to be judged objectively. It really helped as far as the players accepting one another on their merits as opposed to worrying about where they went to school, whether they were black or white, Christian or atheist."

It wasn't a surprise Shula made the moves. Shula was signed by Cleveland as a skinny defensive back for the Browns in 1951 and played for the man who would become his coaching idol, Paul Brown. At the time, the two competing conferences were the All-America Football Conference and the NFL, and neither league specifically stated the banning of blacks. But from 1932, the date that is considered the beginning of modern professional football, until 1946, there were no black players in either league. Brown changed that. That year Brown signed fullback Marion Motley and guard Bill Willis, two prime black talents. There was a violent reaction in some quarters of the nation at the time, including protests, and owners and other coaches throughout both leagues voiced their displeasure about the signings to Brown, but he ignored the outburst. Still, Brown wasn't stupid. He worried about the well-being of the two men and knew he could push social boundaries only so much. When the Browns traveled to play Miami that year, Motley and

MELTING POT   87

Willis were left behind. A Florida state law prohibited any athletic competition between blacks and whites.

One of Shula's finishing touches inside the Dolphins locker room was to put black hair care products like Afro Sheen and hair picks inside the individual lockers of the black players. (Interestingly, in the late 1980s and into the 1990s, when the Green Bay Packers were reintegrated by African-American players, this time in larger numbers, players paid a black barber to travel two hours from Milwaukee to cut their hair.)

Shula asked the white running back Csonka about putting the black hair care products in the locker. "How's that working out?" Shula asked. A surprised Csonka deadpanned, "How would I know?"

Shula wasn't seen as perfect in his handling of racial issues by every black player he coached. Shula had been tough on Bubba Smith, a young black star player for the Colts. Shula's main objective was to get Smith to become a leaner and meaner force. Shula explained in the 1972 book *The Miami Dolphins*: "I was tougher on him than I've ever been on a player," Shula said. "The reason was simple. Bubba was a great athlete who was too fat. When the blubber came off, he became one of the finest players in the game—but it was hard on him and he resented it."

After Shula's departure, Smith had some choice words for Shula. "I don't think he understands black men," Smith told the media. "Me, for instance. I can't function right when somebody is always hollering in my ear."

The problem with Smith's assertion was that Shula hollered in *everyone's* ear and didn't care what color the ear was. It was the greatest sign of equality when Shula yelled at his black and white stars alike. Shula was, in fact, one of the few head coaches in the sport who made an effort to change the racial climate of the NFL for

the better. Shula's racial gestures were appreciated by black players on the Dolphins, even though his moves certainly had other
motives—like his mentor Brown, Shula, above all, wanted to win.
He wasn't going to let even the draining cataclysm that is racism get
in the way of that mission. What Shula did was still significant and
his addressing of racial issues remains a vastly underrated aspect of
his legacy. Simply, what Shula accomplished had been rarely tried
in that time. "We were believers in the one-team concept," Shula
would say years later. "There was no black voice or white voice. Just
our voice."

When Marlin Briscoe arrived in Miami after being traded from
Buffalo in 1971, he expected more of the same ugly racism he'd witnessed as a quarterback and receiver in the NFL. He'd been called
nigger on the field by opponents and ignored or ostracized by whites
on his own team. Briscoe also knew of the stories of the handful
of other black men playing the position, such as his friend James
Harris, who on several occasions needed police protection before
games after receiving death threats.

Briscoe was originally picked by the Denver Broncos in the four-
teenth round of the 1968 draft. The Broncos promised Briscoe he
could train at quarterback for at least three days during training
camp. The Broncos coaches kept their word, but that didn't stop
Briscoe from being moved to the defensive side of the ball once the
three days passed. It's likely Briscoe would have stayed on defense
except in September 1968, during a game against Boston, the starting quarterback broke his collarbone and the backup was tossing
passes into the turf. Briscoe started the season as the number eight
quarterback on the depth chart, meaning he was destined for the
segregation two-step: the forced switch from quarterback to another
position. It was the fourth game, and Coach Lou Saban tired of
seeing his offense struggling. It is in these desperate moments when

practicality momentarily overwhelms the powerful gravitational force of bigotry. Trailing by 14 points, the risk of being socially ostracized was outweighed by the risk of potentially getting fired, so Saban put Briscoe in the game. Briscoe's first pass was a 22-yard completion that hit his receiver square in the chest, the point of the football smacking the pads loudly. The touchdown came for the Broncos on an 80-yard drive. At its conclusion, Briscoe ran 12 yards for the score. There was no jubilant celebration from him (or for him). He calmly walked back to the sideline.

The following week, on October 6, 1968, in a game against Cincinnati, it was Briscoe who became the NFL's first starting black quarterback. It happened forty-seven years after Fritz Pollard became the first black coach in professional football in 1921, three years before Hall of Famer Deacon Jones was told by an owner there would never be another black head coach in the sport in 1971, and fifteen years before Art Shell proved that owner wrong and became the second in 1983. Despite just a handful of practices, and little true support from most teammates, Briscoe finished the season with 14 passing scores, a team rookie record that stood until 2011 when Cam Newton had 17 passing touchdowns his rookie season.

Once Briscoe saved the Broncos' season from disaster, the social norms reset and the segregationist leanings of the sport began to reassert themselves. When Denver's quarterbacks had a meeting at the team facility, Briscoe wasn't invited, only hearing of the meeting from a friend. Briscoe went to confront Saban. "What more did you want me to do?" Briscoe asked. Saban was quiet. "We're going in a different direction," Saban explained. He was reluctant to look Briscoe in the eye while talking.

Briscoe was released by Denver following that exceptional rookie performance and would never play quarterback again.

Briscoe did what almost all other black NFL players who had

hoped to quarterback did: he held his tongue, switched positions, and then worked to be the best. In Buffalo, he became the Bills' top wide receiver and dominated the conference. Again, a weird twist of fate intervened when the Buffalo coach was fired and Saban was named the new coach of the team. Briscoe knew what was next. He was traded.

Briscoe walked into that Dolphins locker room apprehensive, and Miami's reputation as a city didn't help. To many blacks across the country, the city represented one of the hardened segregation bunkers in the nation. Miami was indeed boastful of its separate water fountains and bathrooms, and that warped pride was like a warning beacon to black athletes pondering playing their sports there. Legendary player Larry Little—a key contributor to Shula's Dolphins—grew up in the Miami area and remembers illicitly taking a quick drink out of a white water fountain to see if the myth of superior white water was true.

Not long before Shula took over the Dolphins, a young fighter named Cassius Clay arose at five A.M. many mornings and ran from his inner-city Miami home to the outer rim of Miami Beach. Clay was often stopped by police and sometimes questioned several occasions in one run. They didn't believe he was jogging and phoned Clay's trainer, Angelo Dundee, to verify his story. When Clay became perhaps the most famous of all American athletes, later changing his name to Muhammad Ali, he'd remember those moments as some of the most humiliating of his life.

Dolphins linebacker Doug Swift, a white player who grew up in New England and went to Amherst College, remembered what it was like for black Dolphins players in the Miami area. "I think Miami was a little bit of a stifling atmosphere for blacks," he said. "I don't think they felt part of society in Miami. I think Miami was pretty much all white, southern folks or white Miami Beach types.

The black population [was] pretty much in poor shape." Indeed, black Dolphins players were often stuck in a strange netherworld in Miami. Football player salaries, while far from exorbitant, still made them far wealthier than large swaths of the black Miami population, yet they were separate from and unequal to whites.

This was Miami, and Briscoe expected the worst, yet he found a Dolphins locker room that, while not totally racially harmonious, was not racially poisonous, which was the case inside almost every other NFL franchise. "It was so different from any other team I'd played on or knew," Briscoe remembered. "No other team was like Miami's when I got there. It was the first time I saw black and white unite."

"We didn't have the problem, we didn't have the dissension on our ball club," said offensive lineman Wayne Moore. "We didn't, and honestly, I think it didn't matter to us. Because we were so in tune to getting the job done. We didn't care [about] the color of your skin because we all had one thing in mind, and that's to win the biggest game of all time, the Super Bowl. And by winning the Super Bowl, you get more money. And see all our skins were different colors. We had Spanish, we had black, we had white, but the color on our mind was the same. It was green. It was green—to get that money and get that trophy."

CHAPTER EIGHT

THE MAN WHO FIRED FLIPPER

Joseph Robbie was raised far from Miami's racial divisions and Cold War turmoil, in the actual cold of Sisseton, South Dakota. Only the state of Alaska might be more of a polar opposite to Miami. Robbie's father was a Lebanese immigrant and his mother a combination of Irish and Swiss. His family emerged from the Depression charred but breathing. Law school awaited him, as did a failed bid for governor of South Dakota. Robbie's attempt to buy the Dolphins seemed contrived initially, almost airy. Some powerful men want to own private jets; others, like Robbie, look at a football team like a new toy.

Miami was plotted at a fixed point in time and space while Robbie was sometimes adrift, dabbling in politics and law and hobnobbing, and not necessarily in that order. It seemed like Robbie and Miami were a dramatic mismatch. People had no idea just how true that statement would become.

* * *

Robbie was cheap. Robbie was despised. Robbie was also extremely drunk.

In the summer of 1970, just four years after buying and launching the team, he roamed the concrete tunnels of Tiger Stadium, the alcohol circulating inside his body. He'd been drinking throughout the Dolphins' first exhibition game against the Detroit Lions, and it was taking grand effect. Robbie drinking heavily was far from unusual. Robbie getting lost was. The players, coaches, and front office personnel waited for Robbie on the team bus a short time after the game's conclusion. Five minutes became fifteen and fifteen became twenty. A search party was sent to find Robbie and he was discovered wandering the innards of the stadium looking for the bus. He was inebriated and furious. His loud voiced boomed through the hallways. That didn't change the following day once the team was back in Miami. Robbie blamed the Dolphins' first-year public relations director, Mike Rathet, for his Tiger Stadium walkabout. "Get in here!" Robbie screamed. Robbie was wearing his thick black glasses and a collared short-sleeved shirt. Rathet entered the owner's office.

Robbie reminded Rathet of the incident the previous day, and the more Robbie spoke, the angrier he became. "You're responsible for making sure I'm taken care of!" Robbie yelled.

Many of the Dolphins players, front office personnel, and others had at least one story about Robbie's drunkenness. Some had many. Talk show host Larry King, the Dolphins' radio analyst from 1969–1971, called Robbie "a slovenly drunk." After games, players would visit Robbie's box where he'd watch the Dolphins from high atop the Orange Bowl. Robbie would start drinking hours before the game started—usually Bloody Marys around nine in the morning—and all throughout the day. At the game's conclusion, sometime in the late afternoon, Robbie would be found slumped over in his chair. If possible, he made it to a long table before passing out. "How'd you like the game, Joe?" Morris would ask, knowing he'd get no response from an unconscious Robbie. Other players would join the questioning and uncontrollable chuckling would emerge.

Some of Robbie's drinking stories were less amusing. NFL legend Bobby Beathard was the team's pro personnel director for six years starting in the early 1970s. Beathard worked with Robbie and Shula to coordinate the acquisition of players. Robbie's alcoholism infuriated Beathard and forced Beathard to limit his contact with Robbie to certain hours when he suspected the owner wasn't completely inebriated. Most of the time that was the morning hours, before Robbie headed off to the Jockey Club.

Writers who covered the Dolphins speak of Robbie's drinking in terms usually reserved for people who climb Mount Everest or land on the moon. When *Herald* columnist Pope drank with Robbie, he was stunned at how Robbie would doze off in an inebriated haze—in mid-sentence—and then a few minutes later awake and continue the conversation exactly where he left off.

Elizabeth Robbie once told a journalist how her husband would pass out in the backseat of their limousine drunk. "Mrs. Robbie," the driver would ask, "what should I do when we get to where we're going, dump him on the sidewalk?"

Robbie's extreme personal weaknesses dimmed what was a hearty intellect. "Joe was obviously a troubled guy in some ways," says Shula, "but he was also brilliant." Twice in Minnesota, Robbie was arrested for driving drunk. On one occasion, in 1959, he admitted to drinking three martinis and a highball (whiskey and carbonated water). Despite the heavy alcohol, Robbie insisted his driving was unimpaired and challenged the blood alcohol level of .159, which had been measured with a blood alcohol breath tester, resulting in the measurement over the .150 legal limit. In court proceedings, Robbie demanded a jury trial, and the one-note portrayal of himself as a good man horribly wronged sat well with the jury members. They believed Robbie, and he was acquitted, which stunned the arresting policeman. It was the only such case out of almost 150 the officer had reversed.

This was only part of life under Joe Robbie, a life detailed by Hyde and other writers. A friend of Robbie's and former business partner once said of him: "Joe is difficult in adversity and impossible in success." Robbie wasn't just a drunk. He was also an impossibly cheap man, and in the initial few years of his Dolphins ownership, Robbie's financial gracelessness became legendary. In 1968, most scouting budgets of professional football franchises rarely dipped below $100,000. Miami's was $42,000. Office products like paper clips and stationery were counted and monitored. If too many disappeared—and that number was an arbitrary one—secretaries and office workers were questioned. Players watched in stunned amazement as Robbie angrily confronted locker room attendants and equipment managers (the circulatory force of any football team) if too many towels were washed or missing. Equipment like helmets and shoulder pads were treated like pieces of gold. Incredibly, Robbie asked assistant coaches to tape their outgoing calls. Robbie listened to the tapes to see if the calls were worthy of the expense. If they weren't, the coach received a stern lecture. Robbie would literally spend hours listening to the tapes. He called them a "feasibility study."

Business managers in the Dolphins organization were valued less than the paper clips. At one point during the early part of his tenure, Robbie fired four of them in four years. One was dismissed because he believed some of the secretaries deserved more money. In the offices, where the coaches and personnel worked, over a dozen people squeezed into two rooms. There was one telephone for them all. Secretaries who worked for Robbie so rarely heard the words "thank you" that when they appeared in a note, they framed the note.

Dolphins executives and players were just as infuriated and befuddled by the actions of Robbie as anyone. Joe Thomas was an undervalued aspect of the Dolphins, helping to pluck talent from all across football, some of it from the blue-blooded college football powerhouses, other talent off the scrap heap. Wherever it was, Thomas went to find it. At some point, however, Robbie didn't want to pay for the travel expenses of Thomas and his talent scouts. So Robbie ordered that Thomas could go anywhere just as long as he didn't stay overnight at a hotel. In 1968, scouts had restrictions on how far they could fly because of the expense of airfares.

(Over a decade later, one of Robbie's top lieutenants would provide one of the juicier and perhaps most accurate quotes ever spoken about Robbie. Don Poss worked for Robbie for two years in the early 1980s. Poss said of Robbie: "He has the greatest propensity for shooting himself in the foot of any person I've ever seen. Given a right decision and a wrong decision, he will always opt for the wrong decision and you've got to argue for the right one. I have no animosity toward Joe Robbie. I just don't respect him because of the disrespect he has for most other human beings. That was the main reason I decided to pull the plug. I just couldn't handle watching people let themselves be beat up by him.")

Eventually, anger over Robbie's cheapness subsided into head shaking and the guessing of what was next to come. They soon had their answer and it had to do with ice. It's an invaluable substance to football teams. It cools bodies on sweltering days and reduces inflammation of swollen joints and limbs. Sometimes the packets of ice Miami players needed weren't delivered to the team complex because Robbie hadn't paid the company.

In an effort to save money, the team set up training camp at a bleak site in St. Petersburg. The team put thin sod atop a layer of oyster shell as a cost-cutting maneuver. It wasn't uncommon for the shells to protrude through the turf and cut into players' skin. Some would drive post-practice to the ocean and drown their cuts in the salt water, believing it soothed and cleaned.

No true locker room existed, so players were forced to sleep with their pads, shirts, and jockstraps next to their beds—the smell of sweaty clothing invading their dreams. Since the team could buy Chinese food so cheaply, the hotel served it in gargantuan amounts despite the obvious lack of health and gastrointestinal benefits. So much was shoveled at the players that linebacker Wahoo McDaniel joked: "From now on they'll have to carry me to practice in a rickshaw."

The player payroll was a far thornier issue than diet. Most NFL teams paid poorly, but the Dolphins paid less than most. Defensive end Stanfill's salary his rookie season was $20,000. That was a problem, but not as big as another one. It wasn't unusual for players' paychecks to not clear. In some instances, players literally raced to a local bank to get in line first, fearing there wasn't enough money in Robbie's account to cover the entire team. One month, in the fall of 1967, one of the team's business managers fronted $11,000 of his own cash to meet player payroll. Coaches weren't immune from Robbie either. Wilson paid for the plane tickets home for players who had been released from the team. He was never reimbursed.

What the Dolphins did with equipment and facilities they also did with players. The Dolphins took in the tired, the poor, the huddled masses. The team recruited gym teachers, ex-cops, bouncers, punks, thugs, and creeps, as well as a few brilliant professional players and outstanding characters. McDaniel was an ex-wrestler who bragged about once drinking a quart of motor oil. The *Miami Herald* said the team collected the jetsam and flotsam of the NFL.

By 1969, just a few years after purchasing the team, Robbie was already viewed as a small-time chump among the aristocracy that was NFL ownership. Houston Oilers owner Bud Adams said that Robbie was "running a $2 million operation like a fruit stand." In NFL circles, he was an oddity. In the city of Miami, he was easily one of the more disliked men the city had seen in some time. Nothing alienates people like a wealthy man who asks others to tighten belts when he himself does not. So Robbie's penchant for cheapness was no longer a team secret. It was leaking out into Miami communities quickly and without mercy.

The city prided itself on at least the appearance of chic, and Robbie was cramping that style. "Everybody knows Joe Robbie," Raleigh Tozer, a former Dolphins employee fired by Robbie, told *Sports Illustrated* in December 1969. "You walk down Biscayne Boulevard in front of the Everglades Hotel and eight out of 10 people will say, if asked, 'Joe Robbie? Why, he's that son of a something on the 11th floor of that building.'" After being asked if he hated Robbie, Tozer said, "No, I don't hate him. If I hated him, I could have had him killed. I declined. I'll take care of him myself. Without a gun. He'll break one day. Every time I see him, I say, 'Hello, Joe, you son of a something, how are you?'"

A portion of the chilled reception to Robbie was rooted in snobbery. "Nothing infuriates the natives of Miami Beach more than to be confused with Miamians," a Miami Beach Chamber of Commerce member once said. To many Miamians, Robbie was from a part of the country they knew nothing about and didn't care to. Some of the negative reaction was also seeded in vulcanized bigotry. His Lebanese background was a topic of conversation around the city and in the media. "Whoever heard of an Arab running anything in Miami?" wrote *Sports Illustrated*. In that same story: "Robbie is secret because he is Lebanese . . ." He was described as having a "bent nose" and "furtive eyes." Another person said of Robbie, "Did you ever hear of a Lebanese losing money?" And the latter was a *supporter* of Robbie's. But again, this was Miami, where appearances deceived, and below the sunshiny exterior something always simmered contrarily.

The hatred of Robbie at times became irrational. Once a mayor from Dade County wondered aloud about Robbie before a Miami-area journalist: "What's the matter with that man? We bumped into each other a little while ago and he didn't even say hello." Robbie was being judged for even the ridiculously small things.

Yet it was also inarguable much of the damage to Robbie was self-inflicted. The epitome of his cheapness might have come when he fired Flipper, the beloved movie star dolphin and team mascot. The team used Flipper as a celebratory aid, and after every Miami score he'd bounce and shake in a 16,500-gallon tank (that included 3.5 tons of salt) located in the end zone of the Orange Bowl. The team had selected the dolphin as a mascot by asking fans to submit suggestions, and a thirty-three-year-old housewife won two lifetime season tickets when her dolphin pick won. "I really don't know why I picked the dolphin, except that the dolphin is supposed to be an intelligent animal and the name just came," she said. Others had picked dolphin as well, but she won by correctly guessing the score of the 1965 University of Miami–Notre Dame game, which ended in a tie. "My daughter Holly Ann has this eight ball that makes predictions," she said. "When we asked it about a tie, the answer came up, 'Definitely.'"

The problem for Robbie came when Flipper's tank needed repair and the city of Miami refused to fix it, understandably, thinking the wealthy owner of the team should pay the bill. Robbie declined, and Flipper was suddenly homeless. His tank was removed from the stadium, and Robbie's place as a target of ridicule in Miami was sealed. The Flipper fiasco led to the *Sports Illustrated* headline: "This Man Fired Flipper."

What made Robbie's financial pettiness more noticeable were the actions of some other owners in that era who put their financial spines into the teams. Teams like Pittsburgh. Jim Mandich, after his life-altering stay in Miami, finished his career in Pittsburgh. The Steelers worked a deal with Mandich. He'd be paid a bonus if he played on the bloody and thankless special teams units a certain number of times. After several games, Mandich went to Coach Chuck Noll. "I can't do this," he told the Steelers coach. "My body is giving out." Noll understood and allowed Mandich to skip special teams play. Mandich thought his potential bonus had evaporated since he failed to meet the minimum number of plays. At the end of the season, the owner of the Steelers, the legendary Art Rooney, approached Mandich and handed him a check as Mandich was cleaning out his locker. It was Mandich's bonus with a little extra added to the pot. A stunned Mandich looked down at Rooney. "I didn't earn this," he said. Rooney waved him off. "It was an honor having you here," Rooney replied.

The fact Robbie started to fight back against the media portrayals of him (particularly against the Miami newspapers) only alienated him further because of the awkwardness of his various responses. In one of the Dolphins' 1969 game programs, he lashed out at the press by writing a faux and sarcastic diatribe against newspapers by using journalist Edwin Pope as a target and foil. It wouldn't be the last time Pope and Robbie would openly feud. They'd get into a shouting match in the middle of a hotel lobby in Buffalo. "First you try to run me out of town," Robbie said, "then you ignore me."

In the game program, Robbie posed as a journalist covering journalists.

The first thing I did was call Ed Pope, sports editor of the *Herald*, and tell him I was covering the newspapers.

"Strange," said Ed, "nobody has ever done that before."

"It's long overdue," I agreed. "How is the public to know whether you people are doing an accurate job or not if no one watches over you?"

"Well, exactly what is it you want to know?'

I consulted my notes. "First thing, can you please tell me your total budget, your salary and the salary of every writer on your staff?"

"I'm sorry . . ."

"Also the salaries of your rim men, correspondents and copy boys?"

"We consider that confidential."

"But it's of great interest to the public. I'm checking out rumors that Miami sportswriters' pay is the lowest in the league, next to Denver."

"We don't give out that information."

"But," I argued, "pay has a direct bearing on product. Can you at least tell me how much expense money you give your photographers when they cover Dolphin games out of town?"

"We don't send photographers on Dolphin road trips."

"Oh," I said. "Cheapskates," I wrote in my notebook. "Let's get off finances," I suggested. "Can you tell me why last Sunday you elected to run an eight-column 72-point italic head on your strip story instead of a 72-point Bodoni italic?"

Robbie finished up his serving of sarcasm with this last shot: "I would have liked to talk longer, but I had to cut it short. I had a deadline for my first article. It's very complimentary, actually. It's entitled: Expansion City Sportswriters Getting Better—But Still Have Room to Improve."

Shockingly, the smart-ass-ness of the game-day program story didn't go over well with the media. Soon, the skirmish between Robbie and the press escalated into a full-blown battle. When a *Herald* reporter started to detail the Dolphins' financial issues, the newspaper received an angry letter from Robbie who said he disliked the paper's "morbid fascination with the club's finances." The reporter didn't receive flak from his bosses. He instead got a raise.

Robbie's relationship with the press reached an all-time low after he fired the married couple who catered food for the media at the Miami home games. The bill for Robbie was just $110 per game—a pittance for an NFL owner, but it was still too much for Robbie. So sandwiches and other deli items were replaced by hot dogs.

Robbie couldn't understand why people focused solely on his foibles and not his achievements. Robbie also chuckled at Miami's sense of self-importance and flirtation with elitism. Miami had yet to begin its massive transformation into a cosmopolitan mecca and vacation destination for the middle class, college students, and the worldwide wealthy alike. As late as 1964, Miami had almost zero foreign trade, and more recently than that, the airport had no transatlantic flights. Robbie looked around the city and saw increasing corruption, the drug trades, men making their wealth off the backs of immigrants. Large swaths of Miami Beach were run by the mob, the same way Al Capone ran them in the 1930s. The overall deception, the insanity. The new Casablanca, as writer David Rieff once wrote, with all of its incarnations. "Miami is the only city in the world where you can tell a lie at breakfast," said late nineteenth-century politician William Jennings Bryan, "that will come true by evening."

Shula remembers Robbie as feeling persecuted. This was Robbie's irrational rationale: The fact he brought professional football to Miami should have outweighed whatever minor idiosyncrasies his personality wrought. "I'm where I am now," Robbie once said, "for one reason. That's because nobody wants to put their own money up. They want something for nothing. They don't want to take any risks. That's why I have the club. I took the risk."

In another conversation with *Sports Illustrated*, the owner made what sounded like a passionate, desperate plea for understanding. Robbie explains his mind-set of feeling under siege and underappreciated for bringing a professional football team to Miami. It is, in fact, one of the few times Robbie publicly demonstrated a human side to what had become a disintegrating image.

> The whole thing is this. I brought pro football here when
> nobody else would get near the place. I protected football
> in this community. But the club and I have been under
> constant pressure since the day we got here. I didn't
> have to come down here to have people try to prove I'm
> a cheapskate. It's been personally offensive to me. It's
> against my nature, against my family's nature, not to give
> . . . give the shirt off your back if somebody needs it. I've
> been brought up this way. There's no charge that I'm more
> sensitive to than that.
>
> I've been on the board of governors at St. Jude Hospital
> for 10 years. I've traveled every place they wanted me to,
> even on a monthly basis, at my own expense. I've always
> been involved in charities. For nothing. That's the kind of
> lawyer I was, too. The people I represented I represented
> without fee most of the time. These pack rats that are
> trying to gnaw on my bones! No man ever left my office

unrepresented who came in and said he had no money.
The St. Petersburg training camp was unfortunate, but it
would never have happened had I been on the scene. The
incident there has been the cause of all my trouble. As
soon as I got to St. Petersburg I got the club out of there.
The other reasons for our image here have been disloyal
employees . . .

We've had to live by our wits here in Miami. I think
some people have thought that if they could damage or
destroy our financial structure they could move in and
take over. I've been a target because some people resent the
fact that I have control of this ball club and have had the
legal control of it from the first day. I've been vulnerable
because I was not operating from a strong financial
position. Now let me say this. There is not an investor who
has ever put one red copper cent into the operations of this
club. Every cent that has ever been paid in by an investor
has been used to pay the franchise debt to the AFL, and
a $100,000 annual payment debt to be made to the NFL.
Every bit of operating money has been obtained from
income or from banking arrangements I make. I'm the
only one personally liable in this place.

Robbie grew up during the Depression but he still found work,
spending years in the Civilian Conservation Corps building roads
and planting trees. Most of the money Robbie earned he'd dutifully
sent home. He did custodial work and kitchen duties to pay for law
school, and as a lawyer in Minnesota earned under $30,000 annu-
ally, he helped to support the entire Robbie family, which consisted
of eleven children. He did pro bono work for Native Americans
treated poorly by the legal system. Robbie saw himself as a man who

had truly earned his way into NFL ownership. He wasn't gifted into it the way other owners were. He wasn't born into wealth, and Robbie bristled about how his poor upbringing became an albatross instead of a badge of honor. In 1969, *Sports Illustrated* called Robbie "the poorest man to obtain a sports franchise in the last 20 years." It was written, Robbie thought, with unfair disdain.

If Robbie hated that line in the story, he certainly hated the final paragraph: "Because of his guile and gall in deals, the anatomy of which no one is certain, he will leave his mark on Miami. But he is, it seems, a failure in a sense, that is if you appreciate art, whether it is in a jewel heist or in the gray rooms of finance. On the inside Joe Robbie was said to be delicate, cool and brilliant. Now, whether out of desperation, confusion, or maybe because of a lack of style under pressure, he somehow seems to have become—to those who watch him closely—just another prairie pirate with the touch of a blacksmith."

Not long before Robbie's purchasing of the Dolphins and entering the realm of prairie pirate-hood, George Wilson was a champion unaware he was on the verge of disaster.

He'd become Robbie's first choice as coach of the expansion Dolphins. But for the moment he was coach of the Lions and engaged in sophomoric foolishness. Wilson was often a very unserious man who enjoyed his jokes and light moments. This time it was with writer George Plimpton, who spent training camp with the Lions in 1963 as an amateur quarterback and chronicled the experience in the book *Paper Lion*. Plimpton went to a Lions game in 1964 to say hello to some on the team. Before the exhibition game started, in the locker room, Wilson spotted Plimpton. "Get that man into uniform, quick," said Wilson. Wilson was serious. Plimpton was stunned. The game was just a preseason one—and basically meaningless—but it was still an interesting decision by Wilson to have Plimpton revisit his role.

Plimpton had previously worn the number 0, but it wasn't available, so the equipment manager handed him the number 30. It was Wilson's number when he played for Chicago alongside storied football names like quarterback Sid Luckman and runner Bronko Nagurski. Plimpton got completely dressed—the shoulder pads, the football pants, the helmet, everything—and ran alongside Wilson as the two jogged out of the locker room onto the Detroit sideline. Plimpton was nervous, knowing the Lions were prank players of the grandest order. Wilson had planned to actually insert Plimpton into the game but couldn't since the contest was close. Instead, Wilson parked Plimpton near the bank of phones that connected the assistant coaches sitting high atop the stadium to the players and staff on the ground. Prank averted. Not even Wilson would light that prank fuse.

But most of the time, Wilson did. In Detroit he was seen as a player's coach, the antithesis of Tom Landry, who shut down power to the player dorms during Cowboys training camp at 10:30 P.M. sharp and bed-checked with religious ferocity. Wilson had few rules as coach of the Lions. He drank with his players. Practices were run loosely. Discipline was enforced more by the players than Wilson. His system, no matter its elasticity, worked in Detroit. At least for a short window it did. He was named coach of the Lions in 1957 and in his first season went 8–4 and won an NFL championship. It was a high point for Wilson (it was the last championship the Lions have won), but his penchant for running a program loosely would burn him. Wilson traded star quarterback Bobby Layne from the Lions, which stunned the football world. There is no doubt Layne was indeed a problem child off the field. There were strong suspicions Layne was gambling on football, including Lions games. He'd also been arrested for driving drunk (he was later acquitted). Yet players driving under the influence were not unusual for the 1950s (or frowned upon), and there was no proof Layne had been gambling. The main reason Wilson traded Layne was because Wilson had made a huge mistake in judgment: He thought he could win without him. "To this day, I still don't know why they traded him," said former Detroit linebacker Joe Schmidt, who played with Layne. "We really missed Bobby."

Wilson traded Layne twenty-four hours after a 13–13 tie. Layne was furious and blasted his old team in harsh words that over the decades would become the "Curse of Bobby Layne." When leaving, Layne told some of his Lions teammates: "The Lions won't win for the next 50 years." It seemed like the statement of a petulant man who wanted to see the team that traded him fall flat on its face. However, in the coming years, perhaps no statement in sports would become truer. Detroit won only five games that year. In the five decades since, they have a single playoff victory. On the fiftieth anniversary of the Lane curse, in 2008, the Lions became the first team in NFL history to go 0-16. The way Wilson's career was about to unfold, the curse might as well have applied to him too.

Wilson was fired by the Lions in 1965, and as Robbie began his search for the first coach of the Dolphins, it was becoming clear Wilson was the favorite to fill the job. Robbie initially wanted Ara Parseghian, the coach of Notre Dame, but Parseghian wasn't interested. Paul Brown was. The problem for Robbie was that Brown not only wanted financial control but also control of the entire Dolphins organization. Robbie was a survivor, and he knew the eventual outcome of that relationship. He'd be gone. So that negotiation slowed and eventually died.

Robbie was intrigued by Wilson and became even more enthralled when it seemed Wilson was headed to coach Atlanta. Wilson didn't care about control of the Dolphins. He simply wanted to coach and had a reputation as someone who could coexist with almost any owner or executive. The latter aspect was important to Robbie. Robbie and Wilson met late in 1965, and it was clear the union would happen. Robbie also discovered the actuality of why Wilson departed Detroit. When the Lions coaches were fired, management wanted to keep Wilson, but out of loyalty to the rest of the staff, Wilson quit. Not long after that he'd be in Miami.

Several years into Wilson's tenure, the Dolphins were the dregs of the sport—and a joke to most Miamians. Almost as big a farce as decades earlier, in 1946, when a man named Harvey Hester brought the Miami Seahawks of the All-America Football Conference to the city, making them the first professional team there. They were annihilated in practically every game, had their home opener delayed because of a hurricane, played on Monday nights when it wasn't prestigious to do so, drew 242 fans to one home contest, and disbanded just a year later $350,000 in debt.

In the Dolphins' opening four seasons, the team went 15-39-2. In that horrible 1969 season, the Dolphins won three games and sold 17,478 season tickets total (the Orange Bowl seats seventy-five thousand). As an example of their disorganization at the time, after a 33–0 exhibition loss to Kansas City, a game played in a rainstorm, the Dolphins returned to their dressing room, uniforms soaked. When someone tried to open the door, it was locked. They were shut out of their own locker room and forced to stand in the rain another fifteen minutes while one of the janitors looked for the key.

Robbie had seen enough. It was time to make a change. A drastic one.

CHAPTER NINE

SHULA'S BACKBONE

Decades before Wilson's Miami demise, the last will and testament of Dan and Mary Shula, the parents of Don, was created and served as a portrait of their lives. They refused to accumulate debt, abhorred the collection of material things, and wanted to raise their children in a stable home. This was their simple mission. Dan passed away at eighty-two years old. He left everything to Mary, his unwavering trust in her surviving his demise. "I make no provisions for any children I may now have," his will states, "and specifically disinherit any child or children born or adopted by me hereafter, having full faith and trust in my wife that she will adequately provide for them."

Four years later, Mary died at the age of eighty-three after a fight with Alzheimer's. But before the disease took her mind, Mary shaped her will—both the one inside of her and the document itself. She immediately made the decision to make Don the executor of the latter. She trusted Don to make the right choices since—as she once said—he'd made the right choices his entire life. In the will, the subject of the Super Bowl rings Don gave to his mother was mentioned. Mary signed the document with her usual hoop at the beginning of the *M* in Mary and the *h* in Shula.

I direct that all my just debts and funeral expenses be paid out of my estate as soon as practicable after the time of my decease.

I give and bequeath to my son, James Shula, my Madonna statue; Don Shula's Super Bowl ring; my microwave oven; and my stero [*sic*].

I give and bequeath to my daughter, Jane Shula, my small portable color television; my diamond ring; my Super Bowl ring; my string of cultured pearls and earrings; my silver Early American lamp; my aqua bedroom chair; my marble table; my large brass bed; my pots and pans; my fireplace equipment; my 1976 Oldsmobile Cutlass Supreme automobile; my two (2) blue living room chairs; Don's portrait (large painting); my dresser and chest and Mr. Shula's dresser and chest; my blue silk flower painting; my end table; and one (1) Royal Doulton mug.

I give and bequeath to my daughter, Irene Battista, my silver set (teacup and tray); my one (1) brass Early American lamp; my large brass lamp; my brass candelabra; and my brass candlesticks.

I give and bequeath to Dorothy Bartish Shula my Christ head.

I give and bequeath to Joseph Shula one (1) Royal Doulton mug.

The rest of the household goods, including furniture, fixtures and equipment, I give and bequeath to my

daughters, Jane Shula and Irene Battista, to be divided
between them as they see fit.

My son, Joseph Shula, has already received his share
of my estate through property that was transferred to
him in Grand River, Ohio which was thereafter sold by
him. Therefore, I give, devise and bequeath all the rest,
residue and remainder of my estate whether real, personal
or mixed, of every kind and nature whatsoever, and
wheresoever situated, which I may now own or hereafter
acquire, or have the right to dispose of at the time of my
decease, by power of appointment or otherwise, equally,
to my five children, namely: Irene Battista, Donald Shula,
Jane Shula, Jeanette Moroz and James Shula, absolutely
and in fee simple, share and share alike.

Mary's estate was valued at $126,809.28. The debts were practically
nonexistent—left over gas and phone bills, doctor bills, legal fees—a
result of Dan's lifelong insistence that the Shulas live within their
means. Joseph Shula, given only the Royal Doulton mug valued at
$80, refused it. It was decided the mug would be given to Jane, who
accepted it.

Despite surviving the Depression and living an extremely meager
life, at one point earning twelve dollars a week as a fisherman,
Dan had provided for Mary and his children in his death. James,
Jane, Irene, Jeanette, and Don each received a cash distribution of
$20,341.81 from the Shula estate. It is a remarkable achievement
that began thousands of miles away with a family dreaming of a
better life.

According to Shula family narrative, Shula's father came to the
United States at six years old. Immigration records show Dan actually arrived in New York on June 7, 1910. He was ten. Dan and his

family traveled on the *SS Vaderland* in the third-class portion of the eleven-thousand-ton ocean liner. The captain's written declaration upon arrival at the Port of New York also shows it was a different era: "I believe that no one of said aliens is an idiot, or imbecile, or a feeble-minded person, or insane person, or a pauper, or is likely to become a public charge, or is afflicted with tuberculosis or with a loathsome or dangerous contagious disease, or is a person who has been convicted of, or who admits having committed a felony or other crime or misdemeanor involving moral turpitude, or is a polygamist or one admitting belief in the practice of polygamy, or an anarchist, or under a promise or agreement, express or implied, to perform labor in the United States, or a prostitute, or a woman or girl coming to the United States for the purpose of prostitution, or for any other immoral purpose, and that also, according to the best of my knowledge and belief, the information in said Lists or Manifests concerning each of said aliens named therein is correct and true in every respect."

The Shula family history actually began decades earlier. Joseph Miller Sr. and his wife, Anna Toth Miller, came to the United States in 1898. He was twenty-eight and she was twenty. Dan followed, and his official name on immigration documents shows as Denes Sule. He later Anglicized his name to Dan.

The Shula family migration was far from unusual. There were several waves of ethnic Hungarians that immigrated to America, and the Shulas arrived with the second wave at the turn of the twentieth century. Many Hungarians who came to the country settled in the Cleveland, Ohio, area. They worked the coal mines, steel and textile mills, machine factories, and foundries, and they stayed mostly within their own communities. In the city of Cleveland alone, the Hungarian population went from 9,558 in the early 1900s to 43,134 by 1920.

Some thirty miles east of downtown Cleveland is the city of Painesville, neatly situated along the Grand River in Lake County. The entire county was a treasure of resources, with sprawling vineyards, nurseries, and stocked fisheries. The fishing work was particularly rugged. The men were up and working at four in the morning, returned for a few hours in the afternoon, then headed back out to fish again until the evening. The wives called themselves fishing widows because of the unusual hours of their husbands. The commercial season went from March 15 to November 15, but if the men also mended nets, the work was year-round. Damaged nets were hauled with small trucks, spread across a field, mended, and tarred.

Many men in the town worked at one of several popular fisheries once they reached their late teenage years, and this is what Dan did as well. By the time Dan met Mary Miller, a fellow Hungarian born in the United States, Dan was a hardened fisherman. She was familiar with the life, being raised in Grand River, Ohio, a small Lake Erie fishing village on the outskirts of Painesville.

Dan completed his World War I draft card on September 12, 1918, and three years later, after converting to Catholicism, he and Mary were married in Lake County and moved into their home at 615 River Street, next door to the Miller family grocery store. In the coming years, Dan and Mary would experience the great highs of building a stable life and family and the horrors of losing a young child. On August 17, 1922, Mary gave birth to twins, Josephine and Joseph. When Josephine was six, she was riding her bicycle not far from home when her bicycle flipped and she landed on the back of her head. Her death certificate lists the cause of death as "fracture to the base of the skull . . . died in 10 hrs after injury." She was buried at St. Mary Cemetery in Painesville.

Between 1930 and 1937, Dan and Mary had five more children, including Donald Francis Shula, who was born on January 4, 1930, at the family home. (Don's birth was not officially registered until thirty-four years later. His parents filed a delayed certificate of birth with the Ohio Department of Health on April 24, 1964.) Older sister Irene was born in 1926. Triplets Jeannette, James, and Jane were born at Lake County Memorial Hospital on May 22, 1936. Their births became the talk of Painesville, and a story soon appeared in the *Cleveland Plain Dealer* newspaper. "Goo, goo and goo!" the story began. "It's Jeanette, James and Jane signing on (they never sign off) from their nursery in the Daniel Shula household (which they run to suit themselves) in the tiny village of Grand River, northwest of here. Everyone in Grand River will tell you (they could be prejudiced) they're the most adorable triplets in the world." The story ran prominently next to two articles about President Franklin D. Roosevelt.

Over the years, the Shula/Miller families focused their efforts on running a family grocery. It was built slowly from a small store with great ambition to a larger one that became highly popular in the neighborhood. The 1930 Census shows the store valued at $10,000, which was a large amount for the time. Don's father still had to get more work after the triplets were born, so he got a job at the nearby Grow Brothers Fish Company.

Inside the Shula family home was love and discipline, not many outward expressions of the former, but plenty of discussion about the latter. Shula had a series of rules to live by even as a child. One was simple. When he was out playing, anytime and anywhere he saw the streetlights come on, he was to immediately go home. Once, a power failure savaged the neighborhood and the lights failed. Shula stayed out later than normal, and when he arrived home, his mother and father awaited, furious. Shula told them about the power outage, but it didn't matter. He received a harsh spanking. There were to be no excuses. It was a mantra Shula would carry for the rest of this life.

* * *

Shula had made a remarkable journey and, in a way, a very American one. He was the child of immigrants who initially didn't want their son to play football. He went from the playgrounds as a kid to high school, where he became a man, then to a tiny college, where he played football, followed by a brief professional career. Although he wasn't the most talented, he was the most persistent. He moved into coaching, and the same cunning he displayed on the field worked in the classroom with players. It was a brutally quick learning experience, a rush of highs and lows, leading to an incredible moment: the Super Bowl in 1969, as coach of the Colts, against the New York Jets and perhaps the most famous guarantee in sports history.

Joe Namath was colorful and arrogant, but he was also smart. The Jets came from the upstart AFL, considered a far weaker league than its NFL counterpart. Baltimore was a drastic favorite; no one expected the Jets to stay within 2 touchdowns. To many inside football and the media, this game was one of the greatest mismatches in sports history. The AFL was seen as the NFL's little brother, a league still years away from serious competition. When the merger of the two leagues occurred, the NFL was seen as the vastly superior entity, and this Super Bowl would be a coronation of the greatness of the NFL and the smallness of the AFL. Before the game, former star NFL player and Falcons coach Norm Van Brocklin, as many did, mocked Namath and the Jets to the media. "This will be Namath's first professional football game," he said smugly.

Namath was fully aware of how most people had already handed the championship to the Colts, and he decided to be, well, Namath. He publicly toyed with the Colts during the week leading to the Super Bowl, hoping to get the team out of its impressive rhythm that saw it annihilate teams for much of the season. Namath knew exactly what he was doing. He spoke openly to the media about how there were three quarterbacks in Namath's AFL better than Baltimore's Earl Morrall, and Morrall fell into the trap, vowing to make Namath regret his choice of words. Morrall had a right to be irritated. In replacing the legendary and injured Johnny Unitas, Morrall that season led the Colts to fifteen wins, then the most ever for a quarterback.

Namath wasn't done. He made a guarantee that would become national news and NFL lore. "We're gonna win the game," he said, "I guarantee it." That's it. That simple. And with those words, Shula's Super Bowl became far more interesting in what had already been an interesting year. Unitas would become maybe the greatest quarterback in league history, but he spent most of that season injured. Shula and Unitas had a solid relationship, but Unitas couldn't bite his tongue as his health improved and Morrall stayed on the field. Unitas knew he was a godlike figure and took full advantage. He was right. The sports editor of Baltimore's *News American* wrote the only thing Unitas hadn't done was walk atop the Chesapeake Bay. "Of course," famous Baltimore sportswriter John Steadman wrote, "he's never tried."

Anytime reporters asked Unitas why he hadn't been inserted back into the starting lineup for Morrall once healthy, Unitas had a stock answer. "Why don't you ask The Man?" he'd say. As the Super Bowl approached, Unitas was pushing Shula to start him. Shula refused. He saw no reason to make the switch. Morrall was coming off a blistering 34–0 win over Cleveland in the conference championship game before the Super Bowl. The overwhelming victory led to Colts owner Carroll Rosenbloom declaring in a television interview that the Colts' performance was the best he'd ever witnessed. He praised Shula and declared he'd never want another person to lead his team.

The sentiment was understandable. Like he would do with the Dolphins, Shula blended older players, younger unknowns, highly skilled talents, blue-collar fighters, and characters into a cohesive, dangerous team. The glue that held Shula's teams together was his own coaching skills and innovations both big and small. One of those innovations led to a humorous moment. At the beginning of the 1964 season, Shula made one of his more subtle but interesting moves as coach of Baltimore. He named player Alex Hawkins captain of the special teams. It sounds unremarkable enough, but at the time, the NFL had captains for defense and offense only; special teams captains weren't named. It was considered a joke. Yet Shula had a purpose for the move. He wanted to emphasize special teams as a key component of the game. Most coaches filled their special teams with psychos and dickheads, but Shula wanted his special team players to be elite and important. So here was Hawkins, special teams captain, before the first preseason game, standing alongside legends Unitas and Gino Marchetti. The game official, as was tradition, introduced himself to the captains. He said hello to Unitas, the offensive captain, and Marchetti, the defensive one. Then he turned to Hawkins.

"Captain Who?" the official said to Hawkins.

And Captain Who became a part of Colts lore.

For the game against the Jets, everything was pointing to a Colts win, and that is probably why the Colts lost. The players began to believe the Jets weren't in the same class and watching film of New York only reinforced that belief. The Jets looked slow and small. Shula tried to warn his players of the pitfalls of being overly confident, but it wasn't enough. This was the only problem with Shula being such a young head coach. Shula hadn't yet learned the tricks and tactics of an experienced veteran. He didn't know how to emphasize the point that arrogance would cause them to lose.

The Colts players weren't the only ones perhaps overly confident. The Associated Press handicapped the game in a story: "Jimmy (the 'Greek') Snyder was admitted into the University of California at Santa Barbara Hospital today. Before he checked in, however, he listed the Baltimore Colts as an 18-point favorite to defeat the New York Jets in the Super Bowl." Eighteen points in any NFL game— let alone the Super Bowl—was an incredibly large number and indicative of how almost anyone who knew anything about football believed the Colts would destroy the Jets.

Rosenbloom certainly believed that. Rosenbloom was a chatty man and snappy dresser. Players remember Rosenbloom on the Colts sideline wearing a dark fedora, long dark overcoat, suit jacket and tie, dark trousers, and perfectly shined shoes. Before the Super Bowl, Rosenbloom scheduled a victory party at his home—a serious violation of football superstitions and protocol. The football gods rolled over in their chariots when Rosenbloom, upon seeing Weeb Ewbank, the coach of the Jets, after the Colts' final practice before the game, invited Ewbank to the Colts' celebration. Not only had the Colts scheduled a victory party before the game, but the owner of the Colts *invited the opposing coach to it.* Ewbank was smart. He declined the invitation by simply walking away from Rosenbloom without speaking a word and then later informed his team of Baltimore's arrogance. Ewbank used the party invitation as part of his pregame speech, ending it with the declaration that the Jets would be having a party of their own after the game. With those words, Shula's fate was sealed.

Namath lived up to his guarantee. Instead of adding weight on the players' shoulders, it gave the Jets a sort of freedom. That entire week, Namath was calculatingly aloof and belligerent. He was one of four players who refused to attend one of the first Super Bowl press conferences, which was Namath's way of telling doubters to go to hell.

The Super Bowl was already becoming extremely popular with the American public, but Namath's guarantee drew extra attention, including from the football-obsessed President-elect Nixon, who was in attendance. The Jets played loose, but also with simple and efficient precision, and grabbed control early. At halftime, the Colts trailed just 7–0, but because they were such heavy favorites, the score felt more like Baltimore was losing by five scores. Shula sensed, even at halftime, the game was slipping away. In the locker room, with the team gathered around him, Shula told the team just before they returned for the third quarter: "We're making stupid mistakes. We're stopping ourselves. You've got them believing they are a better team than we are. Let's go out there in the second half and take charge of the game the way we know we can."

Shula's speech didn't matter. Namath would make his guarantee come true as he beat the best defense in football. It was the Jets, as Ewbank predicted, who had the post-game party. While the Jets celebrated, Shula was in a state of depression. On the bus ride home, players glared silently out the windows, saying little. At the team hotel, one of the injured players who had been hit twice in the head suffered a seizure and was rushed to the hospital. He almost died.

Shula had made the wrong kind of history. The Colts lost to the AFL. One of his players almost lost his life. The defeat began to strain his relationship with Rosenbloom. The year following the Super Bowl, the Colts went 8-5-1 and the strain with Rosenbloom worsened. Rosenbloom hired a new general manager and transferred some of Shula's personnel duties to him. There was, soon, a full-blown war between Shula and Rosenbloom. It is in these moments when Shula's stubbornness hurt him. Shula's will was able to power him to the position of one of the best young coaches in the sport, but he was also, at times, impossibly stubborn, refusing to relent on even the smallest of things. Rosenbloom was similar, only with an uglier temper and little patience. Rosenbloom's praise of Shula seemed like a distant memory. In the end, Shula knew his days in Baltimore were almost over.

CHAPTER TEN

THE BEGINNING

In 1969, Jim Morrison took to the stage of the Dinner Key Auditorium in Miami, a converted Pan Am seaplane hangar. Before the arrival of Jim Morrison and the Doors, fans had scaled the outside of the squat building like cat burglars, scampering into second-story windows. Morrison started the concert in a state of extreme inebriation. Even for him. Morrison erupted into a tirade that seemed to call for the concertgoers to riot, and at one point, Morrison had a simple question for the stunned crowd: "You want to see my cock, don't you?" Apparently, some did, and whether Morrison obliged no one has been able to say fully. The aftermath was swift and, like many things that happened in Miami, became national news. The *Miami Herald*, on March 3, 1969, described the concert this way: "The hypnotically erotic Morrison, flaunting the laws of obscenity, indecent exposure and incitement to riot, could only stir a minor mob scene toward the end of his Saturday night performance . . . It was not meant to be pretty. Morrison appeared to masturbate in full view of his audience, screamed obscenities and exposed himself. He also got violent, slugged several . . . officials and threw one of them off stage before he himself was hurled into the crowd."

It didn't take long for the conservatives in the city to fan the outrage, and soon the incident was portrayed by some as a pivotal moment in the battle of *America v. Hippie*. At the Orange Bowl, a group of teenagers held a gathering called Rally for Decency. Nixon saw it and sent the group a letter of thanks. Four days after the incident, the city of Miami issued a warrant for the arrest of Morrison. Or, rather, six of them: a felony accusation of lewd and lascivious behavior, two counts of indecent exposure, two counts of public profanity, and one of drunkenness. Miami served as the beginning of what would be a mini-revolution, but not the kind perhaps Morrison had envisioned. The city began to feel its collective conservative oats, harkening back to the old days of white rule and traditionalism. Miami had made its mark, and the situation ended in Morrison fleeing the country and *Rolling Stone* magazine penning an article entitled "Morrison's Penis Is Indecent."

That same year, not far from Morrison's excellent adventure, Robbie was perhaps wishing his Dolphins could get half the attention Morrison was. The Dolphins finished the season 3-10-1, and Robbie was facing a dismal truth. Not only were his Dolphins horrible, they were also boring. As Robbie searched the coaching landscape for a new leader, his quest was not just for a winner but someone who could give the Dolphins credibility. There was a run at Notre Dame's Ara Parseghian, who at the time was as respected a name in football as there was—his 1966 team won the national title. He listened to Robbie, then said no. The most painful rejection came from the grandest of football royalty. How exactly University of Alabama's Bear Bryant came to be wooed and eventually offered the job has been told several different ways, but the book *Still Per-*

fect! likely portrayed what happened with accuracy. The Dolphins, desperate, courted Bryant for two weeks. The minority owner of the Dolphins had Bryant stay at the Jockey Club resort during his lengthy stay in Miami. He met key business figures throughout the city and was promised a contract from the Dolphins that would have given him 5 percent ownership of the team in addition, of course, to a large salary. Bryant was treated better than a president or king. It's understandable why the Dolphins puckered up to smooch some Crimson Tide rear end. Bryant had won three national titles by 1965. He was already a legend, and his southern background would appeal to a conservative fan base, some of which considered itself children of the South anyway.

The more Bryant returned the flirtation, the more the Dolphins' sense of self-worth increased. *The Bear is interested in us.* For the first time maybe since the organization took its first breath, there was a sense of pride and a feeling that the Dolphins were on the verge of creating something special. "I was telling myself nobody had ever done both—that is, nobody had ever won national championships of both the college and the pros . . ." Bryant was once quoted as saying about the Miami job. "[And] when the Dolphins talked to my tax adviser he came back and told me it would take an awful long time for me to make that kind of money in college ball or anything else . . ." So why didn't he take the job? He enjoyed the flirtation, but Bryant was never truly going to Miami—the Dolphins were viewed by Bryant and others as several notches below the Crimson Tide.

When the inevitable letdown happened, with the governor of Alabama intervening to stroke Bryant's ego and Crimson Tide pride, Robbie's sense of self-worth was replaced by dread. Robbie became so despondent he decided to confide in *Herald* reporters Braucher and Pope.

Pope had a question: Why don't you make this simple and go after a huge name—why don't you try to hire Shula?

Robbie was slightly taken aback and then he wondered: *Damn, what if I could pull that off?*

Braucher called Shula in what was effectively a circumvention of NFL rules. Shula was under contract and no other team could contact Shula without permission from the Colts. While the use of Braucher as a middleman did not technically violate those rules, they essentially did. Everyone involved knew this. Braucher's behavior also wasn't journalistically sound since reporters aren't supposed to insert themselves smack in the middle of news stories, but this was a different era. Reporters hung with their sources, drank with them, partied with them, and sometimes rooted for their success. One of the Dolphins writers was a regular hunting partner with Griese. In that time, what Braucher was doing wasn't considered unusual.

Shula wasn't convinced initially and needed to hear the interest directly from Robbie. Not long before, Shula, unknown to many, had considered the idea of leaving the Colts for another NFL team. Shula wrote in his 1973 biography: "I received a call from another team in the league inquiring as to my availability. It was one of the stronger franchises and they were looking for a head coach. The timing was perfect. We spoke two or three times in general terms. When it began to get serious, I felt I couldn't go on talking with them anymore unless there was something solid to offer. But in the final conversation with them, one of the executives of the club said that rather than pursue the talks any further, they were going to keep the coach they had for at least another year."

Shula flew to Miami, where he and Dorothy were met at the airport by Robbie's wife, Elizabeth. Robbie figured he'd better not be seen with Shula in public just yet. After a flurry of flights and negotiations, Shula agreed to a multiyear contract that paid him $70,000 a year and 10 percent ownership of the Dolphins. At the time, it was one of the wealthiest contracts a coach had ever signed, and it was twice what Wilson earned.

It was done. Shula was coach of the Dolphins. Shula dazzled at his initial press conference with the Miami media. He stood tall, wearing a dark blazer and dark tie knotted tightly around his neck. His hair was combed and parted neatly. He oozed professionalism, which was the opposite of his predecessor. "I'm about as subtle as a punch in the mouth," he said. "I don't have any miracle secrets. I rely on hard work and nothing more."

It all went smoothly except for one thing: Rosenbloom was furious, and as the Baltimore media roasted him for losing Shula, his internal temperature increased. Eventually, Rosenbloom filed official tampering charges against Robbie, and Rozelle, while constantly aware of the public relations hazards, had no choice but to punish Robbie. He handed Baltimore the Dolphins' top draft pick, a number one pick, which was a crushing blow. But Robbie figured: *I got Shula.*

Robbie also fought back by saying this at a press conference: "It never occurred to me either then or now that if a person under contract is told that he can discuss entering a new contract with someone else, the someone else needs permission to talk to the person under contract. Commissioner Rozelle agreed that Shula had obtained permission from the Baltimore Colts to talk to me, but he held that I needed permission to talk to Shula. Think about that for a while. Shula could talk to me but I couldn't talk to him."

Rosenbloom had his draft pick and in part his revenge, but it wasn't enough. Shula's move to Miami initiated an intense hatred of Shula and Robbie that would never ease. When Robbie attempted to initiate a détente with an apologetic phone call, Rosenbloom declared he would never speak to Robbie again and hung up the phone. He literally turned his back on Shula at an NFL owners' meeting later that year.

It was true that all sides were not at their finest in this moment. Robbie used a sportswriter to circumvent NFL rules, Shula allowed him to do so (though Rosenbloom had poisoned the relationship), and Rosenbloom was acting like a petulant child. Yet Rosenbloom had taken things too far. He made it personal in a business where brutal transactions were conducted on a daily basis. Players were axed, coaches were fired, and careers, even lives, were ruined by injuries on a daily basis. Rosenbloom's indignation was remarkable.

From then on, whenever Rosenbloom spoke of Shula publicly, while refusing to speak to him privately, it was to take a shot at him. He pointed out how Shula was 0-2 in the Super Bowl and had also lost the 1964 championship game to the Browns. In 1970, Rosenbloom summed up his feelings on the two men neatly: "I have not talked to Robbie or Shula since this happened. I will not talk to Robbie or Shula ever again. One stole something from me. The other allowed himself to be stolen."

After the Dolphins' Super Bowl loss to Dallas, Rosenbloom again spoke publicly of Shula's inability to win the big game. Rosenbloom's obsession with Shula was almost creepy—it got so bad that Rozelle fined him $5,000 for his continual comments—but Shula kept track of the insults. Every slight was chronicled inside his head. As the Dolphins rolled along, the wins were important to Shula, but there was only one thing that mattered.

Dolphins tight end Howard Twilley once called Wilson "80 percent business, 20 percent fun." The fun percentage may have been higher, since Wilson was known to spend extensive time at Johnny Raffa's

Lobo Lounge drinking beer with friends and coaches at what was essentially the hangout of *Miami Herald* and *Miami News* reporters.

When Shula started winning and the newspapers both nationally and locally attributed that success to Shula's work ethic—and the work ethic he demanded from his players—Wilson took it as a personal affront. His anger remained palpable several years after his dismissal. Much of it stemmed from Wilson's belief that Shula should have been more loyal to Wilson and informed Wilson he was taking the job before it became public knowledge twenty-two days following Shula's signing of his deal. "Shula was making $7,000 a year as an assistant at Kentucky when I hired him at Detroit for $14,000," Wilson said. "I also helped him get the Baltimore Colts head coaching job. I practically wrote his contract for him. Carroll Rosenbloom wanted me to take the job and I had twelve meetings with him about it. But I got him to take Shula."

As the years went by after Wilson's firing, his anger increased. He never used the four season tickets provided to him by Joe Robbie and rarely associated with the team. He was once invited to a team banquet, and because of an oversight in the seating arrangement, he was placed in the rear of the dining room. No one from the Dolphins noticed or acknowledged him. Dolphins radio commentator Larry King, the master of ceremonies, explained at the time the ignoring of Wilson was a simple mistake, but Wilson didn't believe it and left the banquet angry.

All the frustration would come to a head. Wilson was irritated Shula was receiving so much credit for turning the team around. Exactly one day after the Nixon call, in the week leading up to the Super Bowl against Dallas, Wilson went public with his anger in an interview with the *Miami News*, claiming it was Wilson who built the Miami team into a Super Bowl power, not Shula. "I've been silent too long," Wilson said. "As far as I'm concerned, [Don Shula] took over a ready-made team . . . Joe Doakes could have coached that team."

Wilson was now showing those teeth in the most unusual of times. The irony is that it's likely Wilson had tired of coaching before he was fired. There was also the fact he wasn't very good at it. "George is a good guy," one of his Detroit assistants once said. "But down deep, I don't think he even wants to coach. I think he'd be far better off in the front office. He knows football politics and football people, and I think he'd make somebody a good general manager."

Wilson was undaunted, however, and he blasted away at Shula. "I don't think the true story is out on this thing," Wilson explained, speaking of Shula's tenure. "You go over the first three years and you'll see we equaled or bettered the record of any expansion team in pro football. In the fourth season, we were taken out by injuries . . . You go over the roster and you'll see most of the guys who are doing the playing were committed to the Dolphins before Shula ever got to [Miami]."

The fact is, when Shula opened the 1970 season, there were twenty new players on the team, a turnover of about half the roster. Those specifics were only part of Shula's issue with Wilson's diatribe. The other was more philosophical—moral, even. Coaches simply did not excoriate each other in public and they certainly didn't call each other "Joe Doakes"—a colloquialism for "pedestrian" and a refer-ence to a character in a Hearst comic. Shula privately fumed that Wilson was pulling this right before the Super Bowl.

There was something else. Shula had long fought the perception that he was simply someone who took massive levels of player talent, rolled those players onto the field, and let them go. Unbelievably, then, there were some in football who actually wondered how good a coach Shula was. Was it Shula doing all the winning or was it his incredible roster full of Pro Bowlers like Unitas? When Shula took the Miami job, he received a half-teasing telegram from his friend, Norm Van Brocklin, then coach of the Atlanta Falcons. "Congratulations on your first coaching job," it read, "Now you're going to know what the rest of us coaches have been going through all these years." Van Brocklin had underlined the word "first."

Privately, Shula was angry over Wilson's remarks. Publicly, he was different when meeting with reporters. "Hi, I'm Don Shula," he joked, "not Joe Doakes." He'd later smile when then Associated Press reporter Hubert Mizell ended an interview: "Say hello to Dorothy and all the little Doakeses." (At the Super Bowl, Shula would make a Joe Doakes joke at his own expense. When a reporter at one of the press conferences mistakenly called Shula "Tom," Shula had a quick retort. "No," Shula answered, "I'm Joe.")

Shula's ability to smile during the Wilson crisis was part persona and part strategy. Players and the media watch a coach's every movement; every wince, shoulder hitch, and vowel uttered. A tense persona projected weakness and could cause players to experience doubt and the media to question. Keep your cool when before the microphones. That was Shula's philosophy. On Tuesday, just five days before the Super Bowl, the theory would be tested yet again when Shula had another awkward moment. At his morning press conference, he began with a perfunctory opening statement. "We had some good practice sessions in Baltimore," Shula said. He suddenly stopped himself and smiled uncomfortably as some reporters attending the press conference began chuckling. Then Shula laughed as well when realizing he'd accidentally said Baltimore—his former team—instead of the Dolphins. "What I mean is we had some good practice sessions in Miami," Shula clarified, "laying the groundwork for this week when we'll polish our plans and get ourselves ready physically." Shula knew his gaffe would make all the papers and it did. There weren't two more different cities than Baltimore and Miami. Baltimore had established itself as a football powerhouse, and the quarterback for that team, Johnny Unitas, had grown into a legend. The Dolphins were practically football virgins.

And that night, after Shula's press conference, some of the Dolphins players made their own Super Bowl gaffes. Shula had relented to the requests of his captains to extend curfew for a few hours, ending after midnight. Shula trusted his players. He told them in a team meeting to be themselves for the week leading up to the game. "If you feel loose, be loose," he told them. "If you feel tight, be tight. The worst thing you can do is not be honest with yourself."

But Shula wasn't dumb. He warned them about the temptations of New Orleans and also emphasized responsibility and how this wasn't a vacation trip. This was a Super Bowl. He stated this message repeatedly to the players directly and through the media. Actually, Shula floated two messages: watch the temptations and I trust you. Mostly. "There'll be a lot of temptations, a lot of temptations," he told the media in Florida before the team departed for New Orleans. "But I really believe in these guys and I'm convinced they believe in themselves. I don't think the ballplayers will let anything distract them from the business at hand. This has been an excellent group to work with. They all understand and realize what's at stake here and I think they'll act accordingly . . . Listen, the kind of guys you [have] to keep under surveillance for all but twenty minutes a day would find something to do in those twenty minutes."

Because Buoniconti was always honest in answering questions from reporters, he gave a blunt response to a query about how the team was relaxing. "Last Saturday we had a real good practice in Miami but I think we were coming up to a peak a little too early," he said. "When we came back to the practice field Tuesday, the players were very, very loose. For two days we've had excellent practices. I think it's because we had enough time to turn loose, raise a little hell and get our minds off football. It's a long season, twenty games."

Translation: part of their time in New Orleans was spent blowing off steam. They didn't obsessively party. This was, indeed, a professional bunch. But they did party. This was, after all, a football team. One night, during the New Orleans Super Bowl week, a group of Dolphins players crowded into a Bourbon Street bar and, after sitting down, they attracted a number of apparently tall, large-breasted women. "We all figured we had it made—that these tall, beautiful women were going home with us," Csonka remembered. "Then, all of a sudden, one of the [Dolphins players] stood up, pointed at one of them, and yelled, 'She's got a Johnson!' After that, we pretty much tore the place up. The cops were called, and it was a big incident. Apparently the club had signed up a bunch of female impersonators to work the room . . . none of us knew what a drag queen was."

The next day, Shula was furious and launched into a fifteen-minute tirade about the team's lack of focus in a game so big. "And what in the hell," Shula screamed, "is a female impersonator?" Some players covered their faces and laughed uncontrollably at Shula's query.

This was a different Shula from the man who demanded precision—and got it—from the first day he took over the Dolphins franchise two years earlier, in 1970. Shula was beyond a perfectionist. He instructed players where to park their cars before practice. What to eat and where to sit at the table while eating it. There'd be no sitting on helmets or removal of them while practice was ongoing. And Shula insisted his coaches be as demanding as he was. His staff was so talented there were times he didn't need to say much. The coach of the offensive line, the brusque Monte Clark, referred to players who pushed and pulled while blocking instead of powering forward forcefully and aggressively as "Lamaze" blockers. "Sympathy," he'd tell players, "can be found in the dictionary between 'shit' and 'syphilis.'" Shula and his staff would later be considered among the best group of coaches the sport has ever seen.

Shula even had a handful of rules for the team's charter flights. Beer was allowed, even encouraged, but hard liquor was forbidden. No women were allowed on the plane, including the wife of the owner. And he created a first-class section for players who were team leaders.

Shula's first summer practices were a test of the players' endurance. Complaints were not tolerated. He dared his players to walk away. "If it's too tough for you," he'd tell the team, "pack up and go home. We don't want quitters." The day lasted until 11:05 every night and Shula didn't have to enforce the 11:30 curfew because players were too tired to hit the Miami discos.

The Dolphins practiced four times a day in training camp, starting at seven in the morning, the Miami humidity a blanket over it all. Shula constructed the practices so they became incrementally tougher as the heat worsened. It was all by design. The soft would leave. The mentally rigid would stay. At that time, and not really since, what Shula did was basically unprecedented on the professional level. The first practice lasted thirty to forty-five minutes and focused on the kicking game. After that there was breakfast. Then came a thirty-minute meeting to discuss the upcoming morning practice, and that practice lasted ninety minutes, comprised of punishing drills focused on sharpening running the football. The third practice came after lunch, and Shula focused it on the passing attack. After dinner at six, they were back on the field for the fourth and final practice at 7:30, more than twelve hours after the first one. It went over an hour as darkness fell. The players showered—for the fourth time in a day—then headed to meetings at 9:30. The projector lit up as Shula showed film of the earlier practices. The darkness of the room could have induced sleep, but few nodded off, knowing

that a lack of attention could lead to missteps on the practice field
the next hot day and a verbal thrashing from Shula or one of the
assistants. So they stayed awake and listened. And learned. Besides,
most of the players had never used film to review practices. Normally film review was solely for game postmortems, so their amazement at Shula's innovation was stimulation enough.

Shula wasn't a hypocrite. He and the assistant coaches kept their
own taut schedule. Shula was usually awake at 6:30 in the morning
for Mass at seven. He'd eat his sliced grapefruit with coffee while
reading the *Miami Herald*. It was extremely rare for Shula to arrive
at the Dolphins' offices after anyone else on the staff. Shula's week
was mentally rigorous, filled with film study that would sometimes
last twelve hours (with breaks for coffee, food, and the bathroom).

Shula's demand for precision, at times, reached ridiculous propor-
tions. Clark remembered Shula gathering the coaching staff on the
practice field early one morning before the arrival of the players.
Shula instructed the coaches to go through all the warm-up exercises exactly as the players would later. Shula even had the exact
spot for where every player would stand for the warm-ups. Clark
told *Time* magazine, "I've been around organized teams before, but
Shula gives the term another dimension."

He could be blunt and demanding in one part of the day and gentle
in the next. In one game, he chastised player Lloyd Mumphord for
being out of position on pass coverage. "You're giving him far too
much on the outside," Shula screamed at Mumphord. "You've got
Jake Scott to help you inside. Dammit, Lloyd, get out there closer to
the sideline where you belong." That night, at a post-game gathering,
the group relaxed, ate, and drank. At the night's end, Mumphord and
his wife were heading for the door to leave when Shula ran over to
say good-bye, shaking both of their hands profusely. Mumphord was
caught somewhat by surprise at Shula's gesture. The scene showed

how Shula abhorred a lack of discipline on the field but appreciated the family man Mumphord and his wife off of it.

Shula's regimen for the Miami players early in his tenure did receive the rare private grumble and occasional eye roll. Mostly, there was compliance—and gallows humor. Players joked that they removed and replaced so much clothing they felt more like strippers than football players. The transition from Wilson's style—where players all but ran the team—to Shula's system took effect quickly. "[Shula] always reminded us that the football team wasn't a democracy," said wide receiver Twilley. "It was a dictatorship, and he was the dictator, and he was gonna tell us what to do." That extended to all of Shula's staff. When offensive lineman Norm Evans wasn't hitting the blocking sled hard enough for the liking of Clark, it took just a few seconds for Evans to feel Clark's wrath. It didn't matter that Evans had been working so furiously he could barely breathe and sweat ran down his face like he'd been standing in a downpour. "What are you trying to do, Evans?" Clark asked. "The idea is to hit this sled. Hit it, Evans, not hug it. You hit this thing like a schoolgirl."

Evans became enraged but said nothing. He just stared. Clark got closer to Evans's face and, in a highly sarcastic tone, whispered, "You care to try again? Or would you rather rest in the shade for a while?" Evans answered in the affirmative and crouched into a deep three-point stance. He was so angry that his right hand clenched tightly, causing the muscles to cramp. Evans ignored the pain and uncoiled into the blocking sled with such force the heavy piece of metal nearly tipped over. *Whap!* The sound careened throughout the practice field and caught the attention of Shula, who glanced over. He almost smiled. "Better," Clark said.

Csonka was a team leader who personified the brutish style Shula favored. Shula didn't question Csonka's toughness. No one did. When growing up on a farm in Stow, Ohio, a suburb of Akron,

Csonka was known for that toughness even as a small child. One day his father, Joseph, as the story goes, heard the family dog barking excitedly in the back and went to see what was wrong. There sat a three-year-old Csonka biting one of the dog's front legs. "Why are you biting him?" Joseph asked. Csonka replied, "He bit me first."

Csonka built strength by doing farm work—not lifting weights. He dug holes, shoveled cow manure, and moved hay. It was brutal work, and though part of his toughness and physical strength was inherited, the farm work greatly aided his physicality. By the time he was just fifteen years old, Csonka stood 6 feet and weighed over 200 pounds.

Csonka's will and endurance of pain eventually became legendary, even leading to him experimenting with a special protective helmet that contained pouches of fluid designed to provide more cushioning. Yet no helmet prevented Csonka from breaking his nose eight times by his twenty-fifth birthday. (Once, Csonka's nose was so bent it caused team trainer Bob Lundy to say: "Did you see Zonk's nose? It looked like a U-turn.") Dolphins players were constantly amazed at how Csonka dealt with a stubborn case of turf toe, a highly painful injury caused by damaged ligaments under the big toe resulting in stinging pain at even the slightest contact with the ground. The injury kept some players from walking, and most didn't play with it. When Csonka had a nasty dose of it that lasted weeks, he'd jump up and down on it moments before a game, like he was on a pogo stick, the shockwaves of pain surging through his body. Csonka figured he'd get the toe numb and the pain wouldn't be a factor once the game began.

Early in his career, Csonka once endured such a violent tackle it left him unconscious on the sideline and resulted in temporary memory loss. When he awoke and team physician Herbert Virgin asked if he needed help to an awaiting ambulance, Csonka replied,

"I walked in here and I'm going to walk out." Following one hit in which Csonka ruptured his left eardrum, blood running down the side of his face, Csonka's teammate Griese described his running style perfectly: "He attacks the earth."

If the earth had decided to counterattack, it would have been a fair fight. Shula would witness Csonka's indefatigable nastiness with his own eyes when the Dolphins played the Buffalo Bills some years later. Csonka was running the ball near the sideline when safety Pete Richardson approached and attempted to make a tackle. Csonka planted his forearm into Richardson's chest, using it as a fulcrum, and sent him flying backward several yards. The hit was so brutal an official called an unnecessary roughness penalty on *Csonka*.

Later in Csonka's career, the great Dallas defensive lineman Thomas "Hollywood" Henderson had a vicious collision with Csonka that Henderson described this way in Golenbock's book: "I took Larry Csonka on a Near G.O., which means the tight end blocks down and the fullback blocks the linebacker. I stepped across to take on Csonka and I had great position. I had taken on this type of block many times, but I didn't have my back foot on the ground by the time Csonka and I collided. My collision with Csonka went from the top of my head out my ankle, all the force going back down to the ankle. I was putting the foot down, so by the time the force got down there, [it] just snapped. I remember laying in the training room a few days after that and saying to my coach, Jerry Tubbs, 'I'll be back next week.' And I had every intention of coming back, but my ankle was about twenty-five inches around. I think I broke it, but they didn't tell me that. I ended up missing five weeks. I became depressed. I was putting my foot in ice and getting gloomy."

One collision with Csonka did all that.

No one doubted Csonka's toughness. But Shula wanted Csonka to be as precise as he was crushing. In practice, when Csonka lined up to start one particular play, Shula saw an opportunity to drive that message into Csonka the way Csonka drove opponents into the turf.

"Csonka!" Shula screamed. "What the hell are you doing?"

Practice stopped. Players waited as Shula made his way from 40 yards out toward Csonka, who was standing still, shocked. Initially, Csonka thought one of his sons had run onto the field. Shula pointed down toward the ground. "You're lining up a step too wide," Shula told him. "If a linebacker had been coming, you'd have been too wide to block him."

"I always said, when you least expected it," Csonka says now, "is when you got Shula's foot up your ass."

Shula later stood before Csonka, speaking about the offense. Shula looked at Csonka—or, actually, "studied" might be the word—as the two spoke. Shula examined his running back like a new car buyer considering the sticker price. Shula didn't like what he saw. He asked Csonka to lose 15 pounds and play at 235 or less. Csonka was taken aback. "I haven't been that light since high school," he told Shula. Shula let the comment pass, as he did most remarks from his new Miami players. "You will play better at that weight," Shula replied. Conversation over.

"When I first met him, I didn't know what to make of him," Csonka says now. "He was tense, uptight. I don't know if I've ever totally understood Don Shula. He's a very complicated man. In all seriousness, my depths don't run as deep as his. I've always been envious of his ability to look inside a man and figure out what makes him tick."

Shula wanted his players to look a certain way, to dress a certain way. If the players failed to match those expectations, they heard from Shula. Jim Mandich arrived at Dolphins camp in the summer of 1970 as a rookie out of the University of Michigan. He was Miami's first pick that year, number twenty-nine overall, and Shula was looking forward to seeing the man he thought would be a future star. Mandich arrived at camp driving a creaky 1962 Plymouth Valiant, the car painted with flowers, and Mandich sporting bell-bottoms and beads and long dark hair flowing past his shoulders. Buoniconti, the veteran linebacker, saw Mandich arrive.

"Ho-ly crap," Buoniconti said to a teammate, "when Shula sees this he's going to tear this kid apart."

Shula and Mandich met, there was a handshake, and then an immediate comment from Shula. "You're my first draft pick?" Shula said incredulously. To Shula, Mandich looked too much like a hippie. Csonka was standing nearby and saw the stunned expression on Mandich's face as Shula criticized his hair and attire. Two hours later, Mandich appeared back at practice, sporting a high and tight buzz cut, the flowing locks chopped off. His jeans were straight-legged and conservative. Before makeovers were commonplace, Shula had forced his aesthetic mandate on Mandich.

Mandich came to the Dolphins feeling confident. He was captain of Michigan's 1970 Rose Bowl team and wasn't intimidated by the NFL. When Mandich was asked to speak at the rookie luncheon, one of the friendliest players the sport has ever seen happily obliged. "I have observed a number of pretty girls in the area," Mandich said with a sheepish grin. "As a tight end I realize I'm supposed to be catching passes. But considering the young ladies, I have the impression I might be making a few passes as well."

Shula spoke soon after and couldn't resist circumnavigating back to Mandich's comment about chasing skirts. "I can assure you, Mandich, that when training camp opens," Shula said, "the opportunity for making such passes will never come about. You will be very busy in your off-hours looking for a place to lie down."

And nothing irked Shula more than a player who wasn't physically prepared. Players who arrived at camp overweight were like a slap to the face. Shula's top draft pick in 1972 was defensive tackle Mike Kadish from Notre Dame. He came to the Dolphins approximately 20 pounds overweight. Shula was furious. One of the Notre Dame officials attempted to defend Kadish by saying he'd just gotten married, which explained the weight gain.

Shula pounced: "Who'd he marry? A refrigerator?" One year later Kadish was playing his football in Buffalo.

Shula was almost flawless in building his program, but not every player would take to Shula. Jake Scott was a free safety and a free spirit who had no problem telling Shula where to shove his whistle. He arrived in 1969 from the Canadian Football League's British Columbia Lions wearing cowboy boots and driving a new Corvette. Scott's relationship with Shula would go from cordial to professional to antagonistic to a stark bitterness that would last decades. One of several telling moments in their difficult relationship came after the Dolphins' enchanted perfect season, when Vince Costello inadequately filled the massive cleats of defensive coordinator Bill Arnsparger, who left the team in 1973. Scott got into a heated argument in the middle of practice with Costello that was punctuated by Scott screaming, "You fucking moron!"

Shula was standing at the other side of the field but could hear Scott's raised voice and choice of language. Shula yelled across the field, "What's going on over there?" Scott turned and did something no one had ever done to Shula and never did again. "I wasn't fucking talking to you!" he said. Shula would never forgive Scott for the outburst and Scott would never forgive Shula for an incident that would come later in their time together.

Scott aside, most players were amazed, and pleased, at the difference in tone Shula was setting. Wilson allowed Dolphins players to take a swim at a nearby pool if it was too hot for practice. On a bus ride home from Jacksonville, located several hours north, Wilson spotted a bar and ordered the bus to pull over. It screeched to a halt and Wilson drank with the team for an hour. Curfews were flexible. "If you're having such a good time that it's worth the fine," Wilson told the team on occasion, "call me so I can join you." During one particularly terrible practice, Wilson intervened and stopped it. He had the equipment manager, a former Marine Corps drill sergeant, take over. The players were lined up. "Left face!" Some followed the instruction while others turned in the opposite direction. Eventually, they began to march, and they were taken, again, to the swimming pool. "Everyone, fall in." They all jumped into the cool water.

"Curfew is at eleven!" Wilson would yell. Then he'd turn to several of his veterans and wink. It was tacit permission to stay out as long as they desired. And many did.

Wilson had been well liked because he was basically one of the players. Well, liked by most. Even as a rookie, Morris had problems with the way Wilson ran the team. At Miami's team banquet in 1969, just weeks before the start of the season, Wilson told a crowd of fans from the chamber of commerce he'd be satisfied if the Dolphins won half of their fourteen games. Morris didn't care if he was a rookie. A head coach expressing hope to win half of his games infuriated Morris. He spoke to the crowd soon after Wilson. "Did I just hear him say it's okay to lose seven games?" Morris asked. "Well, that's not okay with me. I'm here because I want to go 14-0. If we lose the first game, I want to go 13-1."

"Under George Wilson, you had a very free atmosphere," remembered Buoniconti. "You kinda did what you wanted to do. There was very little discipline. He tried to treat everyone as an adult, as a man. He believed if you're treated like a man, you'll act like a man on the field. But unfortunately, you're not always dealing with mature individuals who know what their roles are. So you had some guys who abused the privilege. Because of that, I thought we were a little disorganized, a little chaotic."

As humorous and incompetent as Wilson could be as coach of the Dolphins, he also had a mean streak. Wilson believed heartily in rookie hazing, and the bigger the status of the rookie joining the team, the more Wilson encouraged veterans to go after the new players. Some of the rookies despised the hazing and Wilson because of it. When Morris was a rookie, he was one of the few that spoke up. "Not right," he'd say when one of the veterans cut in front of him in the cafeteria line. Rookies who refused to sing their college fight song were tossed into a pond located near the practice facility. Morris decided to be a smart-ass when it was his turn to sing. Instead of his college song, he sang three different songs by the Temptations. The veterans recognized what he was doing and threw him into the pond anyway. Like the other rookies, Morris was forced at the annual rookie party to chew tobacco, drink warm beer, and then follow that with pineapple wine. Many of the rookies hadn't even heard of pineapple wine. Morris describes in his 1988 book *Against the Grain* how he became so ill he crawled hundreds of feet from the bar to the ocean to throw up.

Csonka was targeted as well. Veteran players nicknamed Csonka "the Lawnmower" because of his low-to-the-ground style of running. This allowed Csonka to use his power and agility and scoop under defenders the way a bull lowered its head, but older teammates used his style as source material for prodding. Csonka had to sing every fight song from every rookie's school, was sent on sandwich runs at early morning hours, and was forced to get inebriated ten consecutive nights. The irony is that while some rookies enter the NFL with oversized egos and unrealistic expectations of stardom, Csonka was levelheaded, and he accepted the treatment despite the fact he could have pulverized his tormentors.

Shula did not drink with his team. He was instead too busy attempting to create a culture where his players would demand perfection as much as he did. Very slowly, and extremely grudgingly, Dolphins players began appreciating the differences between Shula and Wilson instead of cursing them. The loyalty to Shula quickly intensified.

"When we saw how dedicated he was, it made us ashamed of our dedication," says Csonka. "When we were winning, we wanted to put up our feet and drink beer. But he'd treat a win like a loss. He kept us focused. He worked so maniacally hard it made us want to match his intensity."

Yes, Shula had come a long way, indeed.

In November 1972, Nixon had just won reelection by beating George McGovern, the Vietnam War was ending, and the Dow Industrial Average closed above 1,000 for the first time ever. For Shula, that month meant something else. The Dolphins were 10-0 with four games remaining, and the press was beginning to ask about going undefeated with increasing regularity. He found himself in an awkward position. Privately, Shula thought of the possibility. The idea of winning was the main objective, but if he could make history when so many thought he was incapable of doing something so unimaginable, so daunting, well, that would be just fine. Publicly, for the moment, he'd try to tone down the undefeated chatter.

His players were also privately thinking of the impossible. Not in exquisite detail. Not in their daydreams. But the thoughts were there. The Tuesday after the Jets win, teammates Bob Kuechenberg and Jim Langer, while working out in Miami's weight room (which was basically a shed), began to think that going undefeated was a curse. "Okay, which game are we going to lose?" Langer asked. He went on to say, "We gotta lose one game because sure as hell you don't want to go undefeated because you'd jinx yourself and you'll blow the first playoff game."

"When we had won about eight or nine, and some players were worried now, thinking, *Hey, sooner or later, we're going to lose. Why don't we, you know, think about losing now, so we won't lose one later?*" kicker Garo Yepremian said. "That's the percentages you worry about [because], hey, you win fifteen in a row, you might miss the sixteenth one, which is the most important one, or the seventeenth one. So it was bugging some of the players, and they were joking about it, of course, saying, 'Hey, should we, you know, lose this one this week, or the one next week?' And so forth, but that was all done in jest."

Well, only partially in jest. This is how athletes are. Their superstitions have powerful holds on their lives.

Shula's meeting with the press early in the week during that November was calm and Shula was in a good mood. The team had, after all, won the division with four games left. "We looked at this season in three stages," he said. "First the exhibition season where we got ready to play. Then the league games with a goal to win our division and we've done that. The next stage is the one that means everything: winning the playoffs and the Super Bowl."

Braucher had a question for Shula. "How badly do you want to have an unbeaten season?"

Shula was cautious in his response. "It would be nice later on to look back on a Super Bowl title and an unbeaten year as well. But it's not important enough for us to risk any of our players who need to rest an injury." It was coach-speak. Shula could speak the language well but only for so long. He despised phoniness, so it took just a few seconds for Shula to morph back into himself. "Let me tell you something about unbeaten teams," he continued. "We were undefeated at Baltimore in '67. We were 11-0-2 and our last game of the year was against the Rams out in LA. They were 10-1-2. One of our two ties was the game against them in Baltimore. So if they won [that] one, we'd both have the same record, and they would have the edge on us in points scored in our two games, so they'd go to the playoffs. Well, they completely dominated us. The Fearsome Foursome dropped Unitas seven times. It taught me something about undefeated teams. We were undefeated right up to the last game and we lost everything. An experience like that teaches you what is meaningful. Championships are meaningful."

Coaches often talk to their players through the media, sending them a message, knowing the players read everything. This message was clear: focus on the Super Bowl, not going undefeated. Shula wasn't sure if the message was sinking in but clearly something special was happening. Fleming, who had played for Lombardi and the unified, dominant Packers before joining the Dolphins, told writers Steve Perkins and Braucher after that eleventh win why he thought Miami was winning. He thought the Dolphins and Packers had something in common. "I think both teams have the same type of camaraderie when everybody likes each other," he said. "There are too many situations where you have to worry about why guys block. I'm just happy to be with people like Evans, Warfield and Griese, guys who are pure people, who don't cheat on each other or themselves. This isn't the way it usually is. You have too many people from the North, South, East or West who just can't blend together. I was surprised that Dallas went as far as they did because they have the Dallas Cowboys and they have the blacks and the whites. Here, we have the Miami Dolphins and the Miami Dolphins."

Fleming was speaking of a Cowboys locker room that was extremely racially divided. He knew some of the Cowboys players and their stories, and only years later would the truth about the Cowboys emerge. Some of the black players viewed Landry, the legendary coach, as a hypocrite. Mel Renfro once said: "I can remember when the team would go to an area where there was segregation, Tom Landry used to say, 'Fellas, we know what's going on here. We don't particularly agree with it, but that's the way it is, so we have to do what we can so we don't create unnecessary problems.'

"And sometimes we would joke about it. I'll never forget [teammate] Willie Townes. He called Coach Landry 'Presbyterian Tom.' We'd say, 'There goes Presbyterian Tom again.' Here's a guy who was supposed to be a Christian, and yet he's condoning segregation. He's saying, 'This stuff is happening, and though we may not agree with it, we'll ignore it and stay in our lane.' I'm still a very sensitive person to things like that."

In Miami, on November 27, the Dolphins intercepted 3 St. Louis passes and recovered 3 fumbles and won their eleventh game of the season in a blowout, 31–10, but the Dolphins were actually sloppy in the game, leading just 10–3 in the third quarter. "That shows you the strength of this club," Kiick told reporters after the game. "We looked sloppy and scored 31 points . . ."

Kiick was in good spirits despite losing carries to Morris and healing from a stinging knee injury. He got a nice chuckle, just like the other Miami players, at kicker Garo Yepremian, all 5 feet 8 inches of him, scrambling for a run after his field goal try was blocked. He picked up the ball and bolted but lost 5 yards, those size 7.5 shoes running like a cartoon character's but covering little ground. Kiick was asked how he was handling his reduced playing time, and he was typical Kiick—very blunt and armed with humor.

"It's easy to get depressed," he said, "but winning sure soothes things over. I'm fortunate. I've had my chances to play. Some guys are in a position where they never have a chance . . . I try to look at it from a positive angle. Maybe it'll help prolong my career. I'd never say I should be playing. That would be downgrading Mercury and I'm never going to do that. He's too good a football player. Now Yepremian is another matter. When Yepremian starts running with the football I've got to say I'm better than he is."

There is no one game that symbolizes why the Dolphins were so impossible to beat. No one moment. No single player. No single coach. There were vital parts: Shula, Csonka, Griese, Warfield. There were key plays. There were key drafts and free agent acquisitions. There were many of these elements and that's what separated the Dolphins from any other team then and in the future. They had Hall of Famers, the elite, but it didn't always look that way. Their methodical nature masked extreme talent. Examine the roster and play of other great Super Bowl teams, particularly later, when franchises began to emphasize 40-yard dash times and speed, and there is much more flash. Teams *looked* daunting.

This is perhaps what set the Dolphins apart. Their steadiness, that lack of flash, was perfectly suited to chase perfection. Shula emphasized evenness and control. He did this initially never dreaming of anything like a perfect season. It was just his approach. It was also the approach of his mentor Paul Brown. By the time perfection crept into the corner of their consciousness, Shula's approach had worked perfectly.

Even in an era when life was slower—pre–text messaging, pre–Twitter, pre-twenty-four-hour sports cable news and talk radio—the Dolphins were plodders. That word has negative connotations, but it shouldn't when it comes to Miami. They relied on superior technique and the fact they were better conditioned than their opponents to win rather than overwhelming physical ability. This accounted on occasion for some of their unspectacular wins.

Their twelfth victory, in Foxboro, Massachusetts, on December 3, was a grinding, unimpressive game against the Patriots, but that was Shula's Dolphins. They were a steady punch in the mouth, but that punch was thrown with great precision and planning. The Patriots game wasn't pretty, but it was typical Dolphins as they battered the Patriots on the ground with Morris (113 yards on 15 carries) and Csonka (91 yards on 15 carries) and in the air with Morrall's 201 yards passing. Before the Patriots knew what hit them, Miami had won by 16 points and joined the 1934 Chicago Bears as the only NFL team to win its first twelve games.

Unspectacular, yes, but things began to happen. As the season went on, and the Dolphins kept winning, opposing coaches began outsmarting themselves trying to outsmart Shula. They ran more trick plays and schemes. They were trying to make a point: *I can out-coach you, Shula*. In reality, they were intimidated by him. Foley remembers something else happening late in the year, and he summed it up in one word: "mystique." The Dolphins began to develop it. It spread throughout the team like a virus and then faster throughout the league. Mystique is a dangerous foe in football. Its possessor can move mountains, and opponents suffering from its effects can be pushed with a feather. Mystique is confidence with a dark side. Slowly, surely, this began to happen as Miami piled up wins: Teams began to wonder if the Dolphins could be beat.

CHAPTER ELEVEN

GUTS

Shula once talked about his team having guts. He didn't just mean toughness—though that was definitely also true. Shula meant innards. In the vernacular of twenty-first-century football, it would be called depth. But the word meant more then. Then it meant mental strength and sturdiness. It meant Shula had reliable parts, the parts that weren't necessarily stars, the parts that didn't earn the highest salaries or get their names in the newspapers, but they were nonetheless critical.

This was an elite group of athletes with a businesslike demeanor and blue-collar work ethic—on and off the field. They didn't make a large amount of money, forcing the greatest team in history to work off-season jobs. Manny Fernandez worked as a carpenter for $5 an hour, Larry Little did work as a substitute teacher, and Anderson sold insurance. Anderson made deals by using the single pay phone in the locker room and, incredibly, had a phone installed in his car. The system was set up in his trunk and was 3 feet long and almost 2 feet wide. Anderson would push a button until a light turned green, then manually dialed. He'd do insurance deals during the Dolphins' lunch break. Curtis Johnson was one of the NFL's best defensive backs in 1972. He'd be almost unbeatable at cornerback for the Dolphins, but he never made a Pro Bowl. He later worked for a bank and became a firefighter for the city of Toledo.

The nickname for Mike Kolen was Captain Crunch. He was a linebacker. Of all the hard-hitting players on that Miami defense, few did more damage to opponents than Kolen. Yet he remains a name few today would know.

Different pieces from across the talent spectrum coming together with high velocity. It's almost impossible to completely quantify, but it's likely the Dolphins are the only team in NFL history to go from the gutter to the improbable so quickly. Quite simply, nothing like this had happened before—or since. Few Dolphins have expressed this phenomenon better than Yepremian: "We had a bunch of guys who were free agents, players who nobody else needed or wanted . . . and Coach Shula put us together with some choice draft choices that we had [plus] a lot of character and hard work. And I think with his leadership and all the guys being as hungry as they were, [he] brought up that formula of winning. He didn't have that much talent [on the undefeated team] and he was in a new situation, but he came in and worked us hard. We had so many free agents playing, and he did it [went to a Super Bowl] against people who had all kinds of number one draft choices . . ."

This is a true portrait of the Dolphins, some called castoffs, others called has-beens, a few called elite, Shula bringing them all together . . .

When many Dolphins players from the 1972 team think of Paul Warfield, they remember him in mid-flight. High in the air, arms and legs outstretched, the football landing softly into his hands.

Teammates speak of watching Warfield like it is some sort of sexual experience, the way some romanticize losing their virginity. As time pressed on and memories became clouded with the recent and the right now, the elegance of Warfield would become partially lost. But few were better. Few will ever be better.

Besides his pass catching, what made Warfield elite was his blocking. "When I ran, I liked to cut outside as much as possible near Warfield," Csonka remembers, "because Warfield would cross my bow and smoke the middle linebacker."

It's odd the things some Dolphins teammates remember about Warfield besides his grace and intelligence. Morris remembers seeing Warfield's jersey being often very clean because he'd get so wide open on pass routes, he didn't get tackled. Morris also remembers a 1970 game against Oakland when Warfield caught a deep pass at the Raiders' 40-yard line and did something that would seem impossible. He spun 360 degrees—in the middle of the field—and the Raiders player was left literally standing still and grabbing for air. Warfield ran in for the touchdown, and everyone on the Dolphins, especially Morris, couldn't believe what he just saw.

When Griese saw single coverage on Warfield—a rarity—he automatically called an audible for a pass to him. Warfield could have been an even more prolific pass catcher, but Shula's emphasis on the running game reduced his targets. Warfield never said a peep either publicly or privately about not getting enough catches. "Warfield never bitched," Csonka remembered. "Not once. He blocked his ass off and made the big catch when called upon." Despite the lack of passes aimed at Warfield, he was still extremely dangerous. The numbers were ridiculous. In 1973, he caught just 26 passes but 10 were for scores. If he had caught 60 or 70 passes, he might have scored 20 times.

The reason the Dolphins were special was because each player sacrificed for the collective good. It's something often mentioned by

players and coaches, the way politicians make pledges to lower taxes
or create jobs, but few teams in history have actually achieved such
a state. The Dolphins were one of the few, and Warfield was the
epitome of this selflessness. When Warfield joined the Dolphins in
1970, he had already established himself as one of football's premier
pass catchers. His time in Miami only enhanced this reputation.

Even in the pass-challenged period, when it was routine for quarterbacks to throw the football just 15 or 20 times a game (or less),
the Dolphins were particularly run oriented. Though this further
drained Warfield's receiving numbers, he didn't care. That was the
magic of Warfield. There were no demands for more passes. He
didn't go to the press. He didn't pen books complaining. He bided
his time. He perfected his routes. He took pride in outworking
anyone within his field of vision.

He also blocked with glee and aggression. Warfield was best
known for his sure hands, but the dirty work of blocking was something else that brought him notoriety. The Dolphins, like other
teams, used vicious crackbacks, which was when an offensive player
cut hard at an angle and dived at a player's legs to get him on the
ground. The blocks were known to break legs and shatter knee ligaments and were outlawed by the NFL in 1973. One of the players
cited in the banning of the blocks was Warfield.

Warfield was never dirty, just efficient. His precision was honed
by hours of practice. He'd spend up to an hour, sometimes more,
working on his pass patterns with Griese, and later Morrall, long
after regular practice ended. He was a spectacular athlete, one of
the world's best long jumpers who could have likely medaled in the
Olympics but picked football instead. What made Warfield spectacular was he never took that athleticism for granted. At Ohio
State, he studied anatomy and physiology so he could learn more
about body control. The studying was rewarded, as Warfield became

arguably the best route runner in the history of football, turning sharply at high speeds, shifting his hips in a fake direction to fool defenders. He treated pass catching the way a PhD candidate did a thesis. The book *Still Perfect!* recounts a story told by the legendary Larry King, who was then the team's radio announcer. King was on the sideline near Shula when Warfield came off the field after he had the football yanked from him in a rare mental miscue. As Warfield walked off, Shula asked what happened. "Warfield begins an incredible explanation about the force of his body and the position of his hips and the physical pull on his shoulder," King said, "and the odds of all that happening. Shula finally interrupted him, 'Tell me later.'"

Before the Dolphins, when Warfield was in Cleveland, his numbers were enticing. He led the NFL in 1968 with 12 scores and was averaging more than 20 yards a catch. When Warfield was traded to Miami, he had the same concerns as others who had been traded there. The Dolphins had no history. They had no soul. And as a black player heading to the South, he wondered about his family's safety.

But still, one thing Warfield never did was complain, even as his receiving statistics, once the gold standard, dropped precipitously. He passed the 100-yard receiving mark in a game just once in 1972. In an offense that threw more, he might have done that in every game. He didn't care. The Dolphins were winning.

When Shula first saw Larry Little, he had a question, though it was really a statement: "You're kinda heavy, aren't you?"

Little was slightly taken aback and didn't bother hiding his reaction, though he possessed the acting skills to do so. In elementary school, he played George Washington in the school play. "I didn't cross the Delaware," he once said, "but I didn't tell a lie, either." He was a 285-pound guard, not unusually heavy at all. There was a fine line in the NFL between chubby and stout, and Little didn't think he'd crossed it. Shula apparently did.

"This is what I played at last year," Little responded to Shula's awkward weight query.

"Well, we'll see about this year," Shula said. Then: "Lose 20."

Little didn't think he could lose that much, but strict dieting and an increase in his workout regimen worked and he shed the weight. Little was already a top offensive lineman but Shula was right—losing 20 pounds allowed Little to be quicker and even more devastating. This was part of the brilliance of Shula.

The punter was Larry Seiple. He was self-deprecating, not one of the Dolphins' more physical specimens, not one of their stars. But like other players, he was a critical component on a team made of many small but significant parts. "I wasn't a great athlete," he said. "Never have been. I could do a lot of different things, but I couldn't do them well enough to start; 1968 and 1969 were years where I was moved to tight end. Doug Moreau got hurt and I think Jimmy Cox was hurt. So I ended up playing a lot in '68 and '69—caught a lot of balls. Rick Norton, who was the quarterback, was a friend of mine I played with in college. He made sure I caught the ball a lot, so that's why I caught the ball a lot. I was a slow tight end. I wasn't very big. I couldn't block very well."

Other than that, Seiple was fine. "I knew all that. If I didn't punt I wouldn't have been able to stay in the league . . . I was very fortunate to get with a team that was looking for a punter. I thought I was a pretty good punter coming out of college"—finally, Seiple admits he's good at something—"I didn't feel that I had a very strong leg. I could get the ball high enough that they couldn't return 'em, which was one thing that a lot of people were looking for at that point. I thought I was very unselfish as far as—[Shula] would give me the ball on the 25-yard line to kick it out of bounds inside the 5. That gives me a 20-yard average. But it didn't bother me as long as it helped. Things like that; I just don't feel like I was a great athlete. I was in the right situation at the right time and was capable of lasting a long time, because I could play a wide receiver, or running back, or tight end, or defensive back, fill in here and there in practice, plus do the punting. I think that's what kept me around. As [Assistant Coach] Howard Schnellenberger many times said, 'Jack of all trades, master of none.'"

Defensive end Vern Den Herder was drafted by Shula in the ninth round of the 1971 draft out of Central University of Iowa (now Central College) in Pella, Iowa. The city had a population of under ten thousand people with two of the most notable Pellans being gunfighter Wyatt Earp and John Hospers, who in 1972 became the first Libertarian presidential candidate. Den Herder's aspirations were not to fight bad guys at the O.K. Corral or run for high office. After playing football and basketball at Central, he wanted to study veterinary medicine, and right around the time he'd been picked by the Dolphins, Den Herder was also accepted into the Iowa State College of Veterinary Medicine, a highly prestigious program. He joined the Dolphins anyway, and some time later with just a few weeks left in training camp, when he didn't know if he'd yet made the Miami team, the dean of the veterinary school called. They needed a decision. There were alternates waiting. Den Herder took a massive gamble, telling the school no, but also not knowing if he'd made the team. A short time later, Shula told him he did.

Gene Upshaw played on the offensive line for the Oakland Raiders beginning in the late 1960s. Upshaw was athletic, smart, and brutal, eventually landing in the Hall of Fame and becoming the only player in NFL history to play in three Super Bowls in three different decades for one team. Next to him on that same line was 300-pound tackle Art Shell, who was bigger and stronger than even Upshaw. A former Minnesota player, defensive lineman Doug Sutherland, once said the tandem could block out the sun. They were the most physically intimidating guard-tackle tandem ever. Bob Heinz, a defensive lineman for the Dolphins, went against Upshaw and Shell on more than a few occasions. He survived.

They were football players, great ones, and they were also entrepreneurs and businessmen, in part because they had to be. Players had second jobs in the 1970s NFL because the pay was disgracefully low. Most had one extra job. A few had two. Dolphins players did everything to earn extra income when they weren't getting their heads bashed in during games or surviving Shula's practices.

This was a different time, before players earned millions and sports unions decimated owners in the courts. The owners strangled the players with low pay, and no place was this truer than with the Dolphins. An internal memo from Robbie to his director of scouting detailed the bargain-basement wages. Three key players on the Dolphins were offensive linemen Jim Langer, Bob Kuechenberg, and Larry Little. Langer made $22,000, Kuechenberg $21,000, and Little $30,000. Dick Anderson's first salary was $15,000, his second $17,500, and his third $21,000; eventually, he finally reached $38,000. Today, that's what players tip their personal trainers. Den Herder played for $19,000, and offensive lineman Wayne Moore for a thousand less.

The pay, combined with their drive to succeed, led many of the players to build alternate career paths while simultaneously making football history. As they went 2-0 and then 5-0 and then 8-0 and beyond, they still prepared for a future when football

ended. Buoniconti studied to pass the bar exam. Some players
dabbled in real estate. Others studied medicine. Defensive back
Tim Foley sold Amway.

One moment made kicker Garo Yepremian famous. Or infamous.
Yes, that's the word, infamous. It became one of the most blooper-
ific moments in the history of football. Fifteen years. He spent fifteen years winning games with his kicks. Saving careers. Pats on the
back, footballs through the uprights, 6 field goals in one game his
rookie year. Excellence on top of accuracy. Except he's best remembered for that moment. That crazy moment.

Howard Twilley grew up in Houston, and through the wonders of
television signals bouncing through the atmosphere and landing
God knows where, he watched the Chicago Cardinals play football. Like many kids, seeing pro football players, watching their
athleticism and excitement, made him want to be just like them.
But he was small, even for a wide receiver, weighing 145 pounds
as a junior in high school. He grew to 160 soon after, and then
came his sole scholarship offer from Tulsa and then being picked
by the Dolphins in the twelfth round of the 1966 draft. It was the
team's first year of existence, and the beginning of when the team
would constantly try to trade him or supplant him for someone
faster and stronger. But he stuck. The reason why was one constant:
his toughness. The team's general manager would watch practice,
and he'd joke that he could tell the time by Twilley, who'd hobble
by with one injury or another every five minutes. Injuries slowed
Twilley but never stopped him.

Yes, they tried and tried to get rid of Twilley, but the skinny kid
from Tulsa stuck, impossible to eradicate, and the Dolphins would
later regret that they even tried.

* * *

Once, during a rainy preseason game, Stanfill, a 275-pound defensive lineman, crouched in his stance, waiting for the snap of the
football. He looked across the line at an offensive tackle directly
ahead of him and, just seconds before the play began, said: "Hey,
shoe's untied." The guy looked. *The guy looked.* He looked just as the
ball was snapped.

There was the time when another offensive lineman got into his
three-point stance and Stanfill joked: "You lined up offsides." The
guy thanked Stanfill, lifted his hand, and was called for a penalty.

Stanfill never took himself too seriously—though he could have.
Stanfill would play in three straight Super Bowls, and like many
other Dolphins from this team, his name would fail to be at the tip
of history's tongue.

When offensive lineman Norm Evans played for the Houston Oilers,
he and the other players had a running joke. Whenever a player
would make a mistake—a dropped pass or a blown assignment—
players would sing the 1935 song "Moon over Miami." It was meant
as extreme sarcasm; a player feared being cut and sent to the expansion Dolphins more than the concussions and the long needles used
to dull pain. There was good reason to avoid the Dolphins. The first
year of the team's existence, there were just 12,503 total season tickets sold. In its opening four seasons, Miami went 15-39-2. What
Evans saw in that first season with the Dolphins, when Shula was
just a twinkle in Miami's eye, was an abomination. There were good
teams. There were mediocre teams. There were bad teams. There
were teams so absurdly bad they melted eyeballs. Then there was
100 feet of sludge. And below all that were the expansion Dolphins.

Evans remembered one tryout practice where every truck driver,
high school prom king, and legend in his own mind hoped to

relive past glories. There were few real football players, and even those were being thinned out all the time. In the team's opening scrimmage during that expansion season, the temperature hovered near 100 degrees with thick humidity. Two linemen passed out from heat exhaustion and were taken to the hospital.

Evans was a veteran with a good reputation and experience, and here he was in this expansion hell. Then came the money troubles. Evans and his wife, Bobbie, were having difficulties getting by. It got so bad Evans borrowed $150 from teammate Twilley to pay for food and rent. There was the four-win season. The five-win one. The removal of an appendix. The all-out brawl one game against Chicago players. The ligaments that twisted and strained after one hit that left him in a cast from his foot to his hip. The time Bubba Smith clubbed Evans so hard it twisted Evans's helmet halfway around his head, leaving him peering out the earhole. The feeling of pride for surviving this disaster of an expansion team. The entrance of Shula and the feeling of pride for surviving him and then prospering. His faith a cornerstone of it all, which is why he earned the nickname Pope Norm IV.

The 53 Defense was named because of Bob Matheson's jersey number. He became a historic footnote after a thirteen-year NFL career and two Super Bowl appearances with the Dolphins. When Dolphins players speak of Matheson, they do so with admiration and a smile. He was admired as a player and even more so after Hodgkin's disease took his life.

Center Jim Langer came to the Dolphins the way many other offensive linemen did: unspectacularly. He was signed by Cleveland in 1970, then put on the taxi squad, which was a group of reserves. Here was a future Hall of Famer deemed incapable of playing on the regular team. It is one of the grand examples of how grotesquely wrong personnel decisions can be.

The taxi squad. At the time, Langer was nonetheless excited, since his salary was going to be $500 a week. That was a fortune to someone like Langer. He called his wife, Lynn, who was awaiting word in Minnesota. "Pack your stuff," he told her, "I'm going to be here awhile."

That's what he thought. The rules stipulated that before signing him to the taxi group, he first had to clear waivers. This gave teams a chance to put in a claim. Two hours after the Browns told him he was going to be on the taxi squad, the Dolphins' general manager, Joe Thomas, called to say Miami had claimed him. The call came just a few minutes after one of the Browns players had his car stolen right out of the parking lot. Langer was to report to the Dolphins immediately, and the joy was gone. He didn't want to go. Indeed, he was devastated. The Dolphins were the dregs of the sport. One thought went through his head: *Oh, Christ, this is the end of my career.* He got Lynn back on the phone. "I'm going to Miami," he told her, "so hold everything."

Jesus, the Dolphins. Was Attica filled? It would get worse. Langer, Kuechenberg, and another player named Carl Mauck were fighting for the same position. Clark had approached Langer and told him he wanted to see him pass block, but there was also a warning: Watch Mauck because he likes to head slap. That's what Clark said. He likes to head slap. And he did just that, and what Langer didn't know at the time was that Kuechenberg and Mauck had decided they were going to pummel the hell out of Langer to force him to quit the team. They tried, head slap and all, but Langer was too tough. (Mauck and Langer later became good friends.)

Then there was a final piece of indignity: "I remember signing a contract with the Dolphins. After my $500 offer, I was sitting in a

Holiday Inn immediately the next week after getting to Miami, and Joe Thomas again appeared at the door and handed me another contract that was 350 bucks. And I said, in my limited experience and totally intimidated state, I did ask and say, 'You know, Joe, Cleveland was gonna pay me $500.' He says, 'Well, this isn't Cleveland. This is what we're gonna pay you.' And I said, 'Well, God, I don't have any money.' And I didn't. I was broke flat on my ass, and I said, 'Can I at least get a little extra to get my family down here?' And he said, 'Well, we'll give you $375.' So it's just an incredible thing to go through. As I look back, the insecurity at that point [was] overwhelming. It was a real tough thing to go through at that point. You live day to day not knowing what's gonna happen to you."

Thus one of the great offensive linemen of all time had to beg for a $25 raise and constantly wondered if he'd ever make it in football.

There were so many stories like Langer's on the Dolphins. The unappreciated. The unknown. Later, becoming the indispensable. Initially, Langer played sparingly, mostly on the head-jarring special teams units. The Dolphins saw something in Langer the Browns did not. They eventually made him the starter, and through the 1972 season, Langer battered opponents, opened holes for Csonka and Morris, and, in many ways, redefined the position, his steadiness the new standard. There was Langer playing every down of the perfect season. There was Langer needing blocking help on just 3 of 500 blocks that year. (Later, there would be four knee operations that would lead to screws in his right leg, and he would be able to tell when the weather was changing because of how those knees and ankles felt.) Langer played in 141 consecutive games. *One hundred and forty-one.*

———

Wayne Moore never forgot Shula's speech on that dismal Super Bowl day when Dallas beat Miami. Moore was like a number of Dolphins players. He never forgot. Each block he made as an offensive lineman, each practice, each weight he lifted, each sprint he ran was geared toward making it back. What Shula said weren't just words to Moore and his teammates. It was a mission statement. Moore encapsulates the effect of those words perhaps better than anyone. "'Never forget that feeling. Never,'" he remembers Shula saying. "And we didn't. And . . . all off-season, we had to think about that, and we worked [in] the off-season, and we came back, and we were determined to get back to that Super Bowl. We didn't think we would go undefeated, but we had a goal in mind, and that was to get back to the Super Bowl, and anybody that was in our paths had to be destroyed."

A significant reason the Dolphins won is because of brain and wits. There is no way to measure an NFL team's brainpower and certainly no way to stack one team's smarts against another. But if there were, the 1972 Dolphins would do just fine. The reason Shula was able to push for a disciplined team is because his players had the mental capacity to do so. The Dolphins didn't beat themselves by making mistakes on the field, and it's because of players who had the mental toughness to handle Shula's push for discipline. These Dolphins went on to become doctors, bank officers, teachers; one would begin a lasting campaign to fight paralysis; others would own businesses and, in the case of Jim Mandich, become a broadcaster. Mandich was often spotted around the Dolphins locker room carrying a copy of the *Wall Street Journal* under his arm. He'd make huge catches on the field and debate tax code off of it. He made the College Football Hall of Fame and became a broadcaster for Dolphins games, before succumbing to bile duct cancer at the age of sixty-two.

One of the reasons the Dolphins signed defensive lineman Manny Fernandez was because of his Latino last name. Dolphins executives believed a Spanish-speaking Fernandez would be able to help the team branch out into the Spanish-speaking neighborhoods throughout the city. What they apparently forgot to ask Fernandez was if he spoke Spanish fluently. He spoke almost none. He was Mexican-American, born in Oakland, and played college football at Utah, for Christ's sake. But this was the 1970s NFL in Miami, long before the birth of political correctness.

Before he'd play the game of his life in the Super Bowl, in what was the most dominant performance in the championship ever by a defensive lineman, while also experiencing one of the great injustices in Super Bowl history, he'd make one of the most memorable plays in team history. Fernandez played with 20-200 vision, but against Buffalo was still clearly able to see the handoff about to happen between Buffalo's quarterback and O. J. Simpson. Fernandez timed the interception of the handoff perfectly and grabbed the football away. It led to a Miami touchdown, which won them the game. They had those kinds of games from those kinds of players. All the time.

The Dolphins, one season, were in the Boston area to play the Patriots. One night before the team headed up for the game, linebacker Doug Swift departed to take the admission test for medical school. A short time after, he drove out to practice with the team. Think about that for a moment. While pursuing a flawless season in a brain-rattling sport, Swift was studying to become a doctor and taking entrance exams between practices. His reward for this mental and physical feat? After football, Swift became an anesthesiologist.

In the book *The Miami Dolphins*, written by Morris T. McLemore, he offered a blunt and important look into the brutality of the sport and a glimpse into his philosophy as a player.

"It's a pretty brutal game, I guess," he said. "If you would walk out there and play, just walk in cold and get into it, you'd think the game was insane. But if you practice and train for it, it's a lot less brutal. You get conditioned to it. It's not so important that you get physically conditioned, though that comes with it. The big deal is to get mentally conditioned. Like playing with pain. That doesn't mean anything, put that way, to a pro. If you *can* play, you play. The pain is incidental. The crippling injuries to a linebacker, you know, are in the upper body. The hitting area. If you're incapacitated there, you can't do the job. But the contact . . . a couple of times a year you really get slammed. The only time I get scared is when I'm groggy. You get hit in the head, you know, and you get groggy. You stumble around and you don't know where you are. That's when you get scared. People are yelling and screaming, your teammates are huddling and working hard, and there you are just weaving around. You're trying to understand what everyone is so excited about."

Decades later, the NFL would have a better grasp of the dangers and severity of concussions. Then, however, players suffered through them, not knowing the constant head trauma was perhaps slowly destroying their mental capacities and shortening their lives, and they kept playing, and playing.

Swift then got even deeper. "Sometimes you wonder what the hell you're doing out there. You're at the bottom of the pile [after a tackle] and you're dressed in all that 'armor,' the pads and the helmet, and you're sweating your ass off, and you look down at the artificial grass, man, and you really wonder what the hell it's all about. It sometimes seems like the pyramid thing, you know. You start thinking about that. Maybe you're just building a pyramid for somebody. It's kind of demeaning."

Swift wasn't done. He showed more of his ability to think independently, a character trait that would make him a brilliant

medical professional. He took on pregame prayer, an almost sac-
rosanct tradition in football. "The bullshit that takes place on the
field before the game is ridiculous," he said then. "You're ready to
go and then you have to go through that bullshit. It's like a bad
joke. There's no need for those prayers, those invocations. It de-
presses me. The high schools and all those flags all over the field.
It's unnecessary. I like a good solid prayer. I like the way the rabbis
do it. I'd rather have a rabbi any day. You know how Jews are? To
the point. 'God, bless this field, amen.' That's enough.

"The national anthem is part of the game, part of the tradition.
That's good. But I can't stand the rest of it. All the majorettes and
everything and Nixon sticking his nose in all the time. That gives
the sport a bad name. Political people and civic leaders, they just
use the game to sell their shit. It's depressing. I guess some guys use
all that pregame stuff. Maybe they think, 'If I say a good prayer this
time, or raise the flag right, I'll make some good tackles.' There's
always that kind of character around." (Not everyone in the Dolphins was thrilled with Nixon's seeming eternal presence around
the team.)

Swift then concluded with an apt description of Shula: "Shula
keeps us in a good frame of mind. He gives good speeches. Some of
them. A lot of times, he blows them, but hell, it's hard to come up
with a good one every time. He's crazy, you know. Shula's really wild.
Most people don't see him that way, but he's unbelievable, man. He
gets so *into* the game. As a player, you really appreciate that. He's a
great coach and an interesting person. He's got a lot of energy and
enthusiasm and he's always got time for problems. That's a great ability. To manage a team, you have to find so much time for bullshit.
He's always very up front about things, always very honest with you."

"Inside of Swift, inside that liberal exterior," Shula responded,
"there is an animal struggling to get out."

Swift's thoughts on Shula and the role of a coach show the relationship between NFL players and the sport they loved as well as the relationship between some of the players and the coach they loved and sometimes hated. Many of the players weren't conformists, but they conformed for the greater good. Many of them didn't always agree with Shula, but they rarely publicly complained (Morris aside) for the greater good. Mostly, Shula insisted players follow his instructions to the letter, yet he also allowed them to have their personalities. It was symbiotic—with Shula controlling the symbiosis, of course.

The offensive line was called the "Expendables" by some because each of the five starters had been cut or traded by another NFL team before playing for the Dolphins. Wayne Moore was waived by the 49ers, Evans was picked up from Houston in the expansion draft, Little was traded by the Chargers, Langer was cut by the Browns, and Kuechenberg had an unbelievable story of his own. He was drafted by Philadelphia, hated the team, and actually quit. After doing so, he went to a phone booth to tell his mother, and she handed the phone to his brother Rudy, a player for the Bears who proceeded to call Kuechenberg a coward. That motivated him to return to football, where he played with a semi-pro team called the Chicago Owls before sometimes as few as a hundred people.

A portrait of the Dolphins: some called castoffs, others called has-beens, a few called elite, Shula bringing them all together . . .

PART THREE

THE GREATEST TEAM

CHAPTER TWELVE

UNBEATABLE

"Dear Nigger," the letter started. Succinct. To the point.

It was postmarked in April 1967 from extremists called "Patriotism, Inc." The letter came from St. Petersburg, and its intent was to frighten and intimidate a young man named Ray Bellamy, who had just happened to become the first black football player at the University of Miami. Quit, the letter told Bellamy, or he was a dead man.

Bellamy is one of the sports heroes few people know. He was a wide receiver from Palmetto, Florida, and was the first black college football player in the state of Florida, which had been the second state in the South to integrate its university sports programs (after Texas). At the school he received a brutal reception. Racial slurs were scrawled across the front door of his home. During an on-field drill, white teammates who were against Bellamy joining the Hurricanes smashed into his knee when he wasn't looking. He was arrested in Coral Gables simply for sitting in an idling car with a female white student friend. He was later released with no reason given for his detention.

Florida's battle with the integration of its athletic fields continued in earnest, despite the Dolphins making history with a team that included white, black, and Latino players. It was the strangest contradiction. There were still bigots who refused to accept the modernizing NFL (somewhat modernizing—black players still faced extreme racism in the sport), but as the Dolphins chased history, many Miamians, it seemed, temporarily put aside their prejudices and followed the team with a singular pride. "We were getting support from all over," said Csonka. "Few people seemed to care what we looked like. They cared mostly that we were winning."

Again, there were racial zealots who despised the integrated Dolphins and, in fact, despised integration period. Stowe was the team's backup wide receiver, well liked by teammates, and he also drew a chuckle because he enjoyed dressing like rhythm-and-blues singer Sly Stone. The black Stowe came to Miami from Iowa State and brought his white girlfriend, Judy (the two would later get married). None of the players gave a damn that he was dating a white woman and Shula invited the two to his house for dinner. The players didn't care. The coaches didn't care. But some in the public did. The couple would endure stares and occasional comments when out to dinner or a movie. However, most Miamians didn't obsess over the racial composition of the Dolphins. But that didn't happen below the professional level. Across Miami, and many parts of the southern states, Jim Crow's grip remained firm on high school and college football teams in the South. Those teams refused to integrate or did so at a snail's pace.

Despite integration being accepted within the Dolphins team and throughout the NFL, on the college level, the Hurricanes football team, for decades, stubbornly declined to accept black players. The school also refused to play Penn State in 1946, the *Miami Herald* reported, because the Nittany Lions had two black players on the roster. Miami said not playing Penn State was due to a fear of some "unfortunate incidents" occurring. The truth was twofold. That fear was unwarranted, but the school also liked its Hurricanes white. Four years later, Miami would allow black players to grace its fields when an Iowa team with five black athletes played at the Orange Bowl.

That's the way it went in Miami. The Hurricanes stayed white for decades until Bellamy signed. He joined the team and broke the racial barrier at the University of Miami just five years before the Dolphins would make their run.

Yet the hardened bigots, as they did with the Dolphins, would lose their foothold. Part of the reason was the simple passage of time. And yet, perhaps the biggest reason for Miami's shifting of beliefs was that integrated teams won. The Hurricanes administration saw victories dancing in their bigoted heads and suddenly the color of a football player's skin mattered less.

Bellamy would outlast the racists. His presence would herald the arrival of a steady flow of blacks to the Hurricanes football team, and suddenly sports in Florida looked drastically different. The way Shula would make strides to help integrate the Dolphins, it was Bellamy who not only was responsible for assisting in eroding the prejudices that existed in the city, but his going to Miami marked the end of Jim Crow across all southern football. By 1970, his senior year, the Hurricanes would have fourteen black players. That year, Bellamy would be voted student government president.

He ran under the slogan: "It's not a white or black thing. It's a people thing."

On December 11, 1972, Shula graced the cover of *Time*, which featured the headline: "Building for the Super Bowl." The first two paragraphs of the story hit all the stereotypical Miami highlights.

"Miami, that lotus land of sun, sand, surf and swimming pools, is also a city of golf and mah-jongg, of Shecky Greene and Liza Minnelli—a high-rolling town where lacquered young ladies comb the bars along Collins Avenue through the long, hot winter, trading favors for bread. It is an unlikely kind of football town. Who thinks of apple-cheeked American youth playing a fast game of touch on Jackie Gleason Drive or Arthur Godfrey Road? Who would expect hoarse cries of 'Dee-fense! Dee-fense!' from a bathing suit salesman dressed in robin's-egg blue sports jacket and ocher slacks?"

The next paragraph was even more over-the-top: "Miami expects just that. Lately even the girls have taken to requesting professional football tickets in lieu of cold cash." Notice the not-so-subtle sexism. Even the chicks dig Miami football now! It continued: "Like everyone else in town, they know that the hottest action around is not on the jai-alai courts or out at Hialeah, but in the Orange Bowl. There the Miami Dolphins are grinding up National Football League opponents like so many herring. And irony of ironies, the undisputed hero of sybaritic, leisure-loving Miami is the leader of the Dolphin pack, Coach Don Shula, 42, a rock-jawed Jesuit-trained disciplinarian who would seem to fit the city's image about as well as Frank Sinatra would suit Painesville, Ohio."

The part the magazine got right was the increasing fan interest. The Dolphins had come a long way from the buffoonery of Wilson and twenty thousand people attending games. There is no tangible way to quantify how much fan interest had risen across the city other than ticket sales, and attendance had increased threefold in a matter of a few years. But those were hard-core football fans. The more important measurable was the casual Miamian. The city as a whole had started to pay more attention.

Dolphins fans began to feverishly, and some violently, defend the honor of their team from the bitter tongue of Howard Cosell. According to some fans, during his halftime highlight show in which he'd show snippets of games from around the league, Cosell had taken one too many shots at the Dolphins' schedule, calling it far too easy. This irked some supporters to the point where they mailed a steady stream of nasty letters to Cosell with a few, Cosell said, telling him not to show up to Miami's home game or risk bodily harm. Cosell told the *St. Petersburg Times* on November 28, 1972, that he turned a number of letters over to the FBI and, in typical Cosell form, basically mocked the angry fans. "Most of them know that all the world does not depend on the winning or losing of a stinking football game," he told the newspaper. And you can imagine Cosell saying that in his uniquely Cosellian voice.

"It's a pretty sick thing to find out that because people are complaining about a minute on a damned halftime show," he said, "they can go to these extremes. It's so preposterous on its face that it's almost an absence of maturity to even mention it."

One coach was watching the Dolphins as much as fans were watching Cosell. Alex Webster, coach of the New York Giants, took a copy of Shula's *Time* magazine cover and posted it on the Giants' bulletin board. Webster hoped the fact the media was talking about the Dolphins as a Super Bowl team would motivate his own team. He stated to the New York media how stopping the Dolphins was as simple as stopping Csonka. While Csonka was perhaps the cog, Webster's statement showed how yet another person misunderstood the depth and offensive variety in which the Dolphins could punish defenses. Miami was a powerful team that could win any number of ways, a fact that was and is constantly lost, even now all these decades later.

The weather at Yankees Stadium was made for football, and instead of Csonka, the Giants saw an alternating dose of Morris and Kiick. It was a testament to Kiick; he'd not publicly complained about his loss of carries to Morris, and Shula rewarded Kiick with an increasing number of carries late in the season. Kiick told writer Braucher after the game that the Morris-Kiick rotation, how it worked, was one of the great mysteries of the team. "He says he does it by feel," Kiick explained at the time, "and I've learned to trust his instincts. In fact, this was one of the times I sensed he was going to send me in. We were backed up to the ten-yard line, and I felt I could do something if I got in. I had this definite feeling, and darned if Shula wasn't grabbing me and telling me to go."

One of the clear signs that Shula had succeeded in uniting the Dolphins behind his one-team vision was the fact that Kiick, a onetime doubter in Shula, was now a convert. No, the Dolphins weren't just about Csonka. They never were. He gained only 30 yards on 9 carries against New York while Morris and Kiick combined for 167 yards. (The only controversy from the game was Morris's comment to New York reporters. "It's always fun to beat a team from the Big Apple," Morris said. The comment didn't sit well with Shula, who told Morris to keep his remarks to the press slightly more subtle.)

It was Miami's thirteenth victory (the Dolphins were helped by forcing 6 New York turnovers). Everyone was all smiles, because not only had Miami gone 13-0, but the winning streak tied a thirty-eight-year old NFL record. They were on a roll—an almost unprecedented one. Shula was in a good mood until a New York reporter asked a question that irritated the coach. It's not that it was difficult to annoy Shula—it was actually quite easy—but he had tired of this particular question. He was asked about losing on purpose, particularly about losing one of the late-season "meaningless" games. The idea was that the Dolphins should lose a game in order to lessen the pressure of winning them all and then, the theory went, they could truly focus on winning the Super Bowl.

To the uber-competitive Shula, the idea of wanting to lose was a foreign one. Losing on purpose just didn't register with him and the idea of it made him quite angry. "I just can't buy that attitude," he told writers after the Giants game. "I don't think there's anything you ever gain by losing. I go along with Jack Nicklaus. He once said, 'You know what breeds winning? Winning breeds winning.'"

Shula's quote to the papers was, as usual, a message to his players. He'd heard how some of them were talking about the potential advantages of losing in the regular season. Morrall recalled in a *New York Times* story how, during the week of the Colts game, he heard players talking about the positives of losing that final regular-season game. One player said to Morrall, "Well, if we're going to lose a game, this is the one to lose, because after this week if we lose, we're done." (According to the *Times*, there was a highly entertaining scene after the game involving Morrall. After the Dolphins defeated the Colts, Morrall was being interviewed by a reporter outside the locker room when he was met by his wife, Jane, and one of the couple's five children, Mitch. Turning to Mitch, who was five, the reporter said, "What did you like about the game today?" During the game, Morrall had been picked off by Ted Hendricks, a close friend. To Morrall's mortification, Mitch said, "I liked it when Daddy threw the ball to Uncle Ted.")

Shula had been following Jack Nicklaus closely, as Shula loved to golf and he appreciated the skill Nicklaus possessed. That year, after winning two major championships, the Masters and U.S. Open, Nicklaus had competed in a total of twenty tournaments throughout the world, winning seven, finishing second in four, and, overall, earning fifteen top-ten finishes. Nicklaus has stated several different versions of the quote "winning breeds winning," but this one, from his autobiography, is the most representative: "Fear of any kind is the number-one enemy of all golfers, regardless of ball-striking and shotmaking capabilities. For most, fear of winning is even harder to overcome than fear of losing. Psychologists will tell you that's because, however much such players may believe and tell themselves they want to win, having become so familiar with losing makes them, deep down, comfortable with only that experience. Not knowing what winning is like, they simply are not sure they can handle it, are frightened of what it might do to them. This happened to me before my early successes enabled me to control that kind of fear. That's why I've always said that winning breeds winning: The more you win, the less you fear winning again, or the less frightening success becomes."

Shula fully believed the same. This was, after all, a Dolphins organization that until he arrived was one of the great laughingstocks in all of sports. Shula had changed the culture of losing but wanted to make sure the franchise didn't return to its old habits. One loss could turn into two and two into three. Then the questions from the media would begin, and the players would start to question themselves. No, Shula thought, nothing good could come from losing. Nothing good at all.

CHAPTER THIRTEEN

"THE MONEY SEASON"

That December, the Dolphins received their AFC championship rings, made with thick white gold and a bulging diamond in the middle. Csonka got his ring, looked down at his fingers, and wondered to himself: *What the hell am I going to do with a ring?* The only thing that graced his hands was a Band-Aid on his thumb. Csonka didn't wear jewelry because it tended to get smashed because of the collisions he endured. He accidentally broke his class ring after slamming his hand into a wall, and in general, jewelry ended up in bits and pieces. Indeed, Csonka's hands were always in harm's way. A psychologist once told Csonka he was one of the few people in the world who utilized his sense of touch almost as much as his eyesight. That may be bullshit, but to Csonka, it did explain why he was always banging his hands against walls and doors. Csonka said in a 1972 interview with *Pro Quarterback* magazine: "Must be my Hungarian gypsy heritage. But I think the guy was right. Lots of times I get up at night at home and never turn on the light. I feel my way around. I seem to know exactly where I am."

Csonka didn't wear the ring for another reason. It was a conference championship ring, not a Super Bowl one. Csonka, like his teammates, wasn't interested in conference titles. Been there. And as they went 14-0 by beating the Colts, Shula didn't give a damn about that either. He was matter-of-fact when meeting with the media: "We're delighted to have accomplished what no other NFL team has done. But now we've got to make it 17-0 for it to mean something." That was the message he'd been pushing for weeks and continued to even as the accolades piled high and the pats on the back increased. Shula demonstrated this by making it clear to the Dolphins players he didn't want the game ball. Instead, it was given to Assistant Coach Clark, and the team moved on.

Moved on, maybe, but all these years later, consider what they did during that regular season.

They had two 1,000-yard rushers, a first in league history.

They had three shutouts, second most since the AFL-NFL merger.

They intercepted 26 passes, and Scott picked off 5 all by himself.

The Dolphins rushed for an average 210.8 yards a game, an astounding number, while they held opponents to just 110.6 yards.

Buoniconti averaged 10 tackles a game. He was methodical, efficient, brutal, and brilliant. (Simpson remembers: "Nick was the most underrated player that I played against. Whenever we tried to audible, he seemed to know what our audible was. I can remember on two occasions he literally beat me to the handoff. I would be in my stance sometimes, knowing where we were going, and all of a sudden I'd see Buoniconti either pointing to the hole or shifting a defensive tackle over to the point where we were about to go. You never know how disconcerting it was, because for my career, I was always playing with new or young quarterbacks. I can remember saying to [Joe] Ferguson, 'Audible! Audible! Audible!'")

The Dolphins threw on average just 18.5 passes a game. It was a low number even for the pass-challenged era.

Miami's win over the Colts became huge news around the country and received prominent display in newspapers nationwide, despite a time that was jammed with news of war and political upheaval. "With a 16–0 victory over the Baltimore Colts that displayed their variety of talents," read the first paragraph of a *New York Times* story, "the Miami Dolphins completed today the first unbeaten and untied 14-game regular-season schedule in National Football League history."

The story quoted Morris calling the Dolphins' season thus far "the money season."

Just a few days after Miami beat the Colts, Morris had a few things to say to reporter Al Levine of the *Miami News*. During that game, Shula attempted to get Morris extra carries so he could reach the 1,000-yard mark. It was actually a generous maneuver by Shula, but Morris told Levine: "I don't think I should have run that much on a bad ankle." Fellow beat writer Braucher called Morris a great thespian. "Othello," Braucher said, "was a farmer compared to Mercury."

These exchanges again showed how Morris was considered a mystery to many of the men covering him. Some of these differences were racial; the beat writers were white and Morris was black. Some of it was Morris himself. He was different. He talked differently and walked differently and dressed differently and feared no one and no subject. He was the opposite of the buttoned-down football player, and some in the media didn't know how to handle these disparities.

An understanding of him would have to wait. There was a post-season game to be played against Cleveland on Christmas Eve. The Browns were one of the league's historic franchises and the juxtaposition was striking. Here was upstart Miami, the former dregs of the sport, heavily favored over the Browns, the Ivy League of the sport. Art Modell owned the team, and while he'd become one of the key cogs of the NFL (and despised in Cleveland for eventually moving the team to Baltimore), he was now in the early stages of becoming both famous and notorious. What never left Modell was his sense of humor. "I just hope we can make it through the national anthem," Modell told the press.

Warfield, whom Modell had traded to Miami, was less jovial early Sunday morning on the day of the game. Warfield's family had returned to Cleveland to ready the home for the Christmas holidays (Warfield had kept the house after the trade). Along with the family went the bedroom alarm clock. He awoke in a great panic on the day of the Miami's first playoff game, thinking he'd overslept. Warfield did what many people would when they needed to check the time—he phoned the time service and discovered it was just 5:23 in the morning. Warfield got up anyway to make sure he really didn't sleep past the game's start.

Warfield was a straightforward man who had become the favorite of teammates and writers for his bluntness, yet that week he'd spoken of how playing against his old team didn't mean much to him. "We all knew it meant a great deal to Paul," remembered Shula. "No one bought that." And no one believed Modell's crack about the national anthem as well. The Dolphins knew Modell was highly motivated to beat them and that meant the Browns would be as well. Modell was the owner, but he was also the general manager and almost the coach. Modell wanted to show the trade of Warfield to the Dolphins was the right move.

Warfield told reporters then: "Modell came in with that crack about the national anthem. I wasn't fooled by that. I knew they were trying to lull us into overconfidence, saying they were just happy to be here. [In 1964] when I was with the Browns we played Baltimore for the world title. The Colts were big favorites. All we heard all week was how great the Colts were—and we laid it on them, 27–0. You've got to be leery of teams that low-rate themselves."

Remember, Shula was coach of that Baltimore team, and in team meetings he reminded the Dolphins about the humiliation of that loss.

Warfield had been sleepless because he was playing his old team. Shula was tense in the minutes before the game because he was Shula. Writers caught an interesting glimpse of Shula some sixty minutes before the game against Cleveland. In that time, reporters were allowed into the locker room prior to the contest being played. It was a time to schmooze and get nuggets of information for print or broadcasts. Curt Gowdy was doing just that. Gowdy was one of the more recognizable faces in the media and a popular figure treated with respect by all professional athletes. He was the announcer for Ted Williams's home run in 1960 in his last at bat, the Namath Super Bowl, and the infamous Immaculate Reception catch by Franco Harris that year. Gowdy was in the locker room smoking a cigar and talking to Csonka in front of Csonka's locker when Shula walked by. He noticed the smoke and approached Gowdy.

"Please put out that cigar," Shula asked Gowdy.

Gowdy was taken aback. No one had complained about his cigar in locker rooms before. Initially Gowdy believed Shula was kidding, but then noticed that stone jaw wasn't moving and there was no smile. Anyone who knew Shula for five minutes or less understood that look. The look meant: *I'm not kidding*.

"What's wrong with smoking a cigar?" Gowdy asked.

"I don't want anyone getting upset by the smoke," he said. Then he walked away. Shula had made his pronouncement. There was no need to stick around because he knew his edict would be followed. And it was. The cigar was extinguished, and Gowdy was amazed.

Gowdy turned to Csonka. "That's the mark of a great coach," he said to the runner, "no detail too small."

"No," said Csonka, "he's just getting his game face on."

That was true, but it was also true these playoffs had deepened the creases across Shula's forehead. He'd seen many playoff seasons, but this one felt more intense than some others. The pressure of perfection and the high standards Shula had set didn't come without a price—a loss in the playoffs would render the unbeaten regular season meaningless. Shula had been slightly tenser all week and not just with cigar smokers. Players noticed an extra edge in Shula. It shouldn't have been a shock. No one had done what the Dolphins were about to try. Shula was the first Apollo mission trying to land on the moon.

Shula's apprehension was justified in one sense. The Browns came to play and they did just fine once the national anthem had finished. The Dolphins jumped to a 10-point lead going into halftime, but Cleveland wasn't giving up so easily. Indeed, the close score inspired them. So much had gone wrong for the Browns, including the 3 interceptions thrown by Mike Phipps, a blocked field goal, and a fumbled snap. It was a disaster, yet they only trailed by two scores. Csonka was possibly the most powerful offensive weapon in football, yet the Browns held him to just 19 yards on 8 carries. Cleveland had two big and athletic defensive tackles in Walter Johnson and Jerry Sherk. Johnson was a three-time Pro Bowl pick who was 6 feet 4 inches and 265 pounds, while Sherk would make the Pro Bowl four consecutive years and, by the end of his career, would be considered one of the best defensive players in Browns history. Sherk was brutally tough. Several years later, while playing on Philadelphia's disgusting excuse for a field, a boil on Sherk's foot was scraped off during the game, and a nasty staph infection from the Astroturf entered his system and settled deep in his knee. The disease nearly killed him, but he'd return to play football in a limited capacity the next few years. The two players had a made a pact regarding Csonka. "That big bastard," Sherk told writers, "wasn't going to beat us." They'd make good on that promise.

The Browns continued to believe they could beat Miami and, in the second half, actually led the Dolphins 14–13. It was the first time Miami had trailed in the fourth quarter in a game in over two months. What happened next was typical Miami. No one panicked, and the tension some on the team felt coming into the game didn't heighten but instead dissipated. Csonka may have been nullified, but the Browns would see what other teams did previously. The Dolphins weren't a one-man offense. Warfield ran his almost unstoppable down-and-in pattern for a 15-yard gain, and while Csonka couldn't beat Johnson and Sherk, Morris could, outrunning the Browns for steady and healthy gains. There was more Warfield and eventually a Kiick score and 20–14 fourth-quarter lead. The touchdown drive went 80 yards in 7 plays. A Swift interception sealed the game.

Instead of joy afterward, the Dolphins were frustrated, almost angry. Not shaken. Not flustered. The emotion was a combination of anger and relief. The relief part was that they had gotten a tough, frustrating game out of their system instead of a playoff exit visa. "It may sound stupid," Buoniconti explained to reporters, "but we needed a game like this. Now we know anything can happen."

CHAPTER FOURTEEN

STEEL HURTIN'

The omens for a Miami win were everywhere. First, there was the weather. The game was in Pittsburgh on January 8, yet the temperature was in the 60s with intermittent clouds. It was Dolphins weather, and thus much of Pittsburgh's home-field advantage had been snatched away by Mother Nature.

Other things at the beginning of that day would go Miami's way. A group of hardened Steelers fans used a small private aircraft to drop two thousand leaflets onto the William Penn Hotel where the Dolphins players were staying. "This leaflet will guarantee safe passage out of town to any member of the Miami Dolphins . . ." the leaflet stated in part. "Surrender now and enjoy life with your loved ones rather than face destruction on the field of battle at Three Rivers Stadium." But there was a problem. Because of the wind, the leaflets never reached the hotel and went scattered about the city to little effect.

Not long after that, a quote emerged that may have symbolized Miami the best. It came from Pittsburgh center Ray Mansfield: "The Dolphins have got a lot of talent and their defense is the toughest type to play against. Against a defense that relies on a few great individuals, you'll get dropped for some big losses, but once in a while you can also break for a big gain. But those guys on Miami never get out of position, and you never break a big play against them . . ." Mansfield watched the No-Names pick off Terry Bradshaw twice.

But it was what the Dolphins did on offense that was perhaps more impressive, particularly Little in his fight against defensive lineman Joe Greene. As *Sports Illustrated* reported in its coverage of the game (Morris graced the cover of the magazine), most offenses used two linemen to block Greene (there was a reason he was called *Mean* Joe Greene) and sometimes two linemen and a running back (there was a reason he was sometimes called *Motherfucking Awesome Mean Joe Greene*). Shula and his staff dared to do the impossible: they left Little one-on-one with Greene for much of the game. It turned out to be a smart decision (one of many Shula would make).

There was also some schematic brilliance involved. The Dolphins ran what they called "express" or "sucker" running plays. The line would goad Greene in one direction by showing the flow of the play running one way, then once Greene's momentum got going the back would cut away from Greene. The plays slowed down Greene's attack and had Greene and the entire defensive line second-guessing themselves. Greene once looked at Little and said half jokingly, "What are you guys trying to do to me?" Greene didn't get near the Dolphins' quarterbacks, and in short-yardage situations, the team actually ran *at* Greene. It took massive guts to do that, and the Dolphins weren't in short supply of those.

One of the key plays of the game came from punter Seiple, who ran for a first down after an unplanned fake. Seiple noticed no pass rush, so he ran for a first down. It was that simple. Well, not that simple, but he made it look that way, and it wasn't the first time he'd run that play. In college, while kicking for the University of Kentucky, he ran a fake kick back 70 yards to beat Mississippi.

Csonka later scored on the drive. When Pittsburgh led 10–7, Shula noticed the offense was dragging. So he decided to make a highly risky change. Griese had been recovering slowly from his shattered leg, and in typical Griese form, he approached recovery in an intelligent, methodical, and almost scientific manner. He attended every offensive meeting in the months while he healed. Not most of them. Not the majority of them. All of them. He had a dislocated ankle and broken leg that required a cast, and Griese would hop around the sidelines at most of the practices, watching everything. He also threw the football at times, keeping his arm in shape. To Griese, the injury didn't mean he was done for the year. He stubbornly believed he'd be back that season.

At halftime, with the score tied at 7, Shula approached Griese, who had been sitting calmly at his locker.

"Are you ready to go in?" Shula asked.

Griese wasn't surprised. He sensed a change was coming. After all, what made him such a good quarterback was anticipating the unexpected.

"I'm ready," he said.

Shula walked over to Morrall. This conversation wouldn't be as easy.

"Earl, I'm starting Bob in the second half," Shula said.

Morrall remained calm. "That's your decision," he replied.

"It's best for the team," Shula said.

Morrall didn't get angry and responded with class. "If you need me," he said, "I'll be ready."

"Sure, yes, it was a risk making that change," Shula says now. "If it blew up in my face, I'd have been explaining it for years. It would have been the Super Bowl with the Jets all over again." Morrall was the quarterback then too, when he and Shula were with the Colts. When Baltimore was struggling, Shula considered benching Morrall at the half to put in Unitas, who was also recovering from an injury, but didn't. It proved to be a mistake.

Before the game, Noll had been asked by reporters which quarterback he'd rather see and Noll responded cutely: "I'd like to see all three quarterbacks. But mostly I'd like to see Griese, because that would mean they'd be behind when he came in."

Well, here he was. Griese was rusty and it showed as he threw an interception, but the creakiness was soon gone. If you want to understand why Griese was so talented despite not having the strongest arm, it was because of moments like these. He completed just 3 of 5 passes, but one of them was a laser to Warfield on a play Warfield called the team's "money pattern." It was a simple pass route: run a quick four steps, cut toward the center of the field, and catch the pass. He did that, and it went for 52 yards. His will and decision-making skills were keys to that second half, but the biggest reason they beat Pittsburgh was because of the dominant run game. Morris was on the cover of the magazine, but Kiick, who had his role significantly reduced that season, scored 2 critical touchdowns on two drives that lasted an astounding fifteen minutes. The Dolphins were shoving the ball down Pittsburgh's throat.

The Steelers would go on to become one of the great Super Bowl teams the sport had ever seen, winning multiple titles, but for this game some of them may have gotten a tad cocky. Particularly quarterback Terry Bradshaw, who was gutsy, but he wasn't always viewed—fairly or unfairly—as the brightest star in the Milky Way. Dallas Cowboys player Thomas "Hollywood" Henderson once famously and viciously said that Bradshaw couldn't spell "cat" if you spotted him the *c* and the *a*.

What Bradshaw did that definitely was not smart was discuss with reporters before the game how maybe the Steelers were the team of destiny. In their previous game, the Steelers had beaten Oakland on a last-second play that became known as the Immaculate Reception, and to Bradshaw, it meant there was an inevitability to Miami losing. "Even with the flu, it's been a good week for me," he said before the game to *Sports Illustrated*. "I got all my learning down and I'm throwing the ball well. I've been in high spirits all week. Before San Diego and Oakland and now again, I've had this feeling. It's kind of like ESP and it's that we can't lose."

On one play, Scott smashed Bradshaw in his face, popping the ball loose. Bradshaw had already been suffering from a severe case of the flu, and the hit made his head feel even woozier. The head trauma caused temporary memory loss, and Bradshaw couldn't remember all the plays. Bradshaw's substitute didn't fare as well, and by the time Bradshaw returned, Griese had given the Dolphins a 21–10 lead. Bradshaw's attempt at a comeback fell short, and the Dolphins were going back to the Super Bowl.

One of the best moments of that game, and perhaps in the Dolphins' story, came in the final minutes as the offense was attempting to run out the clock. Griese entered a huddle that was borderline chaotic. Teammates started barking suggestions at him for what play to use next; there was chatter, expletives, and small conversations breaking out. Griese decided he'd heard enough.

His voice rose above the clamor. "Shut up!" Griese yelled. There was silence. Csonka loved it and smiled. Once Griese felt order had been reestablished, he made a quick remark before calling the play. "Now," he said, "let's get this drive going."

It was official: Griese was back.

The Dolphins had not just won 21–17, they dominated, the score not indicative of that domination. Their success ended Pittsburgh's 8-0 home winning streak that season. Shula had been confident going into the game and proved it several times when inside the Pittsburgh 10-yard line he went for first downs on fourth-and-short yardage instead of kicking a field goal. "I had to make more fourth down decisions than anytime this year," he'd say after the game. "You have to gamble if you're going to be world champions."

Shula had taken another risk. Fleming was the best blocking back in the NFL but was viewed as a risk in the passing game due to hands of stone. Shula again studied tape and again noticed a potential advantage. The Steelers tended to pay little attention to the tight ends, instead focusing on shutting down an offense's running game and big-play receivers. Shula knew they'd ignore Fleming as well, and he was right. Fleming had averaged less than 1 catch a game during the regular season but burned the Steelers for 5 catches for 50 yards. Following the win, Fleming had fun with a media that had written it was more likely for Diana Ross to catch a football in a big spot than him. He reminded reporters that this was his eighth playoff ring, many of which he earned with the Packers. Indeed, he had earned so many rings, it was uncomfortable to wear them all at once, so he took some of the diamonds from several of the rings and transferred them to a medallion, which he hung around his neck. "This will be my fourth blocking Super Bowl," he said sarcastically. "How many tight ends have been in four Super Bowls? One. Marv Fleming."

Noll stated one of the reasons the Steelers couldn't generate a pass rush was because many of the defensive linemen were suffering from the flu. The more likely reason was the 63-degree temperature. It was Dolphins weather. "The sun came out," said Fleming, "and they got tired."

Greene, unlike Noll, provided no excuses, and he offered the strangest of compliments to Morris. "They ran the ball at me and I'd say they did a pretty good job," he'd later tell reporters. "When you look at the films, you'll see me flat on my back an awful lot. I wasn't really surprised but it did prove that it can be done." Greene added: "I saw Mercury Morris quoted in the paper earlier in the week saying that when he lived in Pittsburgh he did a lot of running from the cops. I have to admit he runs pretty well."

Greene made a statement after the game that perfectly symbolized the view of the Dolphins, not just then, but even now. "I wasn't effective at all," he said. "I wasn't a factor at all. If I could've played a better ball game it might've been different. Miami's a lot better ball club than I thought. Films have a way of deceiving you. They didn't look as good as they were. They showed us they were a lot better than we thought they were."

Years later, Csonka would sum up why the Dolphins won that conference championship game. "It was two things," he said. "First, the Steelers were really cocky. They thought they were going to kill us. You could tell from some of the things they were saying before the game, on the field, how we had no shot against them. The other thing, the big thing, is that we outsmarted them. We took that game from them because we were smarter. Player by player, they could probably jump higher, lift more weight, but we took that game because we were smarter and *a better team*."

A better team. Morrall exemplified this by his classy handling of the halftime benching for Griese. "We needed points on the board and Bob Griese got them for us," Morrall said. "I'm not unhappy about the second half. I came down here as a backup quarterback and I know what my role is."

It is difficult to imagine a player having that attitude now, when the attention is focused heavily on an athlete's individual statistical greatness. A player today benched in the second half of the AFC title game would live tweet his dissatisfaction, rip the coach on Facebook, and complain on SportsCenter.

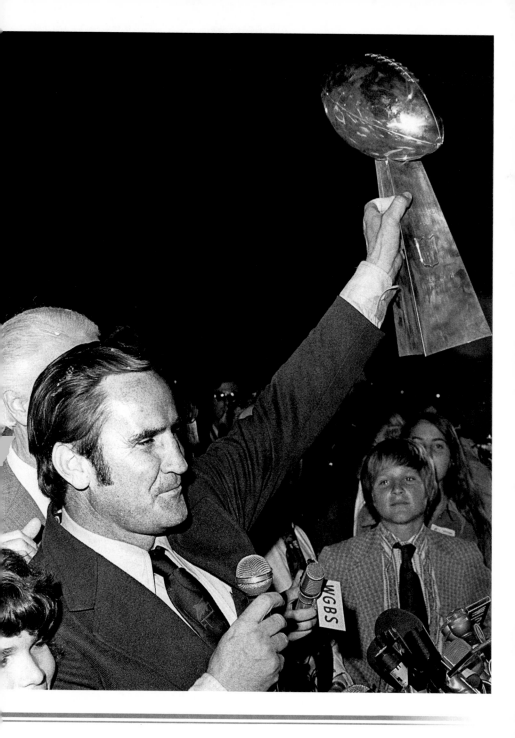

Coach Don Shula holds up the Lombardi Trophy after Miami's Super Bowl win that sealed the unbeaten season. Tens of thousands of fans greeted the Dolphins when the team landed in Miami after Super Bowl VII.

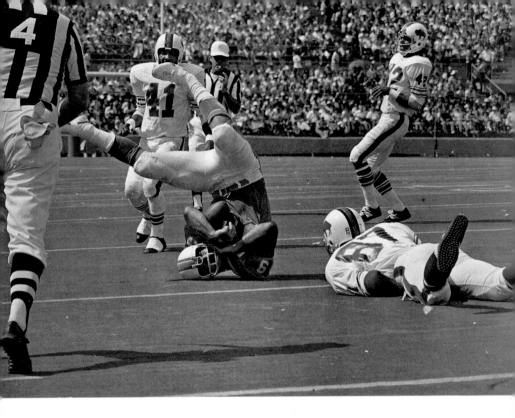

Larry Csonka is perhaps the toughest player in NFL history. He would become almost as famous for his repeated broken noses as he would for his Hall of Fame running skills.

Mercury Morris entered a crowded Miami backfield and provided explosive running that transformed the Dolphins into a more potent offense.

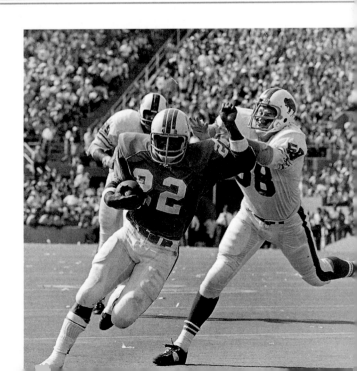

Quarterback Earl Morrall helped save the perfect season when starter Bob Griese was injured.

The Dolphins won Super Bowl VII over Washington to seal their perfect season. The only blemish: kicker Garo Yepremian's flub led to Washington's sole score.

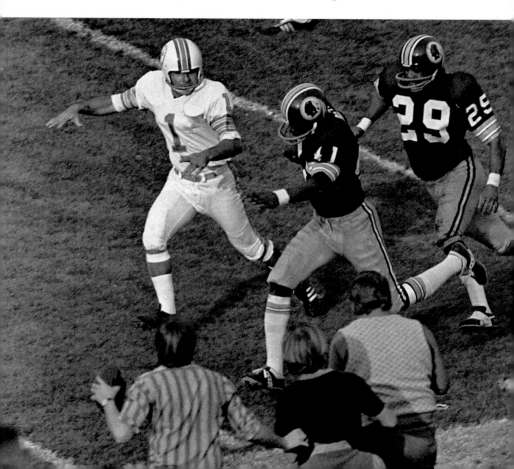

Paul Warfield is the most graceful wide receiver in NFL history. He was a member of the 1970s All-Decade team and provided a dangerous, deep threat for the Dolphins.

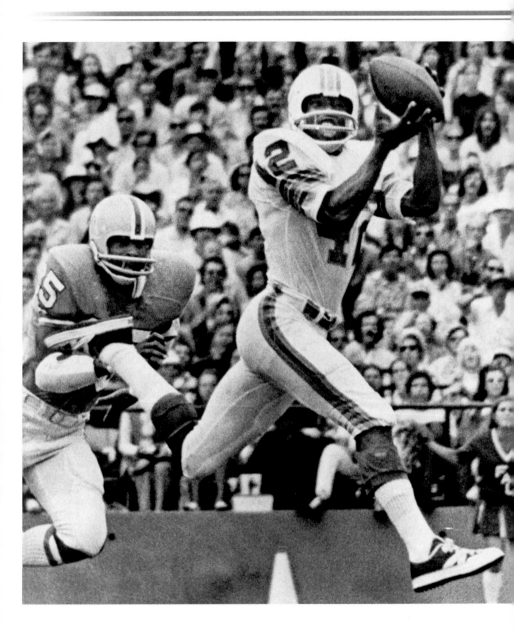

Shula and his staff were some of the most innovative coaches in football. Many also consider Shula to be the greatest motivator the sport has ever seen.

Before their groundbreaking 1972 season, the Dolphins were a laughingstock and one of the biggest losers in football, ignored by Miami sports fans. That changed after Shula took over the team.

Shula would become incredibly popular in Miami, and he remained a huge presence in the city decades after the unbeaten season.

Shula and Pittsburgh coach Chuck Noll after the Dolphins beat the Steelers to advance to Super Bowl VII. It was one of the few big games in which Noll was outcoached.

Tight end Jim Mandich makes a critical catch in Super Bowl VII. Mandich would go on to become one of the most popular Dolphins in team history.

Washington quarterback Billy Kilmer threw for just 104 yards and had three turnovers against Miami's No Name Defense. That season, the Dolphins allowed just eighteen touchdowns in fourteen games.

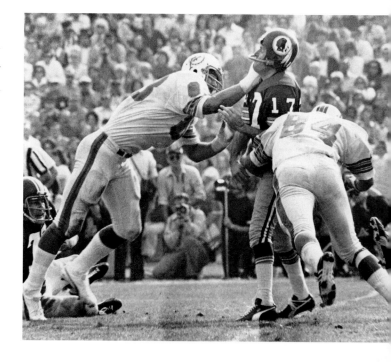

Shula's intensity helped to push the Dolphins from the dregs of the NFL into the best team in league history.

Shula celebrates with Miami players as owner Joe Robbie, right, looks on.

The game meant something particularly special to Shula beyond the obvious reasons. The Dolphins going 16-0 meant they passed the previous NFL record set by the 1948 Cleveland Browns of the All-America Football Conference. That team won fifteen straight. Shula knew this because he had watched that Browns team from the stands as a sophomore at John Carroll University. He saw his favorite team establish a special mark in NFL history, and now, as a head coach, he had surpassed that mark.

A key portion of *Sports Illustrated*'s summary of the 21–17 Dolphins victory over the Steelers stated this: "The Dolphins' gutsy victory supplies further vindication for a team that has been beset by skeptics. While Miami has now won 16 in a row, the most any team ever won in one season and only one game short of the all time streak (compiled over parts of two seasons), the Dolphins have been pooh-poohed for waltzing through an easy schedule. Which they have. Which isn't their fault. The performance against Pittsburgh is something else again, though, for it demonstrates that the Dolphins can beat a good opponent when the schedule provides them with one."

The plane ride back to Miami was joyous but not overly so, which is not difficult to imagine from a group that took pride in remaining steady and singular-minded. Flight attendants offered either champagne or red wine, and many players picked the latter, because champagne had too much of a celebratory feel. The Dolphins knew their true mission was to win the Super Bowl. So while they were excited to win the conference championship game and allowed themselves time to appreciate what they'd accomplished, they also knew there was one more thing to do.

The pilot announced over the intercom that Washington had beaten Dallas, which meant the Dolphins would be playing the

Redskins in the Super Bowl. The reaction was met with violent indifference. Griese grabbed a pillow, adjusted his seat, and went to sleep.

When their plane landed at Miami International Airport, approximately four thousand fans were there to greet the team. As the players disembarked, each received an ovation, and Shula didn't miss an opportunity to tell the fans what he'd told the players for weeks. "All we want to be now," Shula said, "is 17-0."

The Steelers game had changed the minds of many NFL observers. Prior to it, the Dolphins were viewed as a lucky team taking advantage of an easy schedule. That, of course, wasn't accurate, but it was the common view among more than a few both in and covering the sport. The Steelers were seen as one of the toughest teams in the NFL (and later would be considered one of the tougher dynasties ever). One game changed everything, at least in terms of public perception. The league was now seeing the Dolphins had a core of tough guys that went beyond Csonka and a few others.

In some ways, Jake Scott epitomized the toughness of the Miami defense and its intellectual stoutness. It cannot be overstated how effective and bloodying this defense could be, and Scott was one of the main leaders. Scott would bump heads with Shula and eventually come to almost despise the coach, while Shula would see Scott as a problem player, difficult to control. "We had discipline problems in '72 . . ." Shula would say many years after his confrontations with Scott. "Jake Scott wasn't always easy to deal with."

That was true, but it is also no coincidence that as the Dolphins began their trek toward perfection, Scott was on a path toward an impressive career. The Dolphins had picked Scott in the seventh round of the 1970 draft after he had spent one year in the Canadian Football League following his departure from Georgia as a junior when juniors weren't allowed into the NFL. How the Dolphins acquired Scott—and how he took revenge on them—became a part of the legend of Scott's rebellious nature. Upon drafting Scott, the Dolphins' general manager, Joe Thomas, bragged to the media they were able to get a first-round talent for seventh-round money. Thomas was able to get Scott to accept a $10,000 pay cut. Scott never forgot Thomas's words or that the Dolphins were publicly touting they got him for practically nothing. Years later, when the World Football League would begin signing Dolphins players, Scott bluffed the Miami brass into thinking he too had an offer from the new league. Not wanting to lose Scott, the team panicked and gave him a five-year $600,000 contract. He became the first defensive back to ever make six figures. Revenge, indeed.

His impact on the field was immediate. He wanted the same type of precision from the coaches that they required from players. It was perhaps this type of reverse demand—player wanting coach to be perfect the way Shula's staff wanted the players to chase perfection—that caused the initial strain between Shula and Scott. Shula was the boss and Scott sometimes didn't believe anyone was the boss of him.

Shula wasn't the first coach Scott irritated. Scott's relationship with University of Georgia coach Vince Dooley became strained at the end of Scott's college career. The Bulldogs had an outside shot at a national championship game if they played in the 1968 Orange Bowl, but Dooley thought that was unrealistic and prematurely agreed to play in the Sugar Bowl. Dooley's decision was disastrous, thanks mostly to Bulldog players spending more time partying that week than preparing for the game. They were beaten 16–2 by Arkansas.

Scott wasn't your average football player; he was just different. He was extraordinarily principled, often to the point of extremism.

After that game, he refused to have an association with Georgia as long as Dooley was a part of the school. Four decades after Dooley's decision, and after Dooley retired as athletic director, Scott accepted an invitation to be an honorary captain for the rivalry game against Georgia Tech. Scott was one of the best defensive backs in the history of the powerful SEC and eventually made the College Hall of Fame, but it took a great deal longer to do so simply because when Dooley attempted to lobby for his entrance, Scott made it quite clear he didn't care about such things and if they put him in he might not show up for the induction.

With the Dolphins, he was the only rookie not asked to sing his fight song. The veterans knew if they did, they were in for a brawl.

Shula was able to decode almost every player on the team using different techniques to motivate them all. Everyone except Scott. "Coach Shula would yell at some players, like me," Dick Anderson once told the *Miami Herald*. "He'd talk calmly with others. He'd joke with some, like Csonka. Jake Scott? Jake, he'd leave alone."

Shula knew the best way to get along with Scott was to say little to him. Others would learn that lesson in a more painful manner. One of the Dolphins' favorite hangouts was Mr. T's. On one night, Mandich and Scott were drinking and playing Pong, a video game released in 1972. The two were playing the game, enjoying a few beers, minding their own business, when a patron walked up behind them and said: "If the Dolphins play this season like you two guys play Pong, the Dolphins are in trouble."

Mandich looked over at Scott. "I could see how angry he was getting," Mandich remembered in an interview. "It was building like a volcano."

It's been a common occurrence over the decades. Football players enter bar. Stay to themselves. Drunken fan approaches, taunts and mocks. Players ignore the fan. The fan continues taunting. Ignore, taunt. Taunt, ignore. Until punches are thrown.

"You guys really stink at this game," the man continued.

Scott finally had enough. Scott stretched his moderately tall frame and stood close to the larger man. Mandich knew Scott hadn't yet lost control of his temper, but if the man kept pushing, he would. The man did. Scott gave him one last chance.

"If you say one more fucking word," Scott warned, "I'm gonna knock you on your ass."

Another word was uttered and the drunken man threw the first punch. Scott, after a flurry of punches to the man's face, shattered his jaw. The man claimed in court that Scott instigated the fight—a clear falsehood, and witnesses backed Scott's story of self-defense and the assault charges against him were dismissed. Scott had won again.

Scott had five screws inserted into his left hand after it smashed into the helmet of Kansas City fullback Jim Otis one year. One game later, he shattered his right wrist. Both hands were put in casts, leading Scott to say: "Now I find out who my real friends are when I go to the bathroom."

When Shula took control of the Dolphins in 1970, the team had yet to have a winning season. His wife once asked: "Are you sure you want to coach there?" He wasn't, truthfully. There was always a small part of Shula that wondered if such a disgraced franchise could ever win, let alone make it to the Super Bowl. But something told him the Dolphins could. Part of it was Shula's extreme confidence in his abilities. There was nothing cocky about Shula. It wasn't in his nature. But there was great confidence wrapped around skill and a formidable stubbornness. All of those aspects of his personality made him an almost insurmountable force. Shula could, of course, be beaten, as his previous Super Bowl losses would attest, but everyone on the Dolphins felt there was no way Shula would be beaten *again*. And, to be perfectly truthful, Shula felt the same.

This was confidence, not arrogance, which had been honed over a lifetime. It was the end result of a close family that encouraged him to aggressively pursue his dreams. A close family and a humble one. Growing up, the Shulas rarely missed church. Don's mother insisted the family wear clean clothes free of rips. She stitched holes shut and reattached buttons. The house, like the family, was modest and unpretentious. Three levels stacked efficiently with a cozy front porch and an inviting small set of stairs leading to the door. The family spent much of its time in the basement, which was painted and neat. Don's mother often cooked there, and like other Hungarian households in the area, the living room was off-limits to the family and used only for visitors.

Don dutifully digested what was a clear message from his family as he grew from a quiet boy to an aggressive and respected high school athlete: work hard. The message often didn't need to be spoken, even though it sometimes was. Don observed his parents—the late hours, the heavy lifting, the early rising, and the absence of complaining. When Shula was twelve, he worked odd jobs earning a dollar a day. At the end of the week, he'd give his mom five dollars and she'd give him fifty cents as an allowance. The rest was kept in a savings account. Years later, she used the saved money to buy Shula a car his senior year in high school. This was the discipline of the Shula family.

In the lives of some coaches and athletes, there is a seminal moment when they knew they are headed to a life in athletics, either on the playing field or coaching on the sidelines. For Shula it was different. He witnessed the work ethic of an immigrant family and neighborhood. The men who toiled fishing and the women who worked in homes, taking care of everything else, and it all sunk in. A single moment? It was more like a young adulthood of observation and then adopting those beliefs as his own once he reached adulthood.

"I knew how hard my parents worked, my father, my grandfather," says Shula now. "They provided for all of us. They taught us the value of a good day's work. I never forgot that lesson. I was just going to do different hard work. My thought was, I could apply that work ethic to sports."

———

Shula's mother and father didn't truly understand football but would get a better understanding of the sport when Shula came home with his nose bloodied and cut. Shula was a smallish junior high schooler who had decided he was tough enough to engage larger and older players. Shula wrote in his 1973 autobiography, *The Winning Edge*, how at one practice, a player caught a pass directly in front of Shula, who moved into position to make the tackle. What Shula didn't know was the player had used a sharp, metallic object to keep one part of his uniform intact. When Shula made the tackle, the object cut into the side of Shula's nose, splitting it open. He was sent to the hospital, and while stitches weren't needed, the gash required extensive bandaging. When Shula got home, a bloodied mess, his mother was waiting.

"Donald, what happened to you?"

"Oh, it's nothing, Mom." Shula was trying to downplay the injury, knowing what was coming.

"What do you mean it's nothing? What happened to your nose?"

"I hurt it playing football."

"Let me see."

"Mom, it's really nothing, I'm okay."

"Don't tell me you're okay with a bandage that big. Your nose must be broken."

"No, it isn't, Mom. I'm okay now, honest."

"Take that bandage off and let me see for myself. What will your father say?"

"All right, I'll show you that there is nothing wrong other than a little cut." He removed the wrapping and his mother looked as if she had seen a ghost.

"Dear God, what kind of a game is this where you get bruised and battered like that? That's it. As far as I am concerned, there will be no more football." Then she told Shula to go wash for dinner.

To most Hungarians, soccer was a respected and culturally understood sport. Football was neither. Shula's parents didn't get it and believed it was more violence than sport. This was the attitude of many immigrant parents. They didn't immerse themselves in America's sporting culture like their children.

And immerse is exactly what Shula did. On the playground, Shula became the one who got all the kids together to play a pickup game of football. He made out batting orders for softball games. In high school, he irritated coaches by sometimes catching players' mistakes before they did.

Shula's parents forbid Shula from playing football, but for the first time in his life, he ignored their wishes and secretly played anyway. Once Shula made the high school team, he revealed to his parents his secret and invited them to watch one of his games. In it, Shula returned a punt 75 yards for a touchdown. They were excited for their son and officially hooked. They never tried to stop Shula from playing ever again.

It would have been virtually impossible anyway. Shula was obsessed with the sport. At Harvey High School, he became almost legendary, known as much for his serious but friendly disposition as his athletic prowess. In the 1947 school yearbook, *The Anvil*, he is called "an athlete strong and competent." Shula played football, basketball, and baseball; ran track; and topped off his high school career as a member of the Arrow Club, homeroom president, and student body vice president. By his senior year, Shula had developed broad shoulders, a thin waist, and a sinewy frame that packed on muscle. Shula was named "Best Build" in a poll by his classmates. "An all powerful back who was directly responsible for many a tally," another part of the yearbook says, "Don was one of the hardest fighters on the team and overcame an impressive array of opposing grid men. Don has a right to be proud of his senior year at Harvey when he achieved the all-Lake Shore team."

Despite a solid high school athletics career, Shula wasn't pursued to play college sports. Shula may have been voted Best Build, but his speed and level of athleticism wasn't extraordinary. There were moments when Shula wondered what he'd do with his life. His intense religious background gave him thoughts of becoming a priest, but when one of Shula's coaches got him an interview with the football coaches at John Carroll University—a moderate drive from Painesville—everything changed. In typical Shula form, he surprised everyone around him. Shula didn't play his freshman year, but the following season he started the second game, gaining 175 yards on 25 carries.

Shula experienced two extreme highs while at John Carroll. His team beat highly favored Syracuse in Shula's final year, a particularly pleasing win since before the game, a Syracuse newspaper smugly asked the question: "Who is John Carroll?" They soon had their answer. The second high was more personal. After the game, Shula learned that legendary coach Paul Brown had been in attendance scouting Syracuse. Brown, in fact, lived just a few blocks away from the stadium. To many from Ohio, the coach of the Cleveland Browns was a more pivotal figure than the governor. Shula wondered if the Browns would ever have any interest in him. He didn't have to wait long for an answer.

Shula saw Paul Brown the way many Ohioans did: as practically a deity. Brown coached Massillon High School to an 80-8-2 record over nine years, a streak that included thirty-five consecutive wins and six straight championships in the state of Ohio from 1935 to 1940. Massillon wasn't just a random juggernaut; Brown had built a system that created disciplined and efficient teams that bludgeoned opponents. Amazingly, Brown established the beginnings of modern football—position coaches, extremely detailed practice schedules—on a high school level. The program became so successful twenty thousand people attended games. Brown left Massillon in January 1941 and, a short time later, coached the Ohio State Buckeyes to a share of the national title with the University of Georgia. When the city of Cleveland got its first professional football team, the franchise hired Brown, and he'd forever change the sport with a series of innovations that were historic, including inserting radio transmitters into the helmets of players to communicate with them when they were on the field and he was on the sideline, administrating tests to see how smart his players were, and using face masks on the professional level.

Brown was a heroic figure, so when Shula stood before him in the summer of 1951, Shula's legs shook slightly, the nervousness washing over him. Shula used to attend Cleveland Browns games as a kid, and unable to pay the full ticket price, he snuck into the high school section where admission was just a quarter. He dreamed of playing for them, and now, years later, he stood before Brown, a draft pick of the team and the man he admired. Shula signed for $5,000.

* * *

There was something about Shula that Brown liked, and it was easy to see what that was. The two men shared similar physical characteristics and limited athletic ability, and were studious, respectful of authority, and highly dedicated. As he did in high school and college, Shula made the most of his talents while trying to make the Browns. In the final exhibition game against the Los Angeles Rams, and with Shula playing defensive back against Tom Fears, an elite receiver, Shula made his impression on Brown and his teammates. But first he made an interesting impression on Fears himself. On one play, Fears made a catch and Shula made the tackle, and as the two fell to the ground, Shula accidently rolled onto Fear's leg. Fear didn't think it was so accidental, and underneath the pile of human debris after the tackle, Fears kicked Shula in the mouth with his cleats. Shula kept cool, knowing if he retaliated and drew a penalty or was tossed from the game, his chances of making the team would evaporate. His level head paid dividends. He later intercepted two passes.

Brown notified hopefuls if they made the team by putting a letter in an envelope to the handful of players competing for jobs. One envelope had a plane ticket and a note that read, "Goodbye and good luck." The other gave Brown's congratulations for making the team. It was an unusual, if not cruel, way of informing players if they made the Browns, but deities can do whatever they want. A petrified Shula got his letter and quickly opened it. He read the first word and his shoulders relaxed. "Congratulations. You have made the Cleveland Browns football team. Report to the stadium on Wednesday morning for a meeting and practice at 9:30."

Shula was there just before seven.

* * *

Shula was the only rookie from that 1951 team to survive the cut. He'd become a likable fixture around the team, even before making it. In one of Shula's first practices with the Browns, quarterback Otto Graham, an eventual Hall of Famer and also an idol of Shula's, came onto the field carrying a large duffel bag containing footballs. Shula was first on the practice field. "Warm me up, will you, kid," he said to Shula. He was momentarily dazed. *I'm throwing passes with Otto Graham.*

As the season went on, Shula maximized every practice repetition, every chance to impress Brown and the coaches. When one of the starters ahead of Shula was hurt just prior to the third game of the season, it was his opportunity to start. The small-town son of immigrants who played his college football at a school some hadn't even heard of was now a starter on the defending champion Browns. It was a turn in Shula's life, and though that first start was unremarkable in its nature, the fact that Shula didn't blow any assignments and was productive caught the attention of the coaches. He had earned their trust, or mostly did. The Browns finished the season with ten consecutive wins but lost in the championship game, and in that contest, Shula didn't play until the final minutes. Brown only trusted Shula so much.

Shula's introduction to the NFL continued at a dizzying pace. Against Philadelphia, just minutes into the game, he tackled fullback Al Pollard. Tackle isn't the word. It was a violent collision that resulted in the foot belonging to the 6-foot, nearly 200-pound Pollard kicking Shula in the mouth, knocking out Shula's front tooth, almost detaching another, and ripping open his bottom lip, which required six stitches. End of game for Shula. A team dentist replaced the missing tooth and capped the other. Shula played the rest of the year.

After that continuing instruction about the physicality of professional football, Shula learned a cruel lesson about the business of the sport. He'd been pursuing an advanced degree in physical education from Western Reserve University. Shula had just finished one of his classes when he stopped at a coffee shop nearby. Shula did his usual morning routine: he purchased a cup of coffee and the morning paper. This morning would be different from the dozens of others. He flipped to the sports section and on the front page was a story that felt like a punch in the gut: Shula was being traded to the Baltimore Colts. The trade occurred on March 26, 1953, and Shula was part of a fifteen-player deal—the largest trade at the time in professional football history. After the initial shock, Shula became angry. Shula knew nothing of the trade, and the first he'd heard of it was at that moment reading the paper. He slammed his coffee cup onto the table, some of the contents spilling out, and a realization washed over him. Shula's hero had blindsided him.

And, just like that, Shula was in Baltimore.

To this day, Shula won't say a negative word about Brown, who remains his hero, but Brown did teach Shula another valuable lesson: that football was a nasty business. "No, I wasn't bitter," Shula says now, though it's hard to imagine he wasn't. Brown was a like a second father to him. "What happens in that situation," Shula said, "is you really see football is a tough business." It would not be the last time Shula experienced that lesson—or delivered it himself to someone who, upon hearing the message, accused Shula of his own betrayal.

One thing that did happen was Shula made slightly more money. His first contract with the Colts was for $6,500, about $1,000 more than what he was paid in Cleveland. The Colts provided the extra cash because they saw Shula as more valuable than the average defensive back drone. The coaching staff wanted to run Brown's defensive system and needed Shula to help instruct the team. Shula did. In a way, it was his first coaching job.

The Colts, at that time, weren't a talented group. A new coach was hired, and he entrusted Shula with calling the defensive plays. Shula was honored, but his lack of experience showed in a game against the Rams. Before one particular play, the Rams brought ten men into the huddle and the eleventh hid near the sideline out of Shula's view. When Shula called the defense, he did so completely unaware there was a wide-open receiver. The ball snapped, Shula went into his defensive backpedal, and the Ram player streaked down the field wide open. Shula still didn't see him and wondered who the quarterback was aiming for as the football traveled high into the air. *Who is that dummy throwing to?* Shula thought. He was horrified after seeing the ball caught for a score.

Yet overall, Shula was a solid player and he impressed the Colts players so much he was named a captain of the defense, which was slightly unusual in that era for a cornerback to earn such an honor. He was a constant motivator, even if sometimes he irritated his teammates. If a team got a big run, Shula would jump into the faces of the defensive linemen. "Dig in!" he'd tell them. Art Donovan, the smart-ass Colts defensive tackle who was also a world-class comedian, would wait until the Miami secondary would give up a pass and then make a remark to Shula, calling Shula by his nickname. "Hey, Shoes baby, you feeling all right?" Shula wouldn't be amused.

Shula was a hard worker and liked by the Colts, but over the next two seasons, in 1955 and 1956, he began arriving to an obvious conclusion. Shula knew he was a moderate talent at best. His limited physical ability was restricted even more because of an ankle injury in the 1956 season that required painkilling injections directly into the joint. His performances continued to slip, leading to his benching and then, eventually, his release from the Colts before the 1957 season. Again, he was crushed, and after a nondescript season in

Washington, Shula had to admit to himself that it was over. And, as quickly as it began, Shula's playing career was finished.

There was one moment at the end, one instance when Shula's Colts career and what he did as a player, as well as what he meant as a player, crystallized. After Shula was released by Baltimore, and before being picked up by Washington, he watched one of the Colts games as a fan. The Colts won, and Shula went to the Baltimore locker room to congratulate his former teammates. Along the way he was stopped by a group of players led by Gino Marchetti. "We got something for you," Marchetti said as he reached out and handed Shula something.

It was the game ball.

Shula got into coaching for the reason many do. Their careers as players had ended—or never fully started—but their love of football was strong. Coaching allowed Shula, and many like him, to engage in the sport once they were no longer competitive enough to play on the professional level. Shula moved quickly through the coaching ranks. First, there was the $6,500 assistant job at the University of Virginia, then the $7,500 position at Kentucky (which included free housing). Wilson gave Shula his first professional job as a defensive coach on the Lions for $11,000 a year. It was the most money Shula had ever made.

Shula put his formidable work ethic into coaching the way he did as a player. He was a relentless studier and, at Detroit, that intensity was rewarded one Thanksgiving Day in a game against Green Bay in 1962. The Packers were the mightiest team in football and the defending champions. That group, years later, would be considered Vince Lombardi's greatest team. On it were nine future Hall of Famers and over half of them were on offense. It was Shula's job to stop them. It was a nightmarish task.

Shula took an unusual strategy against the Packers. Most defenses were so terrified of quarterback Bart Starr's accuracy they feared blitzing him and getting beat by the big play. Shula took the opposite approach. He attacked Starr relentlessly with pressure from all sides, particularly up the middle. Starr was sacked 11 times, allowing Detroit to jump to a 26–0 lead. The Detroit home crowd was so enthralled by Shula's defense the fans booed when the Lions offense came onto the field. The Lions game was Green Bay's only loss, and the Packers would go on to a 14-1 record and the NFL championship game. Two months later, propelled by his mastering over Lombardi, Shula became coach of the Colts. He was only thirty-three years old, one of the youngest head coaches in NFL history.

In some ways, like Shula, it was amazing Csonka had made it to perfection's doorstep too. Before being drafted by the NFL, scouts had told him he was too big to play fullback. Lombardi himself—Lombardi the infallible—passed over Csonka in the draft. "I thought he was impeccable up until that point," Csonka says.

There were few bodies, even in that nasty time when almost anything was legal, that had taken as much abuse as Csonka's. There was the broken blood vessel over his left eye, which spilled blood into the eye cavity and caused a severe reddening that made Csonka's eye look like it had been colored with a bright marker. There was the cracked eardrum that filled with fluid. There was the elbow that swelled to the size of a tennis ball. Oh, and there was the knee that smashed into the concrete-hard artificial turf and filled with blood. Csonka's nickname reflected his various states of greatness, injury, and ability to inflict injury. The first nickname he earned on the Dolphins was "Ding-Ding," and then it was "Lawn Mower," and finally "Zonk"—definitely appropriate-sounding—is what would last.

It was amazing, his pain tolerance, yes, but this was his plan. To constantly play through the pain and provide a sense of infallibility to the running back position despite the brutality of it all. To Csonka, that was his greatest contribution to the Dolphins. It wasn't just about talent and muscle but longevity. "A running back must first of all be durable," he once said. "The ideal back has speed, ability, and durability. Not many have all three. I would rather have a little speed and little ability and a great deal of durability. It is better to gain 450 yards in one year and to be there for every game than to gain 1,000 yards and not know from game to game whether you can play." On playing with pain, he added: "Some guys can't stand much pain. That doesn't make them any less of a man because of it. I just think my pain threshold is a little higher than the average. Being able to play every week is mostly a case of making yourself play with pain."

"You can't chart drive," Csonka says today. "You can't measure heart. That's the lesson of not just my career but the entire Dolphins team. That's what people always need to remember about us."

That Monday after the title game against Pittsburgh, Shula decided to give the Dolphins two days off, but before that, he made what was a controversial decision at the time. Rather than wait and announce his starting quarterback at a later moment, he announced it almost immediately, saying it would be Griese. It was actually a smart decision. "You put the team at ease when you make that decision quickly and forcefully," Shula explains now. "The team can focus on football and the Super Bowl instead of who will be the quarterback."

At the time, the quick decision was seen as a massive risk by the media, but it actually wasn't. Indeed, two teams during the playoffs that year, San Francisco and Dallas, made their announcements at a later time and the decisions backfired, leading to both losing. Shula also knew there'd be no issues with Griese among the players. Morrall was respected but Griese was *cherished*. That was the difference with the Dolphins.

Braucher, the beat writer who covered the Dolphins, recalled the media reaction to Shula's decision in his 1973 book about the perfect season. "Why are you making the announcement so early?" the media asked Shula.

"Because you don't fool around with men the stature of Griese and Earl," Shula responded. That was also part of Shula's decision. He wanted to treat his two quarterbacks respectfully.

"Are you prepared for the second guesses . . . ?" Shula was asked.

Shula, like most coaches, would rather be stabbed in his forehead than second-guessed by media members who never coached a day in their lives. "I'm always prepared for the second-guess," he told writers. "Every situation is different. I'm not the coach at San Francisco or Dallas. I'm the coach at Miami and this is the right way for us to go. Morrall was brought here to back up Bob. That's the way we started out the season and that's the way we'll go into the Super Bowl."

"Nobody on the team is going to question me replacing Morrall," said Griese to writers. "Shula's the boss and he's made too many right decisions over the years for the players to question him. Some guys might question his views on social activities but not on football. How can you?"

And that was the view of Shula by the players. Total and complete trust in him even if they didn't agree on his restrictions to their "social activities," like having sex the night before games (more on that later). They had come to totally trust Shula. Outside of the team, there were questions if Shula was making the right choice, but inside that locker room, there were no doubts. Not a single one.

The practices that week in Florida were many things: crisp, efficient, even fierce. What they weren't were secure. Shula had closed practices to the public out of fear of spying. His paranoia was totally justified. His Super Bowl opponent, George Allen, coach of the Washington Redskins, was well known for attempts at spying on opposing teams. The stories were infamous. Five years before playing Shula in the Super Bowl, Allen was coaching the Los Angeles Rams, and before playing Dallas, a Cowboys executive noticed a suspicious automobile parked within eyeball distance of the Cowboys' practice field. It was suspicious because it was a car . . . near the practice field . . . and all NFL coaches are paranoid as hell. To them a parked car is an opportunity for an opponent to steal secrets. The Cowboys were so paranoid they ran a search on the license plate of the car and traced it to a Rams scout. Or so they said. The Cowboys complained to the commissioner, but he chuckled at the nonsense and refused to take action.

Allen's reputation for spying would reach insane heights; he was once accused by a rival coach of hiring a woman to push a stroller near practice. Inside the stroller wasn't a baby but a little person (the politically incorrect term is "midget") taking notes on the practice.

Shula wasn't on the lookout for unfamiliar cars or suspicious strollers, but he wasn't against sensible precautions against potential Allen tomfoolery and closed practice to all but team personnel. Or so he thought. A petite woman in her seventies approached practice and began watching it through the chain-link fence. Shula politely asked her to leave, but she only went a short distance away and kept watching. He gave up, figuring not even Allen would try something so obvious.

Shula was uptight and the players could easily sense it. Something was needed to break the tension, and the resident prankster, Csonka, with help from Fernandez, had an idea. "To this day," Csonka says, "I can't believe we pulled it off."

Csonka was, and is, a great outdoorsman. That week, before the team headed to Los Angeles for the Super Bowl, Csonka and Fernandez caught a three-foot alligator. Csonka had a crazy idea: put the gator in Shula's shower at the practice facility. Csonka was extraordinary and his prank IQ was just further evidence of this. Not many people would catch a three-foot alligator to begin with. Even fewer would want to bring it home. And only a handful of men on the planet would want to shove the alligator into the shower of their boss as he washed.

After one of the last practices in Florida, Fernandez went to the trunk of his car, where the alligator had been stashed, and while Shula was occupied elsewhere, he took the poor creature to Shula's private shower. The team had been made well aware of the prank earlier and gathered nearby, waiting for a reaction. The water starts to run . . . a few seconds went by . . . a minute . . . one more . . . suddenly a piercing shriek emerged from the shower. Shula ran out of the shower, put a towel on, sprinted through another office, and found Assistant Coach Clark. Shula said something to Clark the two men never thought either would ever hear. "Monte, there's an alligator in my shower! Go grab it!"

Clark didn't move. "That's not in my job description," he told Shula.

Eventually the team's equipment manager corralled the animal from the shower. The next afternoon, Shula wanted answers. "Okay, who the hell did it?" he said to a group of players that included Csonka. A few seconds went by, and Csonka sheepishly raised his hand.

"You did that?" Shula asked.

"I did," Csonka admitted. "But before you get too mad, you need to know something."

"What?" Shula asked.

"We took a vote and you won by a single vote," Csonka said.

"What vote?" a confused Shula asked.

"We voted on whether or not to tape the alligator's mouth shut," Csonka said, barely able to contain his laughter, "and you won."

Shula was initially furious, but he couldn't stay angry. He laughed hard, and when he did, so did all the players. It was a remarkable moment.

(Pranks, it seems, were a part of the Dolphins' DNA. Every Thanksgiving, the team's equipment manager would place a type-written, official-looking letter in the locker of every rookie. It informed the rookies that a free turkey would be handed out at a local grocery store. Most rookies, often borderline impoverished, would rush to the store only to find out there was no free turkey. They had been duped.)

To the players, this week felt different. There was a sense of celebration in the practice before last year's Super Bowl. This time there was a sense of confidence and mission. They practiced almost angrily but also dutifully. Little and Morris, close friends, exchanged glares after a half-speed practice drill in which Morris ran it at full speed and collided with Little's backside. Shula jokingly instigated an altercation. "Wouldn't be much of a fight," Little said. Morris, never one to back down despite being massively outweighed by Little, replied: "Bring your lunch. It might last all day." Yes, the Dolphins were ready.

CHAPTER FIFTEEN

GONZO DOLPHINS

The week leading to the Super Bowl has long been a circus. "Hookers and drunken sportswriters jammed together in a seething mob" is how Hunter S. Thompson once described it. Sounds about right. Not much has changed except now the circus is seven rings and Twitter. Back then, there was less insanity but still moments of stupidity. The photo shoots, the press conferences, the fans calling the players' hotel rooms. Fans looking for tickets. Fans seeking autographs. Fans offering sex for tickets and autographs. It could be a mess. It could reach ridiculous levels of ridiculousness. Not long after the Dolphins arrived at their Super Bowl hotel, Morrall entered the gift shop to buy a chocolate candy bar. Just as the purchase was completed, a radio reporter approached Morrall and asked him what was his favorite type of candy bar. Morrall looked down at what was in his hand. "Nestle's," Morrall said.

The Dolphins learned a few lessons from the Super Bowl the year before and made the appropriate adjustments. The most important were mental. Buoniconti and Morris encapsulated this with remarks to writers at the time. The players' approach was different, and one way they changed was not to be flustered by anything, even the questions they were asked. "You sit with a different set of writers every day," Buoniconti told writer Braucher then, "and they ask just about the same question the other guys have asked you before. It can get a little annoying. But this year we sort of slipped right into it. We knew what to expect. I've got my act down pretty good. When they keep saying I'm the key man on defense, I'll tell them if that was true I ought to be making five hundred G's like Namath."

Fernandez explained the Super Bowl week interviews were "like going to the dentist every day to have the same tooth filled."

"I remember being shocked at the sloth and moral degeneracy of the Nixon press corps during the 1972 presidential campaign," wrote Thompson, "but they were like a pack of wolverines on speed compared to the relatively elite sportswriters who showed up in Houston to cover the Super Bowl."

Thompson, as you might guess, had a few things to say about the state of the NFL in writing his Super Bowl fear-and-loathing story. One of the most poignant—and some would say offensive—were his views on Lombardi. Thompson wrote: "The success of his Green Bay approach in the '60s restructured the game entirely. Lombardi never really thought about *winning*; his trip was *not losing* . . . Which worked, and because it worked the rest of the NFL bought Lombardi's whole style: Avoid Mistakes, Don't Fuck Up, Hang Tough and Take No Chances . . . Because sooner or later the enemy will make a mistake and then you start grinding him down, and if you play the defensive percentage you'll get inside his 30-yard line at least three times in each half, and once you're inside the 30 you want to be sure to get at least three points . . .

"Wonderful. Who can argue with a battle-plan like that? And it is worth remembering that Richard Nixon spent many Sundays, during all those long and lonely autumns between 1962 and '68, shuffling around on the field with Vince Lombardi at Green Bay Packers games.

"Nixon still speaks of Lombardi as if he might suddenly appear, at any moment, from underneath one of the larger rocks on the White House lawn . . . And Don Shula, despite his fairly obvious distaste for Nixon, has adopted the Lombardi style of football so effectively that the Dolphins are now one of the dullest teams to watch in the history of pro football."

(Ouch.)

Buoniconti had fun with the media, but he also bristled at some of the lines of questioning. At several of his press conferences, he became irritated at a media narrative that had been playing out through the week. In the Super Bowl against Dallas, players and coaches from the Cowboys stated how the way they beat the dogged Buoniconti was by running trick plays that had him move in one direction and then the play would shift in another. Buoniconti was asked so much about his role in that Super Bowl—or lack thereof—his annoyance was palpable, and eventually anyone who asked was greeted by, "Next question."

Buoniconti was asked about how one of the magazines had called him the "nonhero" of that past Super Bowl. More annoyance. "That's great," he said. "I'm the only nonhero on a 40-man squad."

He wasn't done venting. Not yet. "Every analysis you get is that the Dolphins lost because Dallas cut me off," he told reporters. "You've got to be an idiot to talk in terms of one individual. Maybe it's a left-handed compliment but it's ridiculous. How can you take one guy on the defense and say this is why we lost the game." Not. Done. Yet. "The theory is really ridiculous because the big plays they busted on us were not cutbacks. Duane Thomas's big run [23 yards] in the third quarter was not a cutback. He took the pitch and just ran. That was the big gainer that broke our backs."

There wasn't a player friendlier with the media than Buoniconti, but there also wasn't a player who would defend the Dolphins or himself with more ferocity either. And this was vintage Buoniconti. He didn't want to forget the humiliating loss overall since it served as motivation, but he also didn't want to remember the specifics of the game. Buoniconti was one of the few Miami players and coaches who had never reviewed the tape from the game.

Morris was succinct and quotable as usual: "Last year we were glad to get in the game and Dallas came to *win* it. Well, we've already been in the game. This year *we* came to win it."

"Maybe in this game you have to pay your dues," Morris added. "We've paid our dues."

And that was it. To the Dolphins, it was their time. No one had forgotten the mission outlined by Shula, and inside every Miami player, a significant change had occurred. That change would manifest in other ways. Dolphins executives asked hotel staff to keep anyone who wasn't part of the Miami team off the floors where the players roomed. There would be no more freaks and groupies roaming the halls. Players were more relaxed. Griese and several teammates went to see the movie *Deliverance*. There'd also be no Saturday-night team dinner with the families, which Shula did the year prior and regretted it. The Dolphins hadn't done anything like that all season and Shula felt it disrupted the rhythm of the team. He wasn't going to make that mistake again. The wives and girlfriends could wait until Monday. In the meantime, there was a Super Bowl to win.

* * *

Much of the press attention focused on Griese, who was making his first start since his leg was annihilated earlier in the season. Writers who were around Griese for the Dallas Super Bowl saw a different player in this one. Griese was more relaxed. His conversations with writers were more congenial, his shoulders less hunched, and he smiled more, though still not much. Griese's way was to stay calm and analytical. More relaxed, yes. Changed? Hell, no. And that's what made Griese so formidable. In a few words, what made him so great. This was a guy who cursed only once or twice a season because he didn't want emotion to overrule analysis; he studied football the way scientists studied the human genome and became healthily obsessed with his job almost year-round. Anyone who knew Griese understood that he was going to change for the better this time.

And he sounded changed in interviews: "I don't have any hang-ups about being a loser in the last Super Bowl. I only recall a loss as long as it takes to learn why we lost it. The Super Bowl is a game, that's all it is. Except if you win this one, you win the world championship. I get psyched up for all the games. I get very much up for the Super Bowl and I get very much up when we play Buffalo. And the layoff I had, that's an asset. I'm stronger because I was out eight weeks. It's a very long season. Last year in the Super Bowl I was very tired. This year my arm is stronger because it was rested . . ." All of this was true. Well, most of it was. No one believed that Griese equated the Super Bowl with a regular-season game against Buffalo. Deep down, Griese didn't believe that either. Remember his reaction after the loss to Dallas in the Super Bowl. Griese was devastated. Any loss to the Bills didn't cause emotional pain. The Super Bowl loss did.

"They say you learn something from every game," Griese said. "I think what you learn in the Super Bowl is how to pace yourself through the two weeks. You're a little bit smarter the second time you go through it. Last year we were told what it was going to be like, but until you experience it, it's a little bit different."

Writers constantly asked Griese what it was like to be on the sidelines injured while the Dolphins won. "How would you feel if you broke both of your hands in an automobile accident and you were in the hospital and you couldn't type," he said, "and while you were in the hospital your newspaper was named the best newspaper in the world? Would you feel like you were a part of it?"

Buoniconti offered some of the best analysis of how Griese's brain works. "In a game he's like a real general in a real war," said the linebacker. "He's distant. He doesn't talk to anybody on the sidelines. I don't think anybody would dream of talking to him or patting him on the back or anything. Maybe he talks to Shula. We have confidence in him because he has so much confidence in himself and *our* confidence gives him even more. It's an ongoing thing, like the old joke—he knows that we know that he knows."

Griese's counterpart on the Redskins, Billy Kilmer, could not have been more opposite. While Griese digested game plans and analyzed every corner of the game, Kilmer was more, well, relaxed. Then again, Kilmer was always relaxed. Kilmer was the most congenial and accessible star player in the NFL who threw a wobbly ball and wasn't a stranger to alcohol-induced wobbly behavior. His teammates were rumored to call Kilmer "Ole Whiskey." The most infamous Kilmer story came when, following a night of alleged drinking, he got into an argument with a waitress and attempted to leave her a hundred-dollar bill for what was essentially a tab of just four dollars. For some reason, an argument ensued, and for an equally strange reason, the police were called, and Kilmer spent a night in jail. Three years after the Super Bowl, he'd be arrested for drunk driving two days before a game against Dallas.

To say Miami coaches and players were unimpressed with Kilmer would be an understatement. It wasn't necessarily disrespectful, just one of the hard truths of football. Coaches looked for weak points and Kilmer was that weak point. If Kilmer got hot, he was dangerous, but there were stretches of games where his passes fluttered either harmlessly or into the hands of opposing players. Kilmer had skill, but the only thing accurate or consistent about him was his beer drinking.

"If I don't set up right, I throw off balance," Kilmer once admitted, "and when I throw off balance, I throw those flip-floppy, flappy-wappy passes."

It got to the point where Miami players no longer hid their giddiness about facing him. Miami defensive back Lloyd Mumphord openly bragged about his eagerness to go against Kilmer. "I like the way he throws the ball up," Mumphord explained to the media Super Bowl week. "When he was with New Orleans, I picked one off for a touchdown and almost had a couple more. I almost had one off him this preseason . . . He doesn't have that much zip. But he tries to throw it anyway even if the receivers are covered." That lack of consistency and accuracy played into the hands of Miami, who gobbled up quarterback mistakes.

The true core of the Redskins offense was running back Larry Brown. In some ways, Brown was the Redskins' version of Morris except faster. Brown was named the league's Most Valuable Player in 1972, one of the more prestigious honors a player could earn. He became the first Washington player to gain 1,000 yards in a single season, made the Pro Bowl four times, and was a nasty cutback runner. No back in football at the time could start in one direction then suddenly shift to another as quickly as Brown. "He was one of those guys other running backs would watch and go, 'Wow, that guy's good,'" Csonka remembers.

Csonka had an equally interesting quote about Brown during that

Super Bowl week. "I admire Larry Brown," Csonka said. "He takes a fantastic beating. I take my beating in little doses because I don't go too far."

Brown also brought back some ghosts of Super Bowl past. The Cowboys used their backs to run straight up the middle, and the offensive line was able to seal off Buoniconti. When the Dolphins adjusted to that at halftime, Landry went to a more outside pitch and screen game. Landry's game plan had caught the Miami coaching staff off guard, and runner Duane Thomas used cutbacks to kill the Dolphins. It would be one of the few chess games Shula ever lost. "The Dolphins are a well-coached young football team," Cowboys player coach Dan Reeves told *Sports Illustrated* at the time. "That makes it fairly easy to prepare for them. Because they are disciplined and well coached, you know exactly what they are going to do. They are not going to come up and play a defense you haven't seen. They *could* come up with a new defense, I suppose, but they are basically a young team and they can't play a lot of changeups. With an inexperienced club, the only way to play good football is to do the same thing over and over again. You can't give them more offense or defense than they can handle."

This time Shula was determined to be the one dictating the pace and scheme. He wasn't going to be caught with his coaching pants down this Super Bowl.

Landry knew the Redskins well and described Washington's offense this way: They do not devour anybody; they nibble. Meaning the Redskins attacked a defense in small chunks and relied on the defense to make mistakes in helping it advance. But what if that defense, like Miami's, made few mental errors?

In the week leading up to the game, Kilmer spent much of his time speaking to almost anyone who came to see him. That's how friendly he was. When reporters arrived at his ground-floor hotel room, they found Kilmer relaxing in bed drinking Coors beer and talking on the phone. When one writer, Steve Perkins, entered the room, Kilmer told him, "The beer's in the bathtub." As Kilmer did interviews, his room phone rang relentlessly. Many Dolphins players had the hotel operator stop calls to their rooms since often it was fans seeking tickets or autographs. They had learned from their experience the year before. Kilmer didn't care. Many of the Redskins players failed to block those distractions, which would become an actual factor in the game.

The Miami players were loose (and even more so when Robbie paid the airfare for the wives of the coaches and players to travel to Los Angeles on Friday), but the one person on the team who wasn't was Shula. There was no doubt he was feeling the pressure of the nasty potential that he could lose another Super Bowl. He was literally losing sleep during the week, and things weren't made any easier when his bitter nemesis, Colts owner Rosenbloom, again said Shula would never win a Super Bowl. It was another cruel punch to the gut, but what Rosenbloom added infuriated Shula even more. Rosenbloom spoke to the *Baltimore Evening Sun* and the column was picked up nationally, including by the *Miami Herald*. Soon, Shula had it in his hands, and after reading it, he wanted to use those hands to strangle Rosenbloom.

Rosenbloom stated that having two notorious rule breakers in the Super Bowl embarrassed the sport and added a nasty blemish to the game. Notice Rosenbloom lump Allen and Shula together, calling Shula a cheat—something Shula had never been called before. It wasn't true, and Rosenbloom offered no specifics to his charges, but in those days, people actually believed what was in newspapers, particularly credible ones like the *Herald* and others. It was unbelievably damaging to Shula.

Unfortunately his son, David, read the story before Shula had a chance to speak with him first. David asked if the accusation was true. Shula told him it wasn't and that he'd never broken the rules. Shula was both heartbroken and infuriated. "When is this all going to stop?" Dorothy asked.

It was the week of the Super Bowl and Shula had to deal with this, which is exactly what Rosenbloom wanted. He wanted Shula distracted, and now Shula was. He phoned Rozelle and complained, explaining what Rosenbloom said wasn't accurate and arguing that it was highly damaging and Rosenbloom should be punished. Rozelle wasn't about to take any action that would draw attention away from the game. He sympathized with Shula but did nothing.

The Rosenbloom fiasco only served to heighten the tension in Shula, but he masked it well. Or rather, he mostly did. One thing that helped him was the uber-tenseness of Allen. For much of the week, Allen complained about all the distractions and displayed a high level of irritation with having to do anything that required him to leave the practice field or meeting room. When both teams arrived in California, four hundred fans greeted the Dolphins at Long Beach Municipal Airport, waving white handkerchiefs and dancing to the music of a small band. Shula flashed a huge smile to the crowd and promised the Dolphins would do everything they could to win. Four hours later, the Redskins arrived, and Allen told the media it wasn't a big deal returning to the city where he once coached and added that "there's no big thing about being in a Super Bowl unless you win."

Allen went to great lengths to isolate his players. The team stayed at a Santa Ana motel that had a unique feature: The rooms and the lobby were separated by a sprawling highway. Washington quarterback Sonny Jurgensen, who was hobbled because of an Achilles injury, crossed the highway on crutches. "I was trying to get from the lobby to my room . . . ," he said, "and a guy in a Volkswagen nearly ran over me."

Allen didn't care about near hit-and-runs. The highway served as a moat to keep the dirtbag sportswriters and other opportunists away from his players as much as possible. He also employed a small force of four security personnel who were posted at various points around the motel. His main sergeant at arms was a former city cop from Long Beach, California, named Ed Boynton. Allen earned the distinction of being the first NFL head coach to hire a full-time security man. His nickname: Double-O.

"To me, George Allen is a little weird," said Kiick. "But then that's his thing."

(Some Redskins players kept their sense of humor despite the extreme sphincter tightening of Allen. Said linebacker Jack Pardee: "I'll wake up Sunday morning about 6 o'clock, drinking coffee and thinking about Bob Griese and Larry Csonka. I don't believe you have to hate your opponent, only get mad at them temporarily." Pardee would carry this attitude later when he became the only person in the history of professional football to coach a college, NFL, United States Football League, World Football League, and Canadian Football League team.)

Both Shula and Allen were addicted to routine and control, and the Super Bowl was a chaotic maelstrom of media interviews, autograph seekers, ringing hotel room phones, wives, girlfriends, mistresses, and broken curfews. The week caused both men gastro-intestinal distress, but only Allen couldn't truly hide his disgust. In one of his final press conferences, Allen vented. "Yesterday we had thirty-one players interviewed for an hour and a half and we had our worst practice," he said. "You'll pardon me for feeling that I should be with my team this minute rather than here."

Allen actually stopped complaining for several minutes to state perhaps one of the more cogent observations about the Dolphins ever made. "The thing that bothers me most about Miami is they execute so well that they're not impressive. They are like a baseball team with six hitters, hitting singles and doubles."

There was also one moment when Allen offered something that resembled a sense of humor. "My first coaching job was at Whittier College. I coached football and baseball. I taught classes in volleyball, badminton, and wrestling. I taught anatomy at 8 A.M. five days a week. I taught a class in kinesiology, which is a study of the action of muscles. Outside of that I didn't have much to do. That's how I got my ulcer."

The humorous introspection didn't last long. "The disadvantage in this game is there are so many phone calls and so many people come to the [team] hotel," Allen said. "Six months from now they [his players] may say, 'I should have paid more attention to the game instead of going down to somebody's restaurant.' One of the reasons the Super Bowl hasn't been an artistic success is there are so many distractions. You can talk about it from morning to night and it doesn't make any difference."

Allen's demeanor wasn't a surprise to some of the writers who followed him closely. He'd utter the phrase "every time you lose, you die a little" around the team complex. One of his favorites was: "When the sun comes up, you'd better be running." On Allen's gravestone was: "The future is now."

On and on it went all Super Bowl week. Allen the serious, Allen the uptight, Allen the bloodletting. "To win this game," he said, "I'd let you stick a knife in me and draw all my blood." In one of his final press conferences for the week, Allen chirped, "This is the first time in twenty-three years as a head coach I have missed a meeting with my team. I hope you fellows don't ask me the same questions today that you've been asking me all week." Some writers rolled their eyes in disgust.

Allen even decided to take a shot at the wives of the players. "If we could arrange for the wives to be in Chicago," he said, not joking, "I'd be happy." The game, of course, was in Los Angeles. Writers weren't the only ones irritated with Allen. *Sports Illustrated* asked one player how Allen's tantrums and dourness were impacting the team, and the player, wanting to remain anonymous, responded: "We should have left him in Washington."

Once, during the week, when Allen started taking questions from the media, a reporter zinged Allen right in the face. "George, do you realize you are talking like a loser?" Allen was slightly stunned, then got more than slightly irritated. "I'm not a loser," Allen responded. "I've never been a loser. I was merely outlining the problem . . ." Later, when Allen was leaving the press conference, he spotted the reporter. "There's a fellow who stung me with [the] negative question," Allen said to him. "Let me tell you, your question will make us have a better practice today."

Meanwhile, one writer called Miami "the happy Dolphins." The team had a loose eleven P.M. curfew (while the Redskins had a hardened one—blowing it led to a $1,000 fine), except on Monday. There was nothing that day, no practice or meetings, so players had a temporary stay. Reporter Hyde would later write how a group of players rented a car and toured almost all of Southern California. By the time they'd hit the bars and the other sites, it was nearly six in the morning. Mandich decided he was too wired to sleep, so he decided to go to breakfast where Shula—of course—was already up and eating. Mandich walked over to Shula's table and sat in front of him. "Hi, Coach," Mandich said. Shula wasn't amused.

Shula's demeanor overall was the opposite of his coaching counterpart, and to some of the writers covering the game, it appeared as if Shula was toying with Allen through the press. While Allen greeted the press with barbed tongue, Shula welcomed them with a smile and jokes. "Good morning, breakfast clubbers," he'd say.

Shula even had a little fun with Allen and the writers. "Allen's made the statement that he's never lost in the rain," Shula said, "so if it rains on Sunday, we're going to forfeit." Laughs among the press. He was just getting started. Shula joked that he was going to protect his players from any possible threat, including the flu and diarrhea. Then he turned to Baltimore writer Cameron Snyder: "Cameron, you're familiar with diarrhea." More chuckles.

When another writer asked if Shula was filming his practices to catch errors and correct them, Shula joked, "No, George is doing that." Even more laughs. Shula was working the crowd wonderfully and exhibiting a calm confidence that Allen did not. "I think we came in more glassy-eyed last year. I like to think we came away from that disaster with something. What is the attitude of the coach? The coach is 0-2 in the Super Bowl and the coach's attitude is damn good."

"I've gone from being described as a yeller and screamer to the quiet businesslike type," Shula said. "I don't know how or when the transition took place. I'm still a little bit of both."

Shula's calm appearance actually started earlier in the week during an impromptu team meeting. He noticed two players, Kuechenberg and Langer, were missing. They weren't in trouble because the meeting was called so suddenly. When the two men entered the room, Shula decided to have some fun. He acted outraged that the players were tardy and instructed them to sit in two empty chairs facing a corner, their backs toward the center of the room and team. Shula's acting was outstanding and actually fooled the players, but when many of the other players began laughing, the ruse was up. Shula laughed heartily as well.

Yet beneath the jokes and relaxed exterior was an extremely nervous and even paranoid Shula. The concerns over him possibly losing another Super Bowl, Rosenbloom's cheap shots, and the potential spying by Allen were corroding his insides. Shula was so worried that Allen might be stealing practice secrets that he switched the Dolphins' practice field to a more secure one, located at a local high school that had a taller and more closed-in fence. And just in case: Shula stationed two team officials with binoculars to scan the area for wayward eyes.

Shula was tight but his players were not. They were, in fact, as focused and relaxed as they'd been all season. The big moment seemed to be overwhelming the Washington players but not the Dolphins. Griese had been keeping a daily diary of the entire week with one of the team beat writers to be published in the local paper after the game. Griese's entry on Wednesday read: "I finally started looking at Washington films last night. Today I'm convinced that we can beat them. After watching their defense on films, I don't see how we can lose unless we do something to throw it away. I could almost predict a win. But I wouldn't do that. Besides, it has already been done once." That was a delicious shot at Namath.

The Dolphins simply weren't this confident the year before against the Cowboys. Not even close. That week, before playing Dallas, Shula was asked if his Dolphins were confident. "They are individuals," he told reporters. "The ones who are always relaxed before a game are relaxed and the ones who are always tense and serious are tense and serious. I think it is a mistake to ask a club to be either one way or the other. What you want the players to do is be themselves and I think our players have been themselves this week."

This time there was no doubt the Dolphins were relaxed, and though they didn't need any help doing this, what ran in the *Los Angeles Times* might have aided them. They awoke one morning to find a full-page advertisement placed by the city of Miami's publicity department. The cost: $823. Despite the racially insensitive language, it was meant as a show of support for Miami players.

"Dolphins scalp the 'Skins! All Miami is rooting for you. GO GET 'EM!" The center of the ad featured a photo of Griese throwing a pass. The team had come a long way in its relationship with the city. They'd officially gone from ignored to laughingstocks to interesting to passionately followed.

Relaxed, indeed. The last part of Griese's diary entry read: "It looks to me like anything we run can be successful against them. Our strength against their strength should work."

No one can prove this, but it seems the Redskins were seeing the daunting task ahead of them. Some of that could be felt in Allen's uptight attitude the entire week, but there were also snippets the Redskins knew in advance they were in for a long day. "I've been checking my notes on Paul Warfield," Redskins defensive back Mike Bass told reporters that week. "I run a two or three page tabulation on all the receivers I've faced—what leg he starts from, what hand is down in his stance, whether he raises up when he's going to run a short pattern. If anybody is going to be a challenge it will be Warfield."

The Super Bowl was shaping up this way: The Redskins were ecstatic to be there. The Dolphins wanted to destroy the Redskins at any cost. There was a difference. Miami saw the contest as a way toward football salvation. There was a desperate and clawing desire to win. "We need this one," said Swift. "We've got to have it. We've gone 16-0 and if we lose this one people are going to remember us as the biggest bunch of hot air in the world."

Said Kiick: "Sixteen and 0 is fantastic. Sixteen and one isn't. It's a shame it all boils down to one game. It's not the money so much. The money will be gone in a few years, but the ring will always be there."

Wrote the *Miami News*: "The [game] is going to affect Miami's position on the planet either way. If they lose, they will be bums who trundled along undefeated through a creampuff schedule. If they win, they may see headlines similar to the one in New York after Super Bowl VI [the Cowboys win]—'D, As In Dynasty.'"

"The season," Shula said, "is an instant failure if we don't win this."

It was, without question, a total role reversal from the year before for Miami. They were going to be the aggressors. "The feeling going into the game was, 'We're not losing. No way in hell we're losing.' It was a universal feeling that went across every man on our team," says Csonka today. "I can honestly say that wasn't the case against Dallas. But against the Redskins, we weren't awestruck. We were basically Super Bowl veterans. We were angry, vengeful. We wanted our pound of flesh and the Redskins just happened to be in the way."

CHAPTER SIXTEEN

SHOE SHINERS

Morning of.

Larry King drove to the game with notorious oddsmaker Jimmy "the Greek" Snyder. Years later, Greek would self-destruct following a reprehensible and legendary racial outburst. But at the time, Greek was the most recognized and respected oddsmaker in sports. What he said was considered gospel by many, so King, naturally, as Hyde first wrote, picked his brain and asked why Greek was picking Washington to win despite the Dolphins being the ones who were undefeated.

"They're from the AFL," Greek told King.

"Really?" King said. "But the Dolphins *haven't lost.*"

Greek repeated himself. "They're from the *AFL.*"

The conference was still disrespected by many in the media, and the Dolphins were collateral damage despite being on the verge of doing something no team had ever done before. The AFL was viewed as a bunch of jabronis while the NFL was portrayed as almost stately and aristocratic. Greek was simply parroting this belief.

So were many others. Few NFL experts actually picked Miami. Looking back, it may be the most compelling part of that week. The greatest media football minds of the time couldn't see the Redskins losing. Some thought it would be a rout. "I find myself going for the Redskins," wrote *New York Times* writer Arthur Daley. "Maybe the evangelistic Allen has converted this unbeliever into acceptance of his doctrine that the future is now."

"The prediction here is that the fearsome Redskins defense will force Shula to wait for his reward: Washington 23, Miami 13," wrote journalist Pete Axthelm.

"So, who is over the hill anyway?" asked *Sports Illustrated*'s Tex Maule (yes, that's his real name). "Washington should win Super Bowl VII by at least 10 points and perhaps by as many as 21."

"The Redskins are sure to hand them their shoes and ask that they bring them back by morning shined and leave them outside the door," wrote Jim Murray of the *Los Angeles Times*.

A highly respected writer was saying an undefeated team was going to shine Washington's shoes.

There was no bigger punch to Miami's sternum than another column that ran in the *Los Angeles Times* written by Murray, perhaps the greatest sports columnist who ever lived. His mocking of the Dolphins was read by many on the team, passed around, the anger building with every set of Dolphins eyes that saw it. All of this happening just hours before the game.

One pair of those eyes was Norm Evans. He'd been handed the column by line coach Clark. There was usually little that offended Clark, as he was mentally tough and practically impenetrable. In addition to being the force that pulled together a ragtag group of offensive linemen that was now in the Super Bowl, he was also once an offensive lineman himself, playing for Cleveland in the 1960s, a time when offensive linemen were not allowed to extend their arms to pass or run block. Rules forced the hands and elbows to remain at their sides. Linemen had to be patient and skilled technicians. He didn't get rattled as a player or as coach—until the Murray column.

Clark handed it to Evans. "Go ahead, read the whole thing," he said. "See what the sportswriters think of a team that's 16-0. See how much respect you've earned by getting this far."

Clark was using an old ploy—the media disrespecting a team—to rile up his players, only this time the move was less disingenuous. Clark was angry and Evans would soon be as well. "Ladies and gentlemen," the column began, "we bring you today direct from a record-breaking engagement in the Orange Bowl in Miami, a team that needs an introduction: 40 of the world's least-famous performers, the intruders in the Super Bowl, that funny little team from that funny little conference, the ones with the mahi-mahis on their helmets, the— Psst. What'd ya say yer names was again, kids?"

The heart of the column would get worse for Miami: "What are these fishes doing in the Super Bowl? What nerve! I mean, these aren't the Kansas City Chiefs or the Oakland Raiders. Where's Joe Namath, for cryin' out loud? Who ARE these guys? Who asked THEM? . . . It's a good thing they got their names on their uniforms. But that's not much help. What's a Csonka, Daddy? The sound a hammer makes hitting a railroad tie? What kind of a Kiick is that? A place Kiick? A drop Kiick? An onside Kiick? An offside Kiick? . . . What do you do with a 'Mercury Morris'? Put it in a thermometer? Is 'Griese' a proper name or a hair tonic?"

"What is this, the Super Bowl?" concluded Murray. "Or amateur night?" Murray wasn't being sarcastic. He was serious.

The morning was interesting in other ways. Scott had such a badly injured shoulder that Greek had moved Washington from a 2-point to 3-point favorite based on a prevailing notion that Scott wouldn't be healthy enough to play. Since Scott was one of the toughest players in football, such an idea shouldn't have been considered. The only way he'd miss the game was if his heart stopped pumping blood.

What never stopped was Scott's burning wit, even on the day of the biggest game of his life. As the team was boarding the bus headed for the stadium, Scott was handing out tickets to the game to some friends when, as the Hyde book details, Shula spotted him. "You're going to be late for the biggest game of your career," the coach said.

Scott became instantly irritated, since he'd never been late for anything related to the team, let alone the Super Bowl. Shula boarded the bus and Scott followed. Scott knew Shula was nervous and decided, in responding to Shula's quip, he'd go for Shula's jugular.

"What's the matter," he told Shula, "you thinking about going down as the losingest coach in Super Bowl history?"

Shula was taken aback and angered by the comment, but he ignored it since the game was just hours away. He couldn't afford to dwell on Scott's words. It wasn't the first time the men would collide or the last, and it wasn't even their nastiest of moments. Those would come later.

The morning of . . . Dolphins players awoke confident and unsatisfied. One year earlier, when they awoke Super Bowl morning, it was a different feeling. They were exhaling before the game began. Now they were hungry, and not only because it was time for breakfast.

It was time. It was here. The moment didn't call for perspective. Not yet. The players had made that mistake before, but Joe Thomas allowed himself a moment of appreciation. He'd built teams before. He would do it again all the way up until the day he died of a heart attack. But the Dolphins were partly his masterpiece as they were partly pro personnel man Bobby Beathard's, and now they were here largely because of him. Even if, before the Dolphins reached the Super Bowl against Washington, Robbie had fired him.

It was called a resignation but it wasn't. He was solitary, a braggart, and his differences with Robbie and Shula led to his eventual demise in Miami. As the Dolphins players rubbed the sleep out of their eyes and Shula and his staff searched their brains for any last-minute things they may have forgotten, Thomas was still a part of this team, despite his not being present with the Dolphins. It was Shula who willed Miami to two straight Super Bowls. It was Shula who was the reason they were here. But it was Thomas who had supplied all the pieces. He did it in Minnesota. He had done it again with the Dolphins. The best way to describe how Thomas constructed a team was by using a vegetable: the artichoke. "You build from the inside," he once told *Sports Illustrated*. "At the core is the heart of the team: the tender young rookies, the ones you get in the draft. You build *under* the veterans, and then you keep peeling them off, like the leaves of an artichoke, until you're down to the heart, to the guys who are really going to help you once they're ready." It was a cold but highly efficient way to view building a team.

And that's what Thomas did well. As well as anyone ever did, and like many of the players he accumulated, he'd become lesser known despite such remarkable achievements. This was perhaps the singular thread that tied the Dolphins together from the time Shula took over until this Super Bowl. They were a team with a handful of stars surrounding a core of men who played like them but wouldn't be viewed as such by history. Say the name Joe Thomas now to even the most knowledgeable football fan and you'll be met with a quizzical look.

The Dolphins had Thomas's fingerprints across the franchise. He drafted Kiick in the fifth round when most personnel men in the NFL thought he'd be a backup at best. He traded a guy named Mack Lamb for Little. How lopsided was that trade? Lamb ended up as a footnote, being the first Miami native to play for the Dolphins. Little ended up in the Hall of Fame. On December 13, 1971, *Sports Illustrated* reported this fact in a lengthy profile of a long forgotten man: "Miami needed a middle linebacker. Thomas wanted All-AFL Nick Buoniconti of the Patriots. Boston needed a quarterback. Thomas sent films of third-string rookie Quarterback Kim Hammond in action. The films showed Hammond at his best. Boston asked Thomas to throw in Wide Receiver Howard Twilley. 'No, but I'll tell you what,' said Thomas. 'You can have Hammond and [linebacker] John Bramlett.' After a week of phone calls, the deal was made. Buoniconti . . . is Miami's defensive captain; Twilley is a regular. Bramlett is a substitute at Atlanta. Hammond is in law school."

Thomas logged every mile scouting talent, he found the unknown player, he made the impossible trade. He traded for Warfield. He traded for Anderson. He drafted scrambling quarterbacks like Tarkenton before there were really scrambling quarterbacks.

Thomas and Shula came to dislike each other. There were the usual reasons of ego and power. Thomas was gone, but he watched and knew. This was still his team too.

———

The locker room at Los Angeles Memorial Coliseum wasn't so different from the locker room the Dolphins had gathered in a year before. One thing that was remarkably different: the mood. Dolphins players can admit the truth all these years later. They were simply satisfied to reach the Super Bowl against the Cowboys. They were just happy to be there. They were possibly intimidated by the entire experience. But on this morning everything was different. It didn't matter the opponent. The Dolphins were going to annihilate them because it had been their mission for over a year. Their football lives, their personal lives, in some ways everything they stood for as men, was geared toward this moment. It's likely, with the exception of two teams—the Vikings and Bills, both franchises having lost multiple Super Bowls—no Super Bowl team felt a more primal urge to win the game than the Dolphins. Shula had embedded into their genome after the Dallas loss that nothing else mattered and they had acted accordingly. They were back, in another Super Bowl locker room, changed men, feeling invincible.

Some of the players were stretching on the floor in the locker room when Shula entered. Others sat quietly, their faces blank. Everyone was tense. Evans clenched and unclenched his fists. There was very little conversation. Shula walked in confident and strong. He got the attention of the players with a quick but clear pronouncement: "All right. Let's go."

Players on the ground quickly jumped to their feet. The entire team gathered in the middle of the room. Shula stood before the players, and after a few curt warnings about Washington and reinforcing thoughts on the Dolphins' own strategies, Shula centered his pregame speech on what he had told them so many months before. "You know what it was like to lose this game a year ago. A loss this year would waste everything we accomplished in winning 16 games. That streak means nothing if we don't win today. We all worked too hard to let that happen. Get out there and play the way I know you're capable of playing. Let's go."

The first play was Counter 32 Straight and it went to Kiick, who ran for an average 2 yards. The following play was for 2 yards to Csonka. A third-down pass by Griese went for a loss. After a penalty and

Miami punt, the Dolphins' first series ended. Unspectacularly. "I know this sounds strange," says Shula, "but I felt like the team was very relaxed despite that slower start."

Shula was correct. In a way, the team that was loose all week started the game that way. The team that was tight all week started the game that way too. The first half by the Dolphins has remained one of the most flawless the Super Bowl has ever seen. It was mainly a result of the Dolphins having superior skill, superior coaching, and, perhaps most of all, superior will, but the fact the players were loose allowed them to create what was the football version of a canvas with few blotches.

Sportswriter Maule had predicted a Washington victory, but nonetheless the main paragraph of his game story applauded Miami. "The Dolphins won the game with a nearly impeccable first half; with an extraordinarily accurate passer in Quarterback Bob Griese; with a rhino of a runner, Larry Csonka; and, above all, with a defense that may have been No Names, but was plenty of adjectives. Try tough, tight, dashing and daring for starters. The special stars were Tackle Manny Fernandez, who keyed the line; Middle Linebacker Nick Buoniconti, who intercepted one pass; and Free Safety Jake Scott, who intercepted two passes and was named the most valuable player in the game. As an extra fillip, the Dolphins produced the most valuable Redskin when a Garo Yepremian field-goal attempt turned into the most hilarious play yet seen in a Super Bowl and gave Washington its touchdown."

Poor Garo. Poor, poor Garo. He had no idea how his name would become synonymous with all-time follies and tomfoolery. Before Yepremian would make his own type of sports history, the Dolphins began their systematic, almost robotically merciless deconstruction of the Redskins. What Dallas had done to Miami a year earlier the Dolphins did to Washington. It was so dominant that if not for the Yepremian play, the Dolphins would have shut out the Redskins.

Their win really began with stopping Brown's cutbacks. Fernandez and Buoniconti were the stars, playing that type of floating defensive scheme that allowed them to play off the line of scrimmage and wait for Brown to come to them. The game then flowed in the direction Shula wanted and expected. It ended up in the unsteady hands of Kilmer. Not even Shula imagined the symmetry of the Miami coaching staff's game plan being so perfectly linear. There was little chance Kilmer was going to rescue Washington, and he finished 14 of 28 with 3 interceptions. The longest pass Kilmer completed was for 15 yards. Everywhere Kilmer looked, it seemed, there was a Dolphins defender. Scott seemed to know where Kilmer was going with almost all his passes, and considering the way Scott digested and dissected a quarterback's every move, he likely did.

The fact Scott even played the game, let along earned MVP honors, was jarring news in itself. Scott played with a broken hand and wrist and that badly injured shoulder. Many times in sports, the word "heroic" is drastically overused, and it's debatable whether the word should be used in sports at all since soldiers, firefighters, and police officers, among others, are the true definition of the word. Fernandez likely deserved to be MVP (or at least co-MVP). He was double-teamed and, in some cases, *triple*-teamed. His performance was possibly the best performance by a defensive player in Super Bowl history. But Scott's playing in so much pain with multiple broken bones and a severely damaged shoulder made him among the closest thing to a hero, at least in the Super Bowl.

"Jake was great," said Csonka. "He did that all the time. He always played hard and played at a high level. When you hear people talk about the great safeties in league history, his name is rarely brought up. But the other guy in that game was Manny. At the very least, Manny and Jake should have been co-MVPs."

The fact Fernandez had reached this point was a good story in itself. Coaches around the league knew Fernandez all too well. They couldn't help but notice the large man on game tape blowing up offensive plays, but Fernandez still wasn't a well-known commodity, even among players. As a rookie, when a group of Dolphins players joked about how one of them should knock Namath out of an upcoming game, Fernandez volunteered. A newspaper writer overheard the conversation and reported it. When Namath heard of the Fernandez pseudo-threat, Namath responded: "Who is Manny Fernandez?"

After this Super Bowl, everyone knew the answer. His work ethic brought him to the Super Bowl. He rarely missed practice and in his first five years missed curfew just once, which was an unusually low number. (In fact, curfews were often the source of good humor for the team during the season. At a game in New York against the Jets, coaches were doing bed-checks for wayward curfew busters. When assistant Tom Keane reached Fernandez's room, the doorknob fell off. Keane couldn't get in and Fernandez couldn't get out. Satisfied Fernandez and his roommate, Doug Crusan, had indeed made curfew, Keane left them in the room, doorknob-less.) From the butt of a Namath quip to well-deserved MVP honors, it was indeed quite the trip. Well, almost MVP. The reason Fernandez didn't get the award despite 17 tackles sounds like something from a comedy skit, but it's true.

Back then, just one man voted for the Super Bowl MVP: the redoubtable Dick Schaap. Schaap was a skilled author and a smooth broadcaster, and he had the trust of athletes, pop culture stars, and politicians alike. He wrote autobiographies on Namath and Robert F. Kennedy. Few had more overall talent, but he also committed a remarkable Super Bowl gaffe. Schaap had been drinking heavily the night before and was still feeling the effects when the Super Bowl began. "I think I dozed off before the kickoff, but I woke in time to watch Scott make his [two] interceptions," Schaap wrote in his autobiography. "I wasn't alert enough to watch Manny Fernandez make his tackles."

But he was alert enough to pay off his gambling debts. Hunter S. Thompson, no stranger to discombobulated hazes, had made a bet with Schaap. Sometime halfway through the first quarter, Schaap, sitting behind Thompson in the press box, floated two bills into the lap of Thompson. They were a five and a twenty.

Now the MVP is voted on by a small number of handpicked sports journalists covering the game and done so in a casual manner. NFL officials conduct a poll and the votes are then tallied. Not exactly the building of the space shuttle. Simple operation.

The opposite of smooth and simple was Kilmer. Griese was effortless while Kilmer was chaotic. Everything Griese had seen on film proved accurate. The defensive backs were vulnerable to double moves, and the Miami offense could exploit numerous weak points of the Washington defense. He also initiated his game plan—remember, Griese called his own plays—in which he'd pass on running downs and run on passing downs. What was perhaps most interesting of all was Griese himself. The quarterback was like other Miami players in that on another team his statistics could have been gaudier. Griese in an offense that passed the football more could have put up far more impressive passing marks. Griese didn't care. Winning was the key, and this Super Bowl was proof of his team-first attitude. In the biggest game of his life, Griese threw just 11 passes, a startlingly low number. But again, he didn't care.

There were several sequences that were typical Griese, where his intellect as opposed to his arm sliced apart defenses. And it wasn't just Griese's big brain that helped. Twilley was equally intelligent and knew they might have a unique avenue of attack against Washington. The Dolphins utilized the down-and-in pass route frequently, and Washington knew this fact. The Redskins did their own extensive film work and prepared for Twilley to do it all afternoon. In their practices, safety Pat Fischer repeatedly drilled on attacking Miami's short routes. Fischer stood at just 5 feet 9 inches and weighed 170 pounds. In many ways, he was like some of the Dolphins players, in that he was an overachiever but far more talented than many gave credit. He'd earned a reputation as an extremely aggressive hitter, and while Super Bowl week had temporarily devolved Allen's reputation from a genius to a grumpy old fart, Fischer was an admirer. "He could attract the right kind of personalities," said Fischer. "He could look at diverse personalities and know how to use them. Allen didn't do it with just Xs and Os. He united the team. All of us were going in the same direction."

Twilley highly respected Fischer but also knew his aggressive tendencies could be used against him. Twilley and Griese practiced tricking Fischer. Over and over they ran the route after practice. Then came the game. On third-and-4, Griese saw his chance. The Redskins, as he anticipated, put two men on Warfield. When Warfield left the line of scrimmage, he was almost instantly knocked down. It was, of course, a different time when defensive backs could commit felony assault on receivers and did so regularly without penalty. With Warfield on the ground, Griese turned his attention to Twilley. Griese and Twilley had very little in common other than a perfectionist's streak and comeback from ugly injuries. Griese returned from that gruesome broken leg, Twilley a shattered jaw and excruciatingly painful broken elbow.

There was a great role reversal. On this single play, Twilley would be the star and Warfield the decoy. Twilley ran a three-step down-and-in. Fischer aggressively bit on the route, and Twilley suddenly broke to the outside. In the middle of the play, Fischer realized he'd been duped and bolted to catch Twilley, but it was too late. Griese had him. Griese threw the pass on target and Fischer made a desperation tackle at the 5-yard line, but Twilley was able to dive in for the first Miami score.

While Griese was breaking down the Washington defense, defensive assistant coach Arnsparger was doing his due diligence attacking the offense. There have been many great defensive minds across NFL history and it could be easily argued that Arnsparger was one of the best. Like other big defensive brains, Arnsparger was addicted to film study. The idea was to find any clue, any hint, any evidence of a weakness that could be exploited. Or, perhaps, witnessing on tape what an opponent will know about you. Football has always been a game of countermoves and counterintelligence.

The Dolphins were leading, but Kilmer had gathered his wits and was moving the Washington offense. In just 6 plays, the Redskins traversed 31 yards, Kilmer attacking the edges of the Dolphins defense with short passes. It looked as if the Redskins were on their way to tying the game. Then came a critical third down. Tex Maule wrote of what happened next: "Kilmer lost a battle of wits. Figuring that Miami would be looking for either Brown or [Charley] Harraway in a short-yardage burst, he decided to pass instead. The Dolphins had a surprise of their own . . . Arnsparger called a variation of the weak zone which the Redskins were not expecting. Arnsparger went with a deployment that the Redskins know as the Weak Zone Buck, but in their study of Dolphin films they had noticed that Miami had not used the Weak Zone Buck since midseason.

"Larry Brown looped out of the back-field as a pass receiver. Normally, the Redskins would expect Buoniconti to roll to the weak side and then Brown would take off and try to outrun the weak-side linebacker. But in the Miami version of the Weak Zone Buck, Buoniconti fixes himself in the middle of a shallow zone. Ironically, Brown would run a pattern that would take him right to where Buoniconti lay in wait. The Redskins ambushed themselves."

The scene was like a comedy skit. The Dolphins anticipated a short running play. The Redskins anticipated that anticipation. Then the Dolphins anticipated that they'd anticipate the first anticipation and changed tactics.

Maule added: "Meanwhile, Harraway also ran a pass route, leaving Kilmer without any back-field protection. Walter Rock, the Redskin left tackle, dropped back to take the first Dolphin through, while John Wilbur, Washington's fine right guard, fell back to take the second man. Wilbur expected that to be Bob Matheson, the Dolphins' extra linebacker, No. 53, who is inserted into the game at points such as this to key a defense that now bears his number—the 53 Defense.

"As Wilbur eyed Matheson, Doug Swift, the left linebacker, crashed on a blitz. He zeroed in on Kilmer at just about the same instant as Brown reached Buoniconti."

Kilmer then had an Arnsparger-forced choice: get blasted on the sack or try to force the football to his receiver. He chose . . . poorly. Kilmer should have taken the sack because Buoniconti intercepted the pass, showing a burst of speed he supposedly didn't have, and returned the football to the Washington 27-yard line. Footage from the game shows the Dolphins sideline erupting, urging Buoniconti on.

A Kiick score made it 14–0. The Redskins were beginning to fade. Brown had been battered. As the Dolphins offense took the field, Brown went to the sideline and was examined by team medical personnel, one standing to his right, another kneeling and examining a bruised hand, Brown sitting, his helmet atop his head, the two-bar face mask resting above his eyebrows. Brown's face winced as the medical staff pinched and probed.

Allen had been almost boyish in his enthusiasm earlier in the game. Now he was agitated. The old Allen was back—flinching and nervous—the little ticks beginning to appear. Touch the brim of the hat. Then the back. Then the ear. Stroke the back of the head. Touch the mouth. Then the nose.

Shula was calm. He stood and watched like he was watching his kid play in a flag football game on a Friday afternoon.

The game continued in the second half the way it did in the first, despite Allen doing his best to refocus his team. He gathered everyone around him on the field just before the second half was to begin. "I want every damn guy in here now," Allen yelled. "Everybody listen to this. We got thirty minutes to live. We've talked about character and now we're going to see how much character every damn guy has here. Now let's hit somebody. And let's be proud of ourselves. Let's be physical. First series on offense, first series on defense. Let's go."

The speech would only help so much. Their initial drive ended in a missed field goal. The Dolphins weren't scoring, but they were dominating. There were a handful of exceptions, but mostly Miami had completely shut down Washington in almost every way. Five minutes left. Four. Three. Thousands of fans could be seen on the television screen heading for the exits. Smiles began to erupt on the Miami sideline. Csonka admits he suddenly had a strange notion bounce around in his head.

What if we could somehow win this game 17–0? Csonka thought. Today, Csonka says, "Think about the symmetry. A 17–0 score and 17-0 season. Then the Garo thing happened. That was unfortunate."

The Garo thing.

It happened with about two minutes left in the game. Yepremian was attempting a 42-yard field goal. Again, had he made it, the symmetry Csonka spoke of would have happened: 17–0 in the game and 17-0 for the season. "I wasn't thinking of that when I called for a field goal," Shula says now. "But it would have been perfect."

Yepremian's kick was blocked. How it was blocked—or rather, if it was blocked—remains a source of debate among some of the players even today. Some say Yepremian's kick went directly into the rear end of the Miami center Bob Heinz and bounced off. Heinz insists it wasn't blocked and the football actually grazed his backside. Replays show the football careening off the outstretched arm of Washington player Bill Brundige. Blocked field goal tries happen all the time in football, but what occurred next is quite uncommon. After the kick was blocked, the football skipped backward toward Yepremian, who picked it up. That's not horribly unusual either. The ball bounces back and the kicker picks it up either to fall on it or to run it. Yepremian did none of those things. He instead attempted to pass the football. As he wound up to throw, the football slipped from his hands and cascaded about his shoulder pads, bouncing and bouncing and bouncing. It was eventually batted into the air, where Washington's Mike Bass snatched it in mid-flight and returned it 49 yards for his team's only score.

The Dolphins players on the sideline, particularly the defense, were crushed. They were just 2:07 away from a rare Super Bowl shutout. When the game ended, the Dolphins players celebrated, all except Yepremian. He was mournful, almost depressed, despite the Dolphins victory. "That championship ring will hang heavy on my hand," he told writers at the time.

To say the play crushed players isn't technically correct. There was a feeling on the Miami sidelines that Yepremian's folly had not just obliterated the gorgeous symmetry of the 17–0 score and 17-0 season but possibly put the win in danger. No, the Miami players weren't crushed; they were infuriated. To Yepremian, the idea was to try to make the best of a horrible situation. To the Dolphins players, Yepremian, in the face of adversity, made a cowardly, selfish play. "Fall on it," Csonka says now, "and the play is over. Done. But it's easy to say that in hindsight, I admit."

When Yepremian reached the Miami bench, he walked into a wall of silence and harsh looks. Shula encouraged Yepremian and told him that, in the future, just fall on the football. That's Shula, always coaching. Outwardly, Shula was rational, but inside, he was steaming. The only time the silence was broken on the Miami sideline was when several players decided to voice their opinions on the Yepremian flub. "We lose this game, I'm gonna kill you, you little cocksucker," said Fernandez. Buoniconti, a few seconds later, also caught up with Yepremian, saying he was going to hang the kicker by his tie.

One player took the opposite approach. The deeply religious Evans approached Yepremian, put his hand on the kicker's shoulder, and said softly, "Garo, don't worry about it. God loves you and our defense will stop them."

Fernandez and Buoniconti were the only players to express their anger, but they were by far not alone in feeling it. The anger directed at Yepremian would last years. Lineman Kuechenberg would discuss the issue in 1986—some thirteen years after the moment— and even with that great distance between the two points in time his anger was still palpable. Kuechenberg's words are lengthy but perhaps the best quote about the sudden panic the team experienced after the kick and how the players felt about Yepremian at the time.

"We were abhorred because it just poured out of our guts, I mean, the game, the whole world just fell in right then," Kuechenberg says in the book *But We Were 17 and 0.*

> That was the most one-sided game to ever close with seven
> points. That game should have been 24–0. It was—what
> was it at halftime—I guess 7–0 at halftime but we had
> a touchdown to Warfield of fifty yards called back . . .

Also, we had the ball on the two yard line going in for
a touchdown in the final minutes of the first half, and
we turned the ball over, and then they never got close to
scoring until Garo's debacle, and so really, they shouldn't
have got any points, and we should have had a coupla
more touches, and it would have been a very one-sided
game. However, shouldas and wouldas don't win Super
Bowls, and to their credit they hung in there, and when
Garo kicked the ball low, and it hit our center's butt, and
bounced back to Garo . . .

His cowardice took over, and he wasn't man enough to
fall on the ball. That opened up the gates and unbelievably
they found themselves with an opportunity to tie the
game, and go into overtime. No one on the Dolphin team
appreciated that including Shula. If looks could kill, Garo
would never have finished. He was dead when he came to
the sideline. Silence was deafening. Besides, the problem is,
anybody can kick the low ball. Anybody can make an error
but Garo had the ball in his hands with perfection, with
immortality as a team riding on the line in his grasp. But
rather than fall on the ball and take your lumps . . . you've
got the ball. You've got the game. Just don't give them a
touchdown. Fall on the ball, basically. Rather than that, he
saw those big guys coming at him and he panics, and he
basically says, 'Here, take the ball.' He picked it up and then
old Earl Morrall at least got up off the ground and made a
good attempt to tackle a man whereas Garo never got close
to the guy. He just made a feigned attempt to get over there
and get in the action. So I resented it.

Then after the fact he got rich off it. Shortly after that,
they formed a Garo for Quarterback Club and he was

cheerleading and band-leading that thing, too . . . He
made a song out of it. And I didn't appreciate that.

The fact is Yepremian *was* intimidated by the moment. He had
played just several years of professional football and didn't kick at a
college. He'd never experienced playing in front of large crowds for
stakes like this, and perhaps most important of all, he'd never truly
kicked under great pressure, though many of his kicks did help to save
the perfect regular season. The fact he'd reached this point was a testament to his strong work ethic, but like others in critical moments,
football has the ability to test a man in ways he'd never expect.

"I had a lot of things that I had to overcome," he said in a 1986
interview. "I'd never kicked under pressure. I'd never kicked with
about 60,000 people watching me. I was very nervous. My face
would twitch. My knee would twitch. I was really scared to death."

Despite this mishap, there was still little chance the Dolphins were
going to lose. The Redskins didn't try an onside kick as expected
but instead kicked off. Griese completed an 11-yard pass for a first
down that allowed the Dolphins to continue to eat the clock. Shula
ordered the offense to run the ball three times, reminding the backs
to stay inbounds so the clock continued to wind down, and the Dolphins punted, giving the ball back to Washington at the 30-yard
line with 1:14 left. The game ended as it began: with Kilmer's inac-
curacy. He overthrew Brown. His next pass was high and went out
of bounds. Brown made a catch but was thrown for a loss. The clock
ticked down and the Dolphins started to celebrate on the sideline.
After Kilmer was sacked, every Dolphins player, on the field and
off, started to pump his fists and raise his hands. Five seconds, four,
three, two, one . . .

The Coliseum scoreboard flashed the message: THE DOLPHINS ARE

SUPER. The country had seen perfection. Well, most of the country. Many football fans in the metropolitan New York area couldn't see the game because of atmospheric disturbances that interrupted television signals. Allen wished those disturbances had kept him from seeing the game as well. Afterward, he was beyond depressed. "I can't get out of here [Los Angeles] fast enough," he said. "There will be a lot of hours of agony tonight."

Conversely, several players lifted Shula off the ground and up onto their shoulders. There would be no crying. It wasn't Shula's way. His way was to appreciate the moment. "What was I thinking?" he says now. "I was thinking people can no longer say I can't win the big one."

When Shula was lowered to the ground, fans joined in the celebration. It was a massive group of people, all patting him on the back and shaking his hand. One small boy, about ten years old, also shook Shula's hand. Then after shaking it, stripped Shula of his watch.

"Trust me," Shula said, "I got it back."

There was pandemonium in the locker room. Celebrations broke out in every corner, in front of every locker. In the shower area, Yepremian was shaving. Griese soon stood next to him and began shaving as well. Then came the Griese deadpan humor. "Now, listen, Garo," Griese said, "you got to grip the laces and then you hold the ball to the back of your ear . . ."

Shula emerged from the team plane wearing a dark blue blazer, light blue shirt, and paisley tie. His hair perfectly combed and smile neatly arranged. He stopped in front of the microphones and held up to the crowd a shiny silver object. "This is the Vince Lombardi Trophy for the winner of the Super Bowl," he told the crowd, which numbered in the tens of thousands. "Seventeen and 0 says it all. The world's championship. The best team ever in professional football."

The newspapers that had once mocked them and the writers who picked them to lose to Washington were now as giddy as the city of Miami. The headline in the *Los Angeles Times* read: "Who Said Nobody's Perfect?" A simple but elegant *Sports Illustrated* headline read: "17-0-0."

The opening paragraph of the latter story said: "It was not always easy, and far less dramatic than it might have been, but the Miami Dolphins finally demonstrated rather conclusively that they are the biggest fish in the pro football pond. In the seventh Super Bowl they defeated the Washington Redskins 14–7 before 81,706 sweltering and smog-beset fans in the Los Angeles Memorial Coliseum. This meant that the Dolphins went an entire season without a loss, 17 straight. No other NFL team has ever gone undefeated for a season, and no other club is likely to do it again soon, either. On the record, then, Miami is the best club in pro football history."

In the coming months, more accolades would accumulate. For so long, the media had portrayed the Dolphins as a lucky team, a team that feasted on the weak and the sorry, and now they saw the Dolphins for what they truly were: an efficient, brilliant machine. It took a while, but that realization was finally hitting.

"Bob Griese is like the mad scientist, seated at the controls of a wonderful new machine," wrote the *New York Post*'s Paul Zimmerman.

Wrote Rick Talley of *Chicago Today*: "This Miami team just may be the greatest ever assembled in pro football."

CHAPTER SEVENTEEN

PERFECT

In some ways the NFL should have seen perfection coming. There was a single game that in some ways forecasted the fact Miami had the physical and mental stamina to endure such a rigorous historical achievement. It happened on Christmas Day 1971, and to this day, it remains the longest NFL game ever played.

The game was a divisional playoff contest, and the Dolphins were playing the Chiefs in Kansas City. Miami was still establishing its NFL credentials while Kansas City was a powerhouse, going for its third Super Bowl trip in six years. The Chiefs had eleven Pro Bowl players and their record against Miami was 6-0. Everyone expected the Dolphins to get crushed and that's the way it started. The end of the first quarter saw Kansas City leading 10–0. The problem was when the Chiefs had the Dolphins by the throat, they didn't squeeze hard enough. The Dolphins scored because of several huge Warfield catches, a Csonka score, and a field goal. At halftime, a game that looked to be a blowout was suddenly tied at 10. When the Chiefs opened the third quarter with their best drive of the game and scored a touchdown, the Dolphins responded with a touchdown of their own on a drive the great NFL Films called a "portrait of perfection." Griese demonstrated his accuracy and toughness with pinpoint throws and timely scrambles and tied the score at 17. "We kept trying to cut their head off and we couldn't," said Csonka, "and they kept trying to cut our head off and couldn't."

Back and forth the game went. The Chiefs scored again with 6:46 left in the game for a 24–17 lead. Griese again responded with a scoring drive, and the game was tied at 24 with 1:36 left. No heads chopped off just yet. Thirty-five seconds left. The greatest kicker of his time, Jan Stenerud, misses a 31-yard field goal try wide right. Dolphins heads stayed attached as the game went to overtime. Then missed field goals by both sides. *Tick, tick, tick*. A second overtime. Buoniconti, who'd finish with a startling 20 tackles, continued to dominate. *Tick, tick, tick*. Muscles cramped; fatigue that had set in much earlier dragged on the body as if a sail was attached to it.

Ed Podolak was a star for Kansas City at running back that day. After Buoniconti tackled him once, Podolak looked up at the Miami linebacker and asked, "Do you think this thing will ever end?"

The Chiefs, physically superior in almost every way—or so it was believed—did hitting of their own. They battered Griese, once smacking him in the ribs so hard he stayed on the ground wincing for several seconds, then uncoiled his body and got up. Csonka lost so much weight during the game that he dropped several pants sizes. He would pause several times while on the sideline to readjust his football gear to fit his shrinking physique. Still, despite the impossibly long game, Miami plowed on. Nothing kept the Dolphins down. Nothing.

In many ways, they were ready for this sort of contest. Remember,

Shula had pushed them through brutal conditioning in the unforgiv-
ing Florida heat. He had primed the Dolphins for just this moment.
There was also a Dolphin secret weapon utilized to beat muscle
cramps and fatigue. It was beer. Every Saturday before games, Shula
would grill burgers for the team at his house, and in the middle of
the bash would be a huge vat of beer. Shula believed the electrolytes
in the beer prevented muscle fatigue, though surely the electrolyte
advantage was counterbalanced by the hangover factor.

Whatever worked. The Dolphins were tired, but the Chiefs were
exhausted and it started to show. Then, after all that, came the play
Roll Right, Trap Left. That play for Csonka hadn't been called all
day, and Csonka broke into Kansas City territory and into field-goal
range. Yepremian made the kick and the Dolphins won 27–24.

When the Dolphins returned home later that night, ten thousand
fans were there to greet them. Shula smiled all the way to his car,
which wouldn't start and forced him to hitch a ride with a Miami
fan, a stranger. When Shula arrived home, his neighbors spilled out of
their houses to greet him. There was an impromptu party in the street.

That game would define two franchises and send them in different directions. The Chiefs wouldn't win another division title for
twenty-two years. A proud organization would devolve into a mediocre one. In the season opener the next year, the year of perfection, the Dolphins would beat Kansas City again. It validated the
Dolphins' win.

There are three games throughout NFL history that are considered the toughest games ever played. One was the Ice Bowl, the
1967 NFL championship game between the Packers and Cowboys.
(The wind chill temperature at kickoff was minus 48 degrees. It was
so cold a marching band scheduled to perform was forced to cancel
after the woodwind instruments froze and the mouthpieces of the
brass instruments became so cold lips stuck to them. The same thing

happened with the whistle of one referee. One person in the stands watching the game died from hypothermia.) The second game was the contest between Washington and Philadelphia in 1990, which was nicknamed the "Body Bag Game" after eight Redskins players were injured. The third was the "Freezer Bowl" game between Cincinnati and San Diego in 1982, played in subzero temperatures. Miami's game against Kansas City is in the discussion with those legendarily tough games.

The double overtime win was one of the building blocks for the perfect season. In totality, from both teams, fifteen Hall of Famers emerged from that game—twelve players, two coaches, and the owner of the Chiefs. The Dolphins would attain perfection because of their toughness and ability to survive the longest game ever played: 82 minutes and 40 seconds.

The season after perfect started with a typical Shula moment. In the days before training camp, he lunched with Csonka, who couldn't resist poking fun at the coach he highly respected. "I knew what he was going to say," Csonka remembers, "he was going to tell us we had to work even harder if we were going to win another Super Bowl."

Csonka sat across from the legendary coach and imitated his opening-day speech. Then when Shula met with the team, he did exactly what Csonka predicted. "We have the same personnel as last year," Shula said, standing before his team, "so the improvement will have to come from within." Shula next outlined the difficulty of the challenge. No team had won consecutive Super Bowls since the 1966 and 1967 Packers. With that, Csonka, who was seated toward the center of the room, chuckled. Csonka had told Shula he'd use the Packers as motivation.

Perhaps more than any of Shula's messages that season, the constant reinforcing of the Packers as the sole repeaters was the most effective. Green Bay was seen as royalty, and some Miami players, despite the perfect season, were still sensitive to the past reputation of the Miami franchise for being the place where the downtrodden, the castoffs, and the unwanted were sent to rot.

The opening game against San Francisco was closer than they'd have liked, but one of the Dolphins heroes was Yepremian, who kicked 31- and 53-yard field goals early in the near 100-degree Miami heat. It had been an interesting off-season for the kicker who became synonymous with Super Bowl goofiness because of the failed kick and attempted pass. Writer Hyde documented the aftermath of that kick, beginning with a highly unusual kicking drill some months earlier on the opening day of training camp. Shula had the football purposely thrown over Yepremian's short head as a way to duplicate that awful moment. The drill was semiserious and semicruel, since it forced Yepremian to relive it. He was instructed by Shula to simply fall on the football. He did. Expertly. The second time the ball was purposely snapped high, Yepremian twisted his ankle slightly while falling to cover it up. After that, the drill was no more.

Yepremian had turned his flub into a franchise, much to the chagrin of a few teammates. The city of Miami, always looking for a hero, saw Yepremian as a sympathetic figure. This was also the case nationally. Legendary comedian Bob Hope would come to greatly appreciate Yepremian, having him several times on his show, including a tribute to the NFL's sixtieth year of existence that aired in November 1981. He was on the show with Elizabeth Taylor, Betty White, Olivia Newton-John, Cosell, Namath, and Simpson, among others. Before that, he sang with Hope at the Fontainebleau Hotel during a charity event.

It hadn't, however, been all giggles and Hope. In his autobiography, Yepremian wrote of how in the immediate weeks and months after the failed kick he went into a state of serious depression. Then, Yepremian says, he received a letter from Shula reminding the kicker of his importance to the perfect season. The letter pulled Yepremian from the depths and helped allow him to live his life. Years later, at a golf tournament, Yepremian says he thanked Shula for the letter. Shula had no idea what he was talking about. The letter, Shula would tell Yepremian, must have been written by Dorothy, Shula's wife. It was.

Those two field goals from Yepremian were typical of his contribution to the Miami team. The kicks had won games, and in some of the games that weren't won by him, Yepremian kept things close until Miami's defense or Csonka took over. Both happened against the 49ers. Csonka had 104 yards on 22 carries, and Miami won 21–13.

Then, on September 23, 1973, in California, something extremely unusual happened.

The Dolphins lost.

Miami had won eighteen consecutive games until John Madden's Oakland Raiders. "I hate talking about losing," Shula said after the game. The reality was Shula didn't have to experience the pains of losing much over the past year. It was unfamiliar territory for everyone.

"We're back in the pack at 1-1," Shula added. "Now we have to start over. What we've always been able to do is come away from a defeat a better team, and we'll do it now."

"It was just one game but we took it very hard because we hadn't lost very much at all," said Csonka. "We became spoiled by our own success."

It was understandable, but they wouldn't have to experience much losing that year at all. The following week, Miami beat New England by 3 touchdowns thanks to runs of 24, 70, and 35 yards. If there was one thing that became incredibly clear as the Dolphins moved toward their third consecutive Super Bowl, it was that Morris was developing into even more of a dangerous weapon than last year. That game he only had the football for 15 carries, but the 70-yard run was the longest in team history and his 197 yards total was a team single-game record.

The victory began the start of a solid nine-game winning streak. It was a mark of many of Shula's teams before and after the perfect season. He knew how to get on a roll. On October 7, Stanfill's 5 sacks propelled Miami's 28-point win over the Jets. One week later, the Browns didn't reach midfield in the second half of a 17–9 win. On October 21, the Dolphins were 4-1, returning home to the Orange Bowl to face Simpson's 4-1 Bills. The winner would be in first place in the division, and the Florida media played up the importance of the contest with some believing the winner would represent the conference in the Super Bowl.

Simpson was again capturing the attention of the NFL with 813 yards in his first five games that season. He would go on to rush for a league-record 2,003 yards, the first time a runner had ever eclipsed the 2,000-yard barrier and becoming one of only six runners to ever do it in NFL history. Simpson's greatest ability was running on the edges, using his speed to break to the outside and then outrun everyone. Decades later, his ability to run away would have a different meaning, but back then, that ability terrified defenses, including the brilliant Arnsparger. The Miami coaches, unlike other staffs that had faced Simpson, remained confident. Arnsparger knew he had the players who possessed the speed and agility to cut off Simpson's angles of attack. His defense was on a roll, not allowing a touchdown in three of the team's five games.

What Miami didn't know was that Simpson was just as nervous about the Dolphins as they were about him. "I think what some people don't get about that team is that they were better than the team that didn't lose a game," said Simpson. "They were more experienced, but what I saw most of all was that they were more confident.

"I always felt like I could score on any team. I could score anytime, but the Dolphins were the one team where I sometimes had doubts. They were a frustrating defense to play, and during that season, after they went undefeated, they were even better because of that confidence."

Over the past four decades, in numerous interviews, this is a point many Dolphins players have made repeatedly, and it's a point many football historians have either overlooked or forgotten. "I feel that the year that we went back to back, in '73, we probably had a better football team," said Little. "Because everybody was up for us, everybody was trying to knock us off, we had to face that challenge every week."

"I have no problem with saying that the '73 Dolphins team was the best football team that I've ever seen," said Kuechenberg.

"The best part of coming back in '73 was that the '73 team was stronger in different ways," said Heinz. "We had more power, greater bench strength. In '73 we were respected. The teams we played that year knew we were the champions and we were very, very good. So the teams we played that year were playing at a higher caliber than they would normally play to try and knock us off. It was tougher for us to win."

Simpson would average 163 yards per game that year, but against Miami, with his lateral escape routes sealed and those confident Dolphins swarming him, Simpson was held to 55 yards on 14 carries. The Bills, alleged threats to the Dolphins, didn't score a touchdown and lost by 21 points.

Simpson's argument was an accurate one, and the Dolphins' extra confidence started with Shula. There was something different about him; the burden of not winning a Super Bowl lifted, and he was freer. "I think the way to put it," said Csonka, laughing, "is that he was even more of a hard-ass." But it worked. *It always worked.*

The victories kept coming. They won 30–14 against the Patriots; 24–14 over the Jets; 44–0 against his old team, the Colts. Simpson would get 120 yards in their second meeting on November 18, but Miami would get the 17–0 win, as Simpson didn't score a touchdown, and Miami captured the division. In Dallas, on November 22, after beating the Cowboys 14–7, linebacker Lee Roy Jordan said succinctly what made the Miami defense so formidable: "Miami's defense shifts and waits for the mistake, then they kill you."

The Dallas game and the next one against Pittsburgh were two of the more interesting that regular season. By then, the Dolphins had been so dominant they had already secured a playoff spot, and the two games against the Cowboys and Steelers basically meant nothing. Except they did. It was a test of pride for the Miami players. "We were still pissed off about what the Cowboys did to us in the Super Bowl two years before," Csonka says.

(Another example of Warfield's underrated abilities came in that game against Dallas, when he juked one of the great defensive backs of the day, Mel Renfro, who was a ten-time Pro Bowler, on an inside-out fake that ended with a 45-yard touchdown.)

The Steelers were simply collateral damage of a Miami team on a historic roll. The Dolphins' Dick Anderson had 4 interceptions in that game, returning 2 for touchdowns. It was one of the more dominating performances of a defensive back in modern regular-season NFL history.

The second loss of the season came against Baltimore, and it mostly happened because Shula, not wanting to risk injury to Griese, sat him for the game. Morrall started, exceeding 20,000 passing yards for his career, but the Dolphins fell 16–3. On December 15, the Dolphins beat Detroit 34–7 in their final regular-season game.

Miami finished the 1973 regular season nearly flawless. One of the most telling statistics of its dominance was this: in fourteen games, the Dolphins had allowed only 15 touchdowns. In two regular seasons, they were 26-2, the best in history to that point. And Shula made sure the team didn't fracture any appendages patting itself on the back. As he had done the year before, Shula reminded the team that it all meant nothing unless Miami won the Super Bowl.

On December 23 at Miami's Orange Bowl, it was halftime of the Dolphins' first playoff game, and Miami was leading Cincinnati 21–16. But to Shula, his Dolphins were getting killed, and he wanted blood.

When he stood before the team, some of the players kneeling, others standing, all waiting to see what Shula would say, his initial instinct was to scream. Shula could do that. He could be encouraging, brilliant, and hopeful, but he was also, at times, belligerent and belittling, a screamer. In this moment, he decided to be neither. Csonka watched Shula and waited for an explosion. There was an outburst or two, but in the end Shula relayed some simple instructions.

"Act like the score is 0–0," he said, "we're starting over."

What had caused Shula's anger occurred just a few minutes before the end of the first half. Earlier in the game, Miami dominated. The team's offensive stars of Griese, Csonka, Warfield, and Morris were critical again, as each of them scored. It was suddenly 21–3 and the Dolphins looked to cruise. Then Griese threw an interception, which was returned for a touchdown, and the Bengals added two field goals. That 18-point lead was suddenly down to 5. Thus Shula's halftime consternation.

His instructions to start over took root, which wasn't a stunner since most of them had since he came to the Dolphins. Miami outscored Cincinnati 13–0 in the second half and the final score was 34–16. In some ways, it was a scare they needed.

The night before the Dolphins were to play the Raiders, there was a knock on Shula's hotel room door. It was December 29. The game was in Miami, but Shula kept the team in a local hotel to limit the distractions. The man at Shula's door was Griese. The quarterback had been watching film, which, to Griese, was as vital as taking in oxygen. Griese noticed something, a flaw in one of the Raiders' defensive schemes, and he rushed to tell Shula.

The Raiders were utilizing what was then a partially common defensive system (but is now used by every team). When offenses were in third-and-long yardage situations, the Raiders, anticipating a pass, replaced a slower linebacker with a faster fifth defensive back. It was called a nickel defense, and it allowed the Raiders to better armor themselves against a passing attack. The defense was first used in the 1960s by the Philadelphia Eagles, and Shula was all too familiar with it since he and Arnsparger popularized it to combat four-wide receiver sets.

Griese picked up on a gigantic flaw in the Raiders scheme, a flaw every other player and coaching staff that played Oakland had missed. Griese's brain spit out the algorithms and computations to Shula and Shula followed along closely. The linebacker comes out . . . check. The defensive back goes in. He's faster . . . check. The wide receivers on offense are double covered by defensive backs . . . check. That new defensive back, who subbed for the linebacker, covers the tight end . . . check. If the tight end goes downfield, and the receivers do as well, then the defense has everyone covered, right? Right? No, Griese told Shula in that small hotel room.

Who covered the quarterback?

A sly smile crept across Shula's face.

Imagine the moment. The AFC championship is just hours away and one more win means a third straight Super Bowl appearance. Two great football men, future Hall of Famers, are in a hotel room, a new discovery at their fingertips. Many times, in football, games are won in moments like these. Many times, in football, championships are won in moments like these.

Shula's smile got even wider.

The time to test Griese's theory came early in the fourth quarter. It had been a fairly tight game and the Dolphins led just 17–10. For one of the few times all season, the Dolphins were agitated. Not nervous. The Dolphins didn't get scared. But they did get agitated. In that quarter, the Raiders were also starting to build momentum and were threatening to make a run. Miami had bogged down on offense as well, facing a third-and-7 on the Oakland 45. A punt could drastically change the momentum in favor of the Raiders, so the next play had to be picked carefully.

Griese looked over at the Raiders knowing what was coming next. Out went the linebacker, in came the extra defensive back. Griese remained calm, but he knew what play to call next: the Quarterback Draw. Miami's wideouts went deep, the tight end cleared out, and just like he'd seen on film, there was a massive hole in the middle of the field. Griese wasn't especially fast, but his scrambling was efficient enough. Snap, drop back, parting of the Raiders sea, and he bolted for 17 yards and first down at the Oakland 28. It had worked.

The Dolphins were able to get a field goal from that drive. In effect, the play gave Miami a 10-point cushion, but perhaps more important, it stopped Oakland's momentum. Miami scored a touchdown just a short time later and won the game 27–10. No team had ever won three consecutive AFC titles. The Dolphins had already been perfect. Now they were entering an entirely new realm. Only the Minnesota Vikings stood in the way.

One year after a perfect season. Another press conference, another Super Bowl, another piece of history at stake. And more Shula humor.

Shula met with the team a few days before they left for Houston and Super Bowl VIII. He wanted to get some of the mundane—yet somewhat dangerous—details about travel and hotel stays out of the way. These particulars felt formidable to Shula because in the days leading up to a Super Bowl, as the pressure mounted, the small could overwhelm. Shula was often at his best in these moments, and this would be no different.

He informed the team that this year, as in past Super Bowls, wives would be flown to the game at the expense of Robbie, and, as he had also done many times before, Shula allowed some of his decisions to be openly discussed among the players. He didn't expect much discussion until some of the unmarried players began asking the question: Would Robbie pay for the mothers of the single players?

It was an interesting query and one Shula, who often examined every piece of information, admittedly hadn't considered. Once Shula made it clear Robbie's final decision was to pay for wives only, the discussion was over, and Shula thought the matter was concluded. It wasn't. News of players asking about the mothers was leaked to the press, and it became an issue at Shula's first press conference the week of the game. "How are all the mothers this morning?" Shula was asked by a writer.

Shula was incredulous. Someone was actually making this an issue? Instead of getting defensive, Shula decided to have some fun. "The mothers, the mothers," Shula said. "I like mothers." There was a chuckle among the press. Shula continued. "The policy of the Dolphins for the last three years has been to bring the wives. This came up last year when it was announced in a team meeting. But it wasn't as big a problem as it turned out to be this year because last year they took a charter jet out and the year before, there was also a charter and you were able to put as many people as you could on the charters. This year Joe Robbie decided not to take a charter and instead fly the wives out by commercial jet. In doing this there wasn't any room for extra people. This year when the announcement was made 'wives only' some of the single people brought up the question of the mothers and some single people brought up the question of girlfriends." There were more laughs. In the room were about thirty writers and a handful of photographers. Shula turned a small, cold concrete room full of reporters who were initially prepared to create controversy over a nonsensical matter into one where writers were now laughing at their own potential silliness.

"How many players are involved?" one reporter asked.

"Let's see, Larry Little is single, Jim Mandich is single." There was more laughter, and the earlier uncomfortable squirming by the press in their seats ceased. "The ones that voiced complaint were Marv Fleming, Jake Scott and Mandich, although I'm not sure whether that was a mother or girlfriend in that situation." Chuckles. "Who else do we have? Brisco, Stanfill. Stanfill didn't complain last year because he was married. This year he's divorced." The chuckles got louder. The room was now officially Shula's.

"Can married guys bring their girlfriends?" Shula was asked.

Even Shula laughed at that one. "No, it's not an either or situation."

"Do you have tapes of the meeting with Robbie or were they erased?"

"I hope to heck there were no tapes of that meeting." Shula smiled.

"Does a thing like this cause any concern for you? It wouldn't cause any dissension, would it?"

"I'd rather not have this situation," Shula explained. "It's something that was discussed at the meeting and the policy was set. I'd like to think that Griese's married and he's going to throw the ball to either Fleming or Mandich, who are both single." That got the loudest laugh yet.

"Will the wives be in the same hotel as the players?"

"No," Shula said.

"Will the wives' hotel be off limits to the players?"

"No. We're not going to attempt to follow them around and see where they go," Shula said. "A lot of the players voiced the opinion that they would prefer to have the wives in another hotel and a lot of the wives voiced the opinion that they would prefer to be in another hotel. A lot of them didn't but a lot of them did."

"What about the old Tuesday rule?" a writer asked.

"The Tuesday rule . . . the Tuesday rule. I've never been able to check on that." Some in the press laughed, but others looked around with quizzical stares. They didn't know about the rule. Shula was forced to explain it, which added another comedic element to the ridiculous press conference.

"The Tuesday rule is that players can't be with the wives after Tuesday, from then on you dedicate yourself to the task of getting ready for the game." Shula's statement was basically made with a wink, and the laughter from the writers was now raucous. He continued: "I've mellowed quite a bit. That's gotten down to a Saturday night rule for me."

A few more questions came and then the press conference ended. There were other small fires that week for both teams. The coach of the Vikings, Bud Grant, became infuriated when he saw the team's practice facilities at a Houston high school. "Maybe the worst facilities I've ever seen," Grant said at the time. When players attempted to run the showers, a trickle of water emerged from the heads, and in some cases, nothing did. In the ultimate irony, the locker room had no actual lockers. Grant was so angry he took reporters on a tour of the locker room and gave a blow-by-blow description of its ineptitude. At one point, Grant pointed to a nest of pigeons.

Grant had legitimate points, but his demeanor was reminiscent of one year earlier with Washington's Coach Allen. Grant was uptight and his team was following his lead, just as the Redskins had. This fact did not go unnoticed by journalists covering the event. "In stark contrast to Shula, Viking coach Bud Grant spent most of Super Week acting like a Marine Corps drill sergeant with a terminal case of the piles," wrote Thompson. "Grant's public behavior in Houston called up ominous memories of Redskin coach, George Allen's, frantic pregame bitching last year in Los Angeles.

"The parallel was hard to miss, and it seemed almost certain—both cases—that the attitudes of the coaches had to either reflect or powerfully influence the attitudes of the players . . . and in high-pressure games between supposedly evenly-matched teams, pregame signs like confidence, humor, temper tantrums, and bulging eyeballs are not to be ignored . . ."

Arnsparger's discussions to become head coach of the New York Giants the following season were leaking publicly, and both Shula and Arnsparger were asked about them during the Super Bowl. Laughing about player sex after Tuesday was one thing. A vital assistant coach leaving was another. But for the moment, Shula had to worry about the game itself and the Vikings.

Fernandez initially worried about the Vikings as well. Then he started watching tape and was flabbergasted by what he saw. The tape showed a Vikings team that to Fernandez wasn't near the Dolphins' level. When he zeroed in on the Minnesota offensive line, he was even more taken aback. He watched center Mick Tingelhoff the most. Tingelhoff was one of the great centers of the 1960s, making six consecutive Pro Bowl appearances during the decade. But Fernandez saw an aged and slow Tingelhoff. The guards, he thought, were inconsequential. Miami's offense was better, its defense clearly so, and the Dolphins' coaching staff more so. Fernandez thought, *These guys wouldn't make the playoffs in the AFC.*

Fernandez predicted to teammates the game would be a blowout, even as *Sports Illustrated* predicted for the third time a Miami Super Bowl loss. The cities of Miami and Minneapolis made their bets and predictions. "We will put on the line," Miami City commissioner J. L. Plummer told his Minneapolis counterpart in a phone conversation, "one bag of oranges and all the suntan lotion you can use before March the first. We feel that about the only thing that of course you could reciprocate with is a bag of snow if that's agreeable to you."

Namath, clearly comfortable being in the guarantee business, made another publicly to the press. "If Miami scores on the opening drive," he said, "the game is over." In fact, in all three playoff games that season, the Dolphins had won the coin toss, elected to receive, and scored on the opening drive.

While the Dolphins practiced and plotted, Hunter Thompson drank and vomited. He was writing "Fear and Loathing at the Super Bowl" for *Rolling Stone*, and the end product described portions of the crazy scene perfectly. "For eight long and degrading days I had skulked around Houston with all the other professionals, doing our jobs—which was actually to do nothing at all except drink all the free booze we could pour into our bodies, courtesy of the National Football League, and listen to an endless barrage of some of the lamest and silliest swill ever uttered by man or beast . . ."

He was correct about something else. "The consensus among the 1,600 or so sportswriters in town favored Miami by almost two to one . . ." he wrote. The sportswriters then gambled as much as they wrote and sometimes did it in the open. Thompson was speaking midweek to Robbie about the relationship between national politics, football, and the fate of mutual friend George McGovern, when journalist Larry Merchant tapped Thompson on the shoulder and handed him a fifty-dollar bill in full view of Robbie, who didn't skip a beat and continued the conversation. Thompson had been taking his own bets and giving some of the sportswriters favorable odds. He became a major hub for the gambling press.

The Dolphins' game plan was to utilize the aggressive nature of the Vikings' defensive front line, the most formidable in football, against them. The Vikings overpowered teams with that defense by simply trouncing over them. The Dolphins were to use misdirection plays, get the defense running hard upfield, then scoot Csonka in behind them. Teams had tried this technique against the Vikings and watched it blow up in their faces, but the Dolphins had both the athletes to make it work and the discipline required to keep doing it for the entire game.

Against Dallas in the Super Bowl, Csonka had been contained, and in the Super Bowl against Washington, the story was Miami's defense. This Super Bowl, indeed, the entire postseason, belonged to Csonka. Using the misdirection ploys the Dolphins cooked up before the game, he destroyed the Vikings. The first drive went 62 yards in 10 plays and the next went 56 in 10 plays. The offensive line and Csonka met little resistance. The Vikings began playing tentatively, growing fearful of the misdirection, and when they started to draw back, Griese called for straightforward blocking to take advantage of Minnesota's retreat. It was an almost ideal blend of play calling, athleticism, and intelligence.

"The Dolphins took the opening kickoff," wrote Thompson, "and stomped the Vikings defense like they were a gang of sick junkies."

Dolphins lineman Kuechenberg symbolized the domination of the Miami offensive line by schooling maybe the best defensive lineman of the time in Alan Page. He so frustrated Page that Page threw two right elbows to Kuechenberg's face right in front of an official. Page was ejected. From the Super Bowl.

Csonka rushed for 145 yards on 33 carries, both Super Bowl records. The Dolphins weren't penalized for the first fifty-two minutes and Griese—yet again—subjugated his ego for the betterment of the team, throwing just 7 passes and completing 6. The 24–7 score wasn't really that close. "Super Bowl VIII," said sportswriter Maule, "had all the excitement and suspense of a master butcher quartering a steer."

On the field, as celebrations began, Shula looked for Arnsparger and threw his hands around his assistant coach's neck, almost choking him with a full-strength hug.

Inside the locker room, the mood was celebratory but not overly so. It was actually a strange scene. There was joy but it was controlled. Some reporters were actually taken aback by what they were seeing. One writer approached Evans. "If I didn't know any better," the writer said, "I'd think you guys had lost."

"When you come this far," Evans responded, "you don't have the energy to celebrate. I'm still in shock."

"We're an emotional team," Twilley told reporters, "but we show it on the field. What emotion we had, we left it out there. I don't know about the rest of these guys but I'm too pooped to throw anybody in the showers except myself."

In other words, the Dolphins were so professional even their Super Bowl celebration was polished.

The discussion that emerged after the win centered on if the Dolphins were in the same class as the Packers, the great dynastic team coached by Lombardi. Players from the Vikings and Dolphins were asked repeatedly by the press where the Dolphins ranked in history. "The Dolphins are the greatest team to date," said Minnesota defensive great Carl Eller. "The Packer teams under Lombardi were great, too. But the Dolphins are faster and more versatile than the Packers. They're almost a composite team. It would be hard to match that kind of team again. Ever."

"I played against the Packers their Super Bowl years," said Minnesota defensive lineman Bob Lurtsema, "and I've got to say that Miami is a better all-around team. There's no question about it."

"I'm tired of hearing all that crap about how Green Bay was," said the Dolphins' Langer. "I wish they were still around so we could settle the issue. They seem to be the only team that ever gets lasting recognition for greatness or a dynasty or whatever. Well, I'd like to say that if this isn't a dynasty, if this isn't a great team, would someone mind telling me just what the hell it takes to be one?"

It was a common theme among the Miami players—then and now—that history was somehow overlooking them. That defensiveness would last through the decades, even now, forty years later. It could be tangibly felt in their comments to reporters immediately after the game.

"It's the best team I've ever played with or anybody else will ever play with," said Fleming, who was also once a member of the Packers.

"I don't know if we're the greatest of all time," said Csonka, "but let's just say we're the class of the neighborhood."

"I don't want to say we are a dynasty but we are the best team in the history of pro football," said Little. "If anyone has any doubts now show him to me and I'll have him committed."

"We are better than Green Bay . . ." said Fernandez. "We're probably the greatest team in history."

"We have got to be the best team ever," said Langer. "If we haven't proved that now, I don't know what we have to do to prove it."

This quote from Fernandez in *But We Were 17 and 0* is one of the more poignant synopses of that Miami team.

> I think during the short time that we dominated, we dominated as well as anyone. I don't think anyone played at a higher level of football than we did. I don't think we played any better than we had to. We had a bunch of loose guys who liked to have fun at it. The more we were tested I think the better we performed. Personally, I also think the 17-0 team wasn't as good—we continued to improve. I think we were a better football team in '73 to be perfectly honest with you. We gave up fewer points defensively. Offensively we scored more points.
>
> We lost two ball games but when it came time for the playoffs we dominated the playoffs. We literally beat the hell out of Cincinnati, thoroughly beat up on Oakland and then we went in . . . we [could have] beaten Minnesota by fifty points. We didn't throw the ball in the second half—zero passes. We threw five passes the entire game. We were five for seven passing in the first half. It was total domination. If Bob wanted to put the ball up in the air, I personally think we could have destroyed [them]. They had no luck. They had one drive against us that amounted to anything and that was it. They didn't have anything other than that one touchdown drive. It was a fun game. We were only on the field thirty-seven defensive plays. We gave up a total of seven or eight first downs the whole game and five of those were on the touchdown drive. It gives you an idea of how we totally dominated Minnesota in that Super Bowl.

The *New York Times* headline read: "Dolphins Rout Vikings, 24–7, to Win 2d Super Bowl in Row." When the Dolphins returned home there were ten thousand fans at the airport cheering their arrival.

As the subdued celebration continued, and large men laughed and told stories, the team's equipment manager, Dan Dowe, did something that hardly anyone noticed. But it was one of the more interesting moments of the three-year Miami run. Dowe was then, and continued to be, one of the integral parts of the team, joining the organization during its inaugural season in 1966. The man who would clean up after the Dolphins, get their uniforms ready, wash their clothes, and replace destroyed equipment. It is perhaps the most thankless job in all of sports.

In one of Robbie's final acts of pettiness, in 1985, Robbie forced Shula to fire Dowe over a series of minor infractions. Robbie blamed Dowe for a fight that happened when one of Miami's ball boys went to retrieve the football and got into an altercation with a fan. Dowe, who supervised the ball boys, claimed the fan attacked first and the ball boy was simply defending himself. The fan contacted Robbie, claiming otherwise, and threatened to sue the Dolphins for $1 million. The second reason for Dowe's dismissal was even more unusual. A retired police officer who held a low-level position on the team wanted to fly home on the team plane, but his request was denied. Dowe snuck him onto the team plane anyway. So on Friday, February 15, 1985, Dowe was fired.

"We are stunned, we are in shock," Dowe's wife, Virginia, said to the *Miami News*, speaking of her husband's firing. "After 19 years of service, he gets treated like this. He worked like a dog for 19 years on a $22,000-a-year salary. He was two years short of his retirement. I don't know what will happen now.

"I've been disabled for two years and need to go back into the hospital. I don't know where the money is going to come from in this household."

"You can only take so much crap . . ." said Dowe. "Robbie won't listen to what I have to say, so it's just not worth dealing with it anymore.

"You work seven days a week, 12 hours a day for 19 years and there are no rewards. If you get a watch, it's a Mickey Mouse watch with a hand missing."

Five years after that, in January 1990, the notorious Robbie would pass away, and at his funeral in St. Martha's Catholic Church, packed with three hundred people, including numerous Dolphins players and many in the NFL elite, his contributions as a misunderstood man were documented by the deliverer of the eulogy, former guard Kuechenberg. Robbie was the propelling force behind a new $115 million Joe Robbie Stadium, a facility Kuechenberg called a "single unifying factor" in helping to bridge differences within Miami's multiethnic community. Kuechenberg didn't shy away from addressing Robbie's well-known frugality. "I went to the mat with him three or four times . . ." he said. "Did I get what I wanted? Heck no! I got what I needed . . . and I understand now that we [Dolphins players] were being treated just like anyone else in the Robbie family."

But before Robbie's death and before Dowe became a Robbie casualty, Dowe did something in the aftermath of that second Super Bowl victory that remains an important footnote. He approached a blackboard in the corner of the locker room, erased what was on it, and, with only a handful of people noticing, wrote on it: MIAMI DOLPHINS, BEST TEAM EVER.

Few people saw Dowe write it and most thought it was Shula. Slowly players and journalists saw the note and began wondering who wrote it. Shula eventually made his way in front of the blackboard, where he was asked who put the message there.

"Forty players," Shula responded.

PERFECTION'S END

Perfection is like pregnancy, isn't it?

You are. Or you aren't.

—GREG COTE, SPORTS COLUMNIST, *MIAMI HERALD*

In her kaleidoscopic narrative *Miami*, Joan Didion examines the history of a city alternating between states of elegance and obscenity. Didion navigates Miami's steaming beauty, calculated drug violence, immigration politics, and racial discontent while focusing on its tribal feuding with Cuba. In one part of the literary journalist's book, a name is mentioned that seems out of place. It exemplifies just how meaningful the name had become in Miami's history.

On the one hundred and fiftieth anniversary of the founding of Dade County, in February of 1986, the *Miami Herald* asked four prominent amateurs of local history to name "the ten people and the ten events that had the most impact on the county's history." Each of the four

submitted his or her own list of "The Most Influential
People in Dade's History," and among the names
mentioned were Julia Tuttle ("pioneer businesswoman"),
Henry Flagler ("brought the Florida East Coast Railway
to Miami"), Alexander Orr, Jr. ("started the research
that saved Miami's drinking water from salt"), Everest
George Sewell ("publicized the city and fostered its
deepwater seaport"), Carl Fisher ("creator of Miami
Beach"), Hugh M. Anderson ("to whom we owe
Biscayne Boulevard, Miami Shores, and more"), Charles
H. Crandon ("father of Dade County's park system"),
Glenn Curtiss ("developer and promoter of the area's
aviation potential"),and James L. Knight ("whose creative
management enabled the *Miami Herald* to become a force
for good"), this last nominee the choice of a retired *Herald*
editorial writer.

There were more names. There were John Pennekamp
("conceived Dade's metropolitan form of government
and fathered the Everglades National Park") and Father
Theodore Gibson ("inspirational spokesman for racial
justice and social change"). There were Maurice Ferre
("mayor for twelve years") and Majorie Stoneman Douglas
("indefatigable environmentalist") and Dr. Bowman F.
Ashe ("first and longtime president of the University of
Miami"). There was David Fairchild, who "popularized
tropical plants and horticulture that have made the county
a more attractive place to live." There was William A.
Graham, "whose Miami Lakes is a model for real estate
development," Miami Lakes being the area developed
by William A. Graham and his brother, Senator Bob
Graham, at the time of Dade's one hundred and fiftieth

anniversary, on three thousand acres their father had just west of the Opa-Locka Airport.

There was another Graham, Ernest R., the father of Bob and William A., nominated for his "experiments with sugarcane culture and dairying." There was another developer, John Collins, as in Collins Avenue, Miami Beach. There were, as a dual entry, Richard Fitzpatrick, who "owned four square miles between what is now Northeast 14th Street and Coconut Grove," and William F. English, who "platted the village of Miami." There was Dr. James M. Jackson, an early Miami physician. There was Napoleon Bonaparte Broward, the governor of Florida who initiated the draining of the Everglades. There appeared on three of the four lists the name of the developer of Coral Gables, George Merrick.

Then Didion writes: "There appeared on one of the four lists the name of the coach of the Miami Dolphins, Don Shula."

———

Scenes from a post-perfection city that has long embraced hubris, ugliness, and perfection in one unmistakable embrace . . .

The year 1974: Two years after perfection, the bombs exploded. They kept exploding for months. They exploded under cars. They exploded inside of them. They exploded in restaurants. They exploded in the doorways of Cuban shops in Miami's Little Havana. The terror spread quickly, panic registered in unusual ways, and soon capitalism filled a needed void. A flush and vibrant market was created for remote ignition starters. The technology allowed a car owner to remotely trigger the ignition switch from a safe distance—

say, across the boulevard, outside of the blast radius—thus allowing the driver to forecast his own potential incineration. Anyone who believed going to such extremes was insane could read about a man in a Miami hospital without his legs, the result of close contact with an explosive device.

A civil war had erupted inside Miami, a precursor of the drug wars to come, and detailed in an October 1976 story by Dick Russell. In one bloody stretch there was an average of one murder a week. In an eighteen-month span, one hundred bombs exploded in Miami. Bullets filled the air and Jose Elias de la Torriente was the first to die. He was watching television with his wife when a bullet zipped through the window and ended his life. Torriente was a leader in the Cuban exile community who only a short time earlier had hoped to launch a bold offensive against Fidel Castro. Before his plans emerged from the cocoon of thought, he was dead.

A dark piece of paper was discovered outside of Torriente's home. It contained Torriente's initials and had the number 0 on it. Hours after the killing, a typewritten letter in Spanish reached various media outlets. Torriente was but the first, the letter claimed, and revenge would be taken against those who blocked the "process of liberating their homeland by working only to advance their own bastard ambitions." It was a direct challenge, seemingly, to the Cuban exiles planning to destroy Castro.

"Each in his own time and in a cool and dispassionate way will start getting his zero," the letter finished. "An infinite zero that will adorn their soon to be forgotten tomb . . . Cemeteries are very big and we have more than enough time to fill them."

The letter was signed: "Zero group."

Not long after Torriente's murder, a second letter was sent to Miami's newspapers. Inside was a list of ten well-known anti-Castro exiles with their names marked by the word "zero." Castro was the people's suspect, but as the FBI and other law enforcement officials descended upon Miami, the Castro link was deemed tenuous by investigators. None of the exiles was still a threat to Castro, and the FBI believed the reasoning behind the attacks was a smoke screen. The list itself was not. Four of the ten names on it had been murdered. One man was alive but missing his legs. As a result, some Miamians began arming themselves.

"Everybody's running around with a new .45 and a new mini-millimeter with a big clip," Miami homicide lieutenant Gary Minium told one newspaper. "I mean, we're not used to it. This isn't what we've had or experienced previously. It's completely new to us and hard to understand."

It actually wasn't all that difficult to comprehend. People were terrified. They armed themselves.

Miami fell in love with perfection but not even that unifying force could change what was coming. Or what was still there. The city was still rife with bigotry. The drug wars were coming. So were the riots.

But the core beauty of Miami stayed the same. Legendary Miami crime writer Edna Buchanan described the first time she saw the city from the backseat of a taxicab: "You ascend a slight rise in a silver stretch of expressway and suddenly, there it is across the water, spread out in front of you, all pink, radiant, and bathed in sunlight. The glittering bay sprawls at its feet, its rooftops and Art Deco towers surrounded by vast sky, and drifting clouds glow golden at sunset and rosy at dawn. It is the image of a fairy-tale kingdom full of dreams and legends."

Morris left the NFL in 1976 with $250,000 in savings, two spacious houses, nice cars, investments, and a reputation as a pretty good guy. It was all pretty perfect until the drugs hit. He started freebasing cocaine in 1979 but had first tried snorting it during Miami's off-season some six or seven years earlier. Other Dolphins players used cocaine during the off-season, but they insist there wasn't a drug problem on the team, and once the season began, the use stopped.

Morris was wrongly convicted of cocaine trafficking in 1982 and sentenced to twenty years in prison. His conviction was overturned by the Florida Supreme Court and he was released after serving three years. Few Dolphins would become as well known as Morris after the perfect season. He'd also become one of the more inspirational sports stories of the past forty years, ending his drug use and becoming a motivational speaker and one of the more fiery, if not at times annoying, representatives of the perfect Dolphins.

Perhaps the second-most interesting Dolphin, post perfection, was Jake Scott. Journalist Hyde chronicled in the *South Florida Sun-Sentinel* how Scott became increasingly isolated from Shula and the team, leading to an eventual split and an uncomfortable meeting in an elevator. It stemmed from an incident that happened during the 1975 season. Shula made a stern announcement in a meeting with the players that an attendance at an upcoming banquet was required. That was Shula-speak for "have your asses there." Some players privately grumbled but intended on going anyway. Scott wasn't one to grumble privately. He spoke his mind. He did to Shula and told Shula he wasn't going.

Shula threatened a fine of $5,000. It was, actually, an unfair request. Forcing players to attend a function that had nothing really to do with the team was a step beyond. Most players feared challenging Shula over this. Scott did not. He fumed and asked for a trade and would soon have his wish. In the next year, during the meaningless exhibition season, a request by Shula for Scott to play was denied by Scott, who had an injured shoulder. Shula wanted Scott to take a painkilling injection for the game. Scott was incredulous. Why should he suit up for a crap game that didn't mean anything? To Shula, a painkilling shot wasn't a big deal, and he practiced what he preached. About twenty years earlier when Shula was a player for the Browns, he took painkilling injections for his injured ankle almost every game that year, including the exhibition ones. To Shula, this was simply a part of the game.

Scott wasn't buying into it. The two men argued fiercely one day in the team facility, and about twenty-four hours after that Scott was traded. The two men have barely spoken since, except for one exchange that Shula says never happened and Scott claims did. At a ten-year reunion for the 1972 team, the two men ran into each other in an elevator inside the bowels of the Orange Bowl.

Scott told Hyde that he said to Shula: "We've got to meet next week and iron out this thing between us."

"Fuck you," Scott says Shula shot back.

Shula denies that happened. What is undeniable is that Scott has been mostly a ghost. There are rumored sightings and, like ghosts, it's difficult to confirm if those sightings are actually true. "Every player from our team," says Csonka, "misses Jake."

Jim Brown, the greatest running back of all time, played for one of the best NFL leaders of all time, Cleveland coach Paul Brown. When Jim is asked if there was one coach he'd rather play for other than Paul, he doesn't hesitate. "It would have to be Shula," Jim Brown says. "I know it was a different era, but you could tell how much he respected running backs. Look at all the great ones who played for him. That's no coincidence. That's Shula making good choices and then letting them flourish.

"When you talk to Dolphins players who were on his teams, there's nothing but respect. They talk about him like he's a god. They remain loyal to him because he was so loyal to them. You just don't see that kind of loyalty to coaches anymore or coaches being so loyal to the men who played under them. That tells you a lot about Don Shula."

In June 2011, Pat Riley, the legendary coach and general manager of the Miami Heat, discussed his basketball team's past season. It's the standard fare about a nonstandard team. The Heat had engaged in a grand experiment by putting superstars LeBron James and Dwyane Wade, along with All-Star Chris Bosh, on the same Heat team. Before the season began, and in a moment of testosterone-induced braggadocio, James stated the group would win multiple championships. Instead, once the group reached the NBA Finals, it lost to a more inspired Dallas team. Riley was left to explain why his mouthy group of stars had been beaten by a less talented bunch.

A portion of Riley's response to the media served as yet another example of why the 1972 Dolphins, despite accomplishing the greatest feat in American team sports history, remain the least appreciated. It is also one of the reasons this book was written. People forget. They truly forget what this team did, as exampled by Riley's next words.

"The greatest thing in the history of South Florida sports was those guys coming together," Riley said of James, Wade, and Bosh. "With the exception of the [undefeated 1972] Dolphins. Maybe."

Riley said *maybe* the only team in NFL history to go undefeated, the Dolphins, was as big a story as the three NBA stars arriving in Florida and winning nothing.

He said *maybe*.

AUTHOR'S NOTE

Don Shula got on the phone and his message to me was immediate and blunt. "I'm not talking to you for a lengthy time," he said. "I'll talk, just not long." Then he proceeded to give me what I needed. That's typical Shula. All these decades after practically willing the Dolphins into history and controlling the wills of men, he was trying to control me.

Shula was working on another biography about his life and perfection. My guess is he instinctively didn't want to give me too much as to not interfere with his own book. I didn't mind. *This was Don Shula*. It's his life. It's his legend. But again, he treated me with dignity and class, and I'll always be grateful for him speaking to me.

It's important to remember that at one point in Shula's coaching career it was written by the press that Shula couldn't win the big game. Now, all these decades later, the NFL names one of its awards for coach of the year after him.

I saw Shula in February 2012 at Super Bowl XLVI. Shula was a

tremendous hit the moment he arrived in Indianapolis to partici-
pate in various Super Bowl functions. Former NFL player Warrick
Dunn was also in Indianapolis and was dining at one of Shula's restaurants. "Eating lunch [at] Shula's," tweeted Dunn, "and legendary
coach Don Shula walks in to have lunch also. Pretty cool."

Late in the week, Shula was greeted by New York Giants coach
Tom Coughlin as Coughlin approached a stage prior to his press
conference. You could see from Coughlin's face he was smitten to
see Shula. Coughlin was at the Super Bowl with so much at stake
for him, so much to discuss with the media, yet Coughlin began a
portion of his press conference this way: "It was great to see Coach
Shula here this morning. I made reference . . . when I talked with
[a reporter] . . . I was like, 'How in the world did Coach Shula win
328 games?' It's incredible to even think about that. It was great to
see him here."

Shula being Shula later explained he appreciated what Coughlin
said but couldn't resist correcting the record.

"It's 347 wins." Shula smiled.

I wrote this book because time causes great memory rifts and gaps.
To younger fans and sports journalists, the year 1972 was when Co-
lumbus discovered America. Many other writers and sports fans, at
least in my experience, have shown the Dolphins very little respect.
There's an infamous, crusty, complaining older sportswriter who is
a massive Pittsburgh Steelers backer, and he constantly declares any
of the 1970s Steelers Super Bowl teams would crush the 1972 Dolphins. He forgets that Miami beat the Steelers in Pittsburgh with
Morrall at quarterback in the first half and Griese at quarterback in
the second en route to that perfect season. Little blocked Mean Joe
Greene one-on-one the entire afternoon.

And that's the key word: "forget." This year marks the fortieth anniversary of that perfect season, and it's easy to think of what the team did as an accomplishment a long time ago in a galaxy far, far away. The critics point to the dearth of Hall of Famers and how the Dolphins were a patchwork group cobbled together by management. There is even a great deal of animosity that has developed toward the team over the past few years. It reached an apex in 2007, when Bill Belichick's New England Patriots came close to going an entire regular and postseason unbeaten as well but lost in Super Bowl XLII to the Giants. Morris, in his typical bombastic and fearless style, spoke after the Patriots went undefeated in the regular season. "My feeling about it is as consistent as it has been all year," he said. "It doesn't matter to me whether or not they win them all because it doesn't affect anything we've done. When all the dust clears, the best they can do is stand beside us, and in the end, that's not a bad thing. I will welcome them to the neighborhood with my Mr. Rogers sweater on, but first they have to get to the neighborhood."

Next, Morris went on ESPN, where he was asked why the Patriots weren't yet as good as the Dolphins, and his answer was even more typical Morris. "Actually, because our neighborhood is the finale," he said. "We are in a status called 'unbeaten.' So thus far they are not undefeated. Undefeated is the culmination of being unbeaten. So after you've won all your games regardless of how many that is . . . it's not about how many games you won. It's about how many games you didn't lose. Because that's the criteria for the automatic-ness of going undefeated." Then Morris just got straight obnoxious.

"And unfortunately the only person who knows what they're talking about in this conversation is me," he said. "Because I speak from what's called subjective experiential knowledge. Meaning, I went undefeated. Along with . . . my other teammates. So everything that you're talking about is speculation. There may be a hope that this occurs. A wish that it occurs. The reality is that it hasn't occurred yet. So if in fact they do run this gauntlet that they've got coming up, and they do go through this, and they win every game. And they don't have to do it convincingly. I have more respect for them for the games in which they were on the ropes and they came back than I do the games they buried everybody. Because that's the most important thing, to show the character of what it takes to do this.

"You gotta remember. We did this in 1972, and 1,290 chances later is what we're talking about now. So over the [past] thirty-five years, if [a team] would have been good enough to do it, it would have been done . . ."

Morris's answer to the first question went on for more than three minutes. The interviewer, Michelle Bonner, had to interrupt with a quick "Mercury!" Then she asked Morris why he couldn't give credit to the Patriots for what they'd done thus far. Remember, at the time of the interview, the Patriots had traversed through the regular season unbeaten but still had the Super Bowl to play. To Morris, you're not on the Dolphins' level—not in their neighborhood—until you win *every* game. The thought that anyone would consider the Patriots in the Dolphins' class before the Patriots played in the Super Bowl seemed to irk Morris. "Let me explain something to you," he responded. "If we won sixteen games and then we lost in the Super Bowl, our season would be nothing. So props don't come now, miss." Yes, he dropped a "miss."

"Props come at the end of the day," Morris continued, "when you get your report card. It's not about how you think you did but how you actually did." The real subject of Morris's ire was both ESPN and Bill Parcells. It was Parcells, the former coach of the Giants, Jets, and Patriots, who said in an ESPN story that many of the great franchises in NFL history, including the Dolphins, would have been beaten by the 2007 Patriots.

It was a remarkable interview, and portions of it went viral and became the talk of the sport. Eventually the backlash came and it was strong. Wrote one blogger: "Mercury Morris Please Do Us All A Favor, Shut The F_ck Up !" The words "Mercury Morris" and "shut up" and "pie hole" began to show up in football chat rooms across the Internet and on Google searches for Morris's name.

Morris was defensive, but he wasn't alone among the Dolphins. His attitude reflected a general feeling among the Dolphins players that what they'd accomplished didn't garner as much respect as it should have. They were undefeated. To them, this is an undeniable fact. "We constantly hear about the things our team supposedly couldn't do," Shula said, "instead of what we could."

"The Patriots showed very little respect to what we did," Csonka said. "It was like they were saying, 'Maybe you guys are in our class. Maybe not.' I remember thinking, 'Gee, thanks.'"

(A few exceptions were some of the New York Giants players who beat the Patriots in the Super Bowl game that ended their undefeated season while securing Miami's place in history. Giants defender Michael Strahan told me after the game the spirit of that Miami team helped the Giants win. "I think the Dolphins were a great team that could play with anybody, anywhere," he said.)

Some Dolphins players remain irritated to this day over an NFL Films hypothetical computer showdown between them and the 1978 Steelers, in which Pittsburgh won 21–20. It was yet another sign of disrespect.

The 1972 Dolphins team has long been disrespected. It's a grossly overused word in sports jargon, but it's applicable. Most football historians, sports journalists, and players don't rank the Dolphins near the top of the great all-time lists. In my opinion, the Dolphins could have competed against any other team across history.

Remember this quote from Washington Redskins coach George Allen, who faced the Dolphins in the culmination of the greatest season in football history: "The thing that bothers me most about Miami is they execute so well that they're not impressive. They are like a baseball team with six hitters, hitting singles and doubles."

This is why the Dolphins were so formidable and sometimes disrespected (there's that word again). They were steady, precise, and unrelenting. Many players, fans, and media don't always respect or understand the power of constancy. The Dolphins applied steady pressure on both sides of the ball, and while this wasn't sexy, it was extremely effective. They didn't have flash. They didn't have Lawrence Taylor or Jerry Rice or Ray Lewis or Jim Brown. They didn't have the Steel Curtain or the Doomsday Defense. The Dolphins weren't lightning or nuclear, but they were something just as good: they were perpetual. That's what it takes to be perfect. Not flash but relentlessness.

Morris has always said the 1972 Dolphins had an X factor. He's right. The Dolphins players weren't as big or as fast as today's players or even as some of the great teams from the 1980s, but they had those intangibles and a fierce will, which would have served them nicely against any opponent. "We weren't the all-time greatest athletes," Csonka said, "but we had smarts, drive, and talent. We had a lot of all those things. We also had a great deal of depth. If the Patriots had our depth, they'd have also been undefeated."

The players from that era were tougher, more studious, and respected authority far more than today's. They were nastier, hungrier, and didn't care as much about money or fame. Indeed, if there was a team today that might embody those Dolphins, it would be the Giants team that unseated the Patriots and beat them in the Super Bowl.

Miami's roster is also not as average as has been portrayed by some:

Larry Csonka could play in 1972 or 2022. If he played today, he'd be one of the top backs in football.

Paul Warfield could play in any era.

Griese's extreme accuracy would make him one of the top throwers today in a league where many quarterbacks couldn't hit a house from five paces.

Larry Little would be in the Pro Bowl every year.

Mercury Morris, I believe, is one of the top three most underrated players in NFL history. Morris's shorter career (he played six years with Miami and one with San Diego) and outspokenness over the years has hurt him in the eyes of some football historians, but it was Morris's speed and explosiveness that was a significant key in transforming the Dolphins from a team that lost a Super Bowl to Dallas into a team that would win the next two.

One criticism made against the Dolphins was the team went undefeated in an era when African-American players were still only partially integrated into the sport. It's a historical fact—not stereotype or bigotry—that the influx of African-Americans dramatically increased the level of athleticism in the sport (as in many American sports). Those Dolphins simply didn't have to compete against the speed that would dominate the sport decades later, the argument goes.

Today the NFL is approximately 55 to 60 percent African-American, but in the early 1970s, those numbers were smaller. But not as small as some may think. The roster of the 1972 Green Bay Packers was 40 percent African-American. Some teams had a higher percentage of blacks and some lower, but that was about the average. So the Dolphins went against plenty of black players.

The Dolphins definitely possessed something other teams wouldn't in a mythical showdown across the ages: they had Shula. There are only two coaches that I would rank ahead of Shula. The first is Bill Belichick, and though his legacy took a hit with his second Super Bowl loss to the Giants, he is still the best coach in NFL history. The second is Cleveland's Paul Brown.

But still, Shula did more with less than any coach before him or since. Please, don't misunderstand. The Dolphins had talent, but they weren't overflowing with Hall of Famers like some of the Packers teams from the 1960s, the Steelers teams of the 1970s, and the 49ers teams of the 1980s. Shula lost Super Bowls, but in a short period he took a joke of an expansion team, a team laughed at and despised by many in the NFL, to three Super Bowls and won two, including a perfect season. That is, well, pretty damn impressive.

In fact, the only thing that stopped Miami from perhaps winning one or two more titles was the World Football League. Players knew the breakup of the team was imminent. They discussed it, in fact, just twenty-four hours after winning that second Super Bowl. On Monday morning, linebacker Swift spoke to three reporters in the crowded lobby of the Marriott hotel as fans packed into their cars and headed for the airport. His quote about the Dolphins' future was a sign of things to come: "You can expect to see a lot of new faces on next year's team. A lot of important contracts are coming up for renewal, and you can bet that the guys will be asking for more than management is willing to pay."

The fact is Dolphins players, who had won so much, had reached wit's end in terms of pay. Csonka made $55,000 a year, a pittance for an NFL player even in the mid-1970s, and he was the highest compensated. There were stars on the Dolphins making $30,000 a season while the NFL was making $200,000 for every sixty-second commercial during the Super Bowl and far more money in television and other avenues during the rest of the year. Yes, *all* football players were underpaid, but the Dolphins extremely so, and the new league, which would fold just a few years later, were paying huge contracts.

There were actually only two things that stopped the Dolphins from winning at least one more Super Bowl: the WFL and a player strike called in July 1974. The WFL was supposed to be an alternative to the NFL, and it made a huge splash with a highly unusual move. The league signed Csonka, Warfield, Kiick, Foley, and Kuechenberg to *future* contracts, meaning they would play with the Dolphins in the 1974–75 season and then go to the WFL. Nothing like that had ever been done before. It caused too many obvious problems in the locker room for Shula to handle. One group of players was on its way out the door, on its way to making huge money, but was still with the team. All the consternation led to an unfocused Miami team that lost its opening game to the Patriots 34–24. "We stunk," said Shula.

Of course, they wouldn't stink for long. That's not the Shula way. The Dolphins would finish the regular season 11-3. They were eliminated from the playoffs by Oakland, losing 28–26. That season was Shula's twelfth as a head coach and he had yet to have a losing season. But the Oakland loss did signal one thing: the dynasty was done.

The irony of football today is that there will likely be more challenges than ever to Miami's historical achievement of not losing a game during a season. Newer NFL rules allow offenses unprecedented leeway. Consider that three teams in 2011 scored over 500 points that season, a first. Never before in league history have offenses been allowed so much power over defenses. This will allow teams with great throwing quarterbacks like the Packers, Patriots, Saints, Giants, and one or two others to explode offensively and start 7-0, 10-0, and beyond. From there anything can happen. So expect more runs at history, but as we've seen as recently as the Packers in 2011, it's easier to start off undefeated than finish that way.

How would Shula's Miami teams do against the best in history? They were 32-2 in two years, 43-5 in three. Three Super Bowl appearances in three years, winning two, and in one of those seasons won every game. "I like our chances against any team in history," Shula says now.

So do I.

Twenty years ago, I was actually interviewing O. J. Simpson for another story when eventually he mentioned the undefeated Dolphins. Now, since Simpson proved to be a bit of a—ahem—chameleon, it's unclear if he actually believes what he told me then. Simpson explained that while he was a player, he often went against the Dolphins, and while he didn't think they had the most talent, no team was mentally tougher. "They intimidated people with their intellect and their will more than anything else," he said. "They outlasted you. They were better conditioned and they basically played almost perfect football and forced you to play almost perfect football. But few teams could do that so they outlasted you. Again, it was about that will. The Dolphins basically said, 'Our will is stronger than yours.'"

I kept my Simpson notes and quotes all these years and never used them (I pondered writing a Simpson biography). Simpson's words had intrigued me. I knew of the Dolphins, of course, but not in great detail. I started to study them and found the team utterly fascinating. Since then, I have read every notable (meaning lengthy or close to it) newspaper and magazine article ever written about that 1972 team. Yes, ever written, and also every book, including a children's book about the team. I've interviewed Shula a half dozen times over the past ten years about various NFL issues and always slipped in a question or two (or three, or four) about that Dolphins team. You could always hear the pride in Shula's voice whenever he talked about the team and sometimes the fire in it when he defended the team from those who felt that Dolphins group was overrated. Since that Simpson conversation, I've amassed several hundred pages of notes, about twelve thousand pages of documents, and everything NFL Films ever broadcast on the Dolphins. I dropped in on some of their speaking engagements and press appearances. I quietly stalked the 1972 Dolphins for many years.

One of the questions I have tried to answer about this team arises constantly. Where should this team rank among the all-time great NFL teams? The Dolphins players often get the most irritated over this discussion. "We're the only undefeated team in history," says Shula. "How are we not ranked the best of all time? It makes no sense to rank anything other than number one."

There are always limitations in this argument unless someone has access to a time machine. How do you compare a team that played in the 1970s to one that plays in the twenty-first century? The athleticism of the 2010 Super Bowl champion Green Bay Packers would seem to dwarf the athletes on the '72 Dolphins. Or the Dallas Cowboys in the 1990s with Troy Aikman, Michael Irvin, and Emmitt Smith. Or the 1985 Chicago Bears with Mike Singletary at linebacker. Or those great San Francisco 49ers teams with Joe Montana and Jerry Rice. Wouldn't they obliterate Shula's perfect Dolphins?

It would seem that way, but I'm convinced the Dolphins would hold up well against any opponent from any point across the NFL timeline. The reason why is that strong will so many Miami players and opponents have discussed over the years. The Dolphins also possessed one of the top three coaching staffs from top to bottom in history. They'd be formidable opponents schematically and tactically against the best coaches of today, even the geniuses like Belichick.

I would finish with this: If the Dolphins, as some of their critics suggest, would be destroyed by modern dynasties like the Joe Montana 49ers, the 1985 Bears, or the Patriots, then why has only one team—those Patriots—come close to what the Dolphins accomplished? Why has only one team truly come close to perfection?

Yes, the Dolphins would do okay, thank you very much.

On January 3, 2010, the Dolphins organization celebrated Shula's eightieth birthday. Corporations bought spots for VIPs at $10,000 a table. Celebrities, actors, and U.S. senators came. The Black Eyed Peas' Fergie sang a rendition of "Happy Birthday" to Shula.

Shula wrote for the game-day program given to fans. The cover had a montage of Shula moments and inside was a special section dedicated to him. "It's hard to believe that I'm about to turn 80 years old," he wrote. "I feel great. I'm healthy. I'm playing golf. I'm enjoying life. My wife, Mary Anne, and I are doing a lot of traveling. We're doing the things we've always wanted to do. Eighty years old? It's really just a number to me. But I remember when I was young I thought 80 years old was pretty old. But I really do feel good about where I am in life and I'm thoroughly enjoying it."

Attending the party were thirty of Shula's former players from the undefeated team. The men he used to chide and ride and scold arrived in huge numbers. It is the thing you perhaps have to understand most about this group. The unity that allowed them to be great, that glue, hasn't dissolved. All these decades later, they are a tight group. They still call Shula "Coach" and he still jokes about his powers over them. He talks, they listen. He respects them, they adore him, even though they don't always want to publicly admit it. "I've spent the last thirty years getting Don Shula's voice out of my ears," Csonka told the crowd. "To be asked to come here and talk about him and put him back in my ears, I had to think about it a little bit.

"In all seriousness," Csonka added, "I think now, along with his bride, he's finally started to really enjoy life. I don't say this easily, folks, but the last few times I've been around Don Shula, I've enjoyed it 100 percent of the time. It's a lot of fun reminiscing. He tells very funny stories. He's very relaxed and has a great sense of humor. He wasn't any of those things when he coached."

That's how most of the 1972 Dolphins display their love for Shula. Men often don't tell other men "I love you." And men from that team, some of the toughest the league has ever seen, won't say at a public birthday in front of Fergie and senators "I love you, Coach" despite that being how they feel. Instead, they display that love with stories about how Shula greatly impacted that team and their lives. This is how tough men say "I love you." Shula does the same.

Though there was one moment during the birthday bash and tributes and odes to Shula that the Wall of Manhood was scaled. Kuechenberg was present, and at one point, he walked up to Shula, hugged him strongly, and kissed him on the cheek. The moment, like many things about the Dolphins, was perfect.

ACKNOWLEDGMENTS

I first want to thank Don Shula for speaking with me. I've interviewed Shula many times over the years and he has always been one of the most accessible of all the legendary coaches. The Bum Phillips quote about Shula at the beginning of this book was actually used twice by Phillips. Phillips also said that about Bear Bryant, but I remain convinced no coach in history got more out of personnel than Shula. No, not Bryant either.

Most of all, I wanted to thank the Miami players. In more than twenty years of covering sports, I have never met a nicer group of people. They spoke to me without wanting something in return, which is a rarity in sports today. One of my favorite moments from speaking with the players was talking to Csonka about his passion for the state of Alaska, where he travels often for extended vacations. It was a common occurrence with many of the Dolphins players. They are extremely well-rounded men and can speak on a multitude of subjects. It's this depth and intelligence that likely allowed them to digest so much of Shula's and his assistants' complicated schemes.

Interviews with the players composed the bulk of information for this book.

Quotes from the *Miami Herald* and *Miami News* were used and are attributed. The beat writers who covered the Dolphins in the early 1970s were excellent at their job. Stories from *Sports Illustrated* were also helpful for this book.

Harvey Greene, the public relations guru for the Dolphins, is one of the best in the business and helped me track down many of the players. His help was greatly appreciated.

The Nixon letter to Shula came from the Nixon Presidential Library and Museum. Luckily, Nixon taped everything. I transcribed Nixon's dictation exactly as he said it.

I read every article of substance ever written on the perfect team. I also read every book. Writers Dave Hyde, Joan Didion, T. D. Allman, Morris T. McLemore, Edna Buchanan, David Rieff, Jody Brown, Bill Braucher, Francis and Raymond Lodato, and Steve Perkins were all helpful. The works of those writers gave me helpful insight into the Dolphins and others into the city of Miami itself. Some of these writers wrote their books on the Dolphins in the 1970s while some were more recent. I've followed Hyde's work for a long time. He's one of the finest sports journalists out there. Any information used from those works is properly credited.

I had an army of help for research and editing. The redoubtable Susan Thornton Hobby, my old neighbor turned master editor, did her usual outstanding job. Researcher Seth Berkman was a huge help. As was Jennifer O'Neill, another great reseacher.

My professors at Goucher College: Madeleine Blais, Thomas French, Laura Wexler, and Leslie Rubinkowski, as well as the program director for the MFA creative writing program, Patsy Sims, helped me think of ways to approach this book I would not have otherwise considered. So many big brains among that teaching staff.

Thanks to my agent, John Monteleone, as this is our sixth book together.

And to my wonderful mother, who used her genealogy skills to find hundreds of pages of documents on the Shula family's origins.

To Kelly, always.

NOTES

INTRODUCTION

"That bad, huh?" Nixon White House tapes 235-014, December 9, 1972.

"The Cowboys are a fine football team": Don Shula, *The Winning Edge*, p. 160.

1 "I DON'T EVER WANT TO FEEL THIS WAY AGAIN"

"Hey, you dummy, move over": Shula, p. 171.

"Is this your shit?": Alex Hawkins, *My Story*, p. 152.

"To get to the Super Bowl": Francis J. Lodato, p. 172.

2 TRUCE

Earlier in their marriage: Janet Chusmir, "Dorothy Shula," *Miami Herald*, January 6, 1972.

4 THE THREE WISE MEN

Declassified documents later showed: Joan Didion, *Miami*, p. 34.

Named Nigger: Mercury Morris, *Against the Grain*, p. 34.

7 MELTING POT

Dolphins linebacker Doug Swift: Lodato, *But We Were 17 And 0*, p. 176.

"We didn't have the problem": Lodato, p. 50.

8 THE MAN WHO FIRED FLIPPER

"Get in here!": Hyde, p. 35

12 UNBEATABLE

"Dear Nigger": Bruce Feldman, *Cane Mutiny*, p. 1.

14 STEEL HURTIN'

"I'm ready": Shula, *The Winning Edge*, p. 202.

17 PERFECT

"How many players are involved?": Shula, p. 8.

BIBLIOGRAPHY

Allman, T. D. *Miami: City of the Future.* New York: Atlantic Monthly Press, 1987.

Braucher, Bill. *Promises to Keep: The Miami Dolphins Story.* New York: Dodd, Mead, 1972.

Briscoe, Marlin, with Bob Schaller. *The First Black Quarterback: Marlin Briscoe's Journey to Break the Color Barrier and Start in the NFL.* Grand Island, New England: Cross Training Publishing, 2002.

Brown, Jody. *Don Shula: Countdown to Supremacy.* New York: Leisure Press, 1983.

Buchanan, Edna. *The Corpse Had a Familiar Face: Covering Miami, America's Hottest Beat.* New York: Random House, 1987.

Didion, Joan. *Miami.* New York: Simon and Schuster, 1987.

Evans, Norm, Ray Didinger, and Sonny Schwartz. *On God's Squad: The Story of Norm Evans as Told to Ray Didinger and Sonny Schwartz.* Carol Stream, IL: Creation House, 1971.

Feldman, Bruce. *Cane Mutiny: How the Miami Hurricanes Overturned the Football Establishment.* New York: Penguin Group, 2004.

Golenbock, Peter. *Cowboys Have Always Been My Heroes: The Definitive Oral History of America's Team.* New York: Warner Books, 1997.

Hawkins, Alex. *My Story (And I'm Sticking to It).* Chapel Hill, NC: Algonquin Books of Chapel Hill, 1990.

Hyde, Dave. *Still Perfect: The Untold Story of the 1972 Miami Dolphins.* Dolphin/Curtis Publishing, 2002.

Lodato, Raymond and Francis. *But We Were 17 And 0.* Lake Worth, Florida: IQ Publications, 1986.

McLemore, Morris. *The Miami Dolphins: The Story of Pro Football's Most Exciting Team.* New York: Doubleday & Company, 1972.

Morrall, Earl, and George Sullivan. *Comeback Quarterback: The Earl Morrall Story.* New York: Grosset & Dunlap, 1969.

Morris, Mercury, and Steve Fiffer. *Against the Grain.* New York: McGraw-Hill, 1988.

Nixon Presidential Library and Museum. White House Tape 648A.

Perkins, Steve, and Bill Braucher. *The Inside Story of the Miami Dolphins.* New York: Grosset & Dunlap, 1973.

Rieff, David. *Going to Miami.* New York: Little, Brown and Company, 1999.

Shula, Don, and Lou Sahadi. *The Winning Edge.* New York: Popular Library, 1973.

Thompson, Hunter. *The Essential Writing of Hunter S. Thompson.* New York: Simon & Schuster, 2011.

ABOUT THE AUTHOR

Mike Freeman is a National NFL Insider for CBSSports.com. Before that, he was an NFL writer, investigative reporter, and columnist for the *New York Times*; a columnist for the *Florida Times-Union*; and a sports reporter, features writer, and investigative writer for the *Washington Post*, *Boston Globe*, and *Dallas Morning News*. In all, Freeman has covered professional football for more than two decades. He has twice been named honorable mention in the Best American Sports Writing anthology and is one of only a handful of writers to have multiple top-ten finishes in one year in the Associated Press Sports Editors writing contest. *Undefeated* is his sixth book. He lives in New Jersey.